Love & Loss

Love & Loss

A Story About Life, Death, and Rebirth

A Memoir By
Jane Bay

The events in this book are based on the experiences
of the author. Some Tibetan names and circumstances have been
changed to ensure confidentiality.

Clear Light Publishing
Santa Fe, New Mexico

Copyright © Jane Bay, 2006

Clear Light Publishing, 823 Don Diego, Santa Fe, New Mexico 87505
www.clearlightbooks.com

First Edition
10 9 8 7 6 5 4 3 2 1

Library of Congress Cataloging-in-Publication Data

Bay, Jane.
   Love & loss: a story about life, death, and rebirth / by Jane Bay.—1st ed.
      p. cm.
   ISBN 1-57416-088-5
   1. Youdon, Namgyal, d. 2003. 2. Mothers and daughters. 3. Adopted children—Death. 4. Bereavement. I. Title: Love and loss. II. Title.
   HQ755.85.B387 2006
   294.3'9230922—dc22

                                                2006006268

Front Cover: Namgyal and Jane—Yamdrok Lake, Tibet
            Photograph by Auntie Drakpa
Back Cover: "The Endless Knot" symbol created by Bob Jacobson

Interior Design / Production: Bonzelet Graphic Design
Printed in Hong Kong

For my Dear Friends

This book is dedicated to all my dear friends
whose love and support
encouraged and nurtured
the telling of this story.

May it be of benefit to others.

Acknowledgments

First and foremost, I want to thank all the dear friends who held me in the arms of compassion from the moment of Namgyal's death through the end of mourning my beloved daughter.

To my primary teachers, His Holiness the Dalai Lama, Robert Thurman and Yvonne Rand, I am grateful for the opportunity to study with you and to receive the blessings from your practice of lovingkindness. Special thanks to Arjia Rinpoche, Losang Samten and Sylvia Boorstein for your generous support and encouragement.

My deepest appreciation goes to Tina Mills for her fantastically creative work on all the photographs, especially the cover.

To Tom Hunter, my heartfelt gratitude for all your help with legal matters on both PRECIOUS JEWELS OF TIBET and LOVE & LOSS, and most importantly, for your constant friendship.

Oceans of love and gratitude to Rita and Tommy Sullivan for taking such good care of me. Thank you from the bottom of my heart.

Many thanks to Allan Kausch for skillfully editing and proofing the manuscript, to Anne Merrifield for her efficient proofreading, to Debbie Raike for typing the first draft, and Kristine Hanna for reading through several drafts and giving feedback on the writing.

Thanks to Harmon Houghton and Marcia Keegan at Clear Light Publishing for their steady commitment to bringing the book to fruition. Also thanks to Lee Moore for her insightful editorial comments, and Carol O'Shea for her efforts.

And last, but certainly not least, a special thanks to Krystie Bonzelet for her terrific design of the material that turned hundreds of individual emails into an intimate, accessible book.

Contents

Love & Loss

A Story About Life, Death, and Rebirth

LOVE & LOSS—A Story About Life, Death, and Rebirth is something of a sequel to my book Precious Jewels of Tibet—A Journey to the Roof of the World in that this story begins where Precious Jewels ended. It is the story of my relationship with Namgyal Youdon, my Tibetan daughter, and the consequences of her life and death on my life.

Namgyal was thirteen years old when I met her at the Tibetan Children's Village (TCV) in Dharamsala, India. I was traveling with my spiritual friend, Losang Samten, who was at the time, a monk at the Dalai Lama's Monastery. We had made a pilgrimage to the sacred Buddhist sites in India: to Bodhgaya, Varanasi and Sarnath, and ended our journey in Dharamsala at Namgyal Monastery, the home of the Dalai Lama.

A smiling civilian guard opened the wrought-iron gate at the entrance of the Tibetan Children's Village and motioned for us to proceed up the road to the creamy yellow administration buildings ahead. Losang and I stepped out of the jeep and ascended the steep steps to the main office. TCV was founded in 1960 to provide a modern education in Tibetan culture, religion, history and languages to the hundreds of Tibetan children who are being smuggled out of Tibet, those who have lost their parents living in India, and those whose parents have not been able to provide for their children in exile. It is an orphanage and a school. There are several thousand children at this branch, from babies to high school age. It looked like any other school, with swings, jungle-gyms, outdoor tables and benches, and children playing basketball on the playground. I had brought a video camera and filmed my surroundings to the delight of a dozen kids who quickly gathered around me.

Losang introduced me to the Sponsorship Secretary, Mrs. Tashi Lungrig, then left saying he would meet me later that evening for dinner at the Tibet Hotel where I was staying. Mrs. Lungrig and I began our tour on the walk up the terraced steps, past several dormitory buildings.

"The older children are still in class," she advised, "so we'll go to the 'Baby Home' first. Most of these children are two or three years of age."

"Great, I love babies."

"Do you have children?" she asked.

"No" I said, "I've had two husbands, but unfortunately, I was never able to have children."

Mrs. Lungrig said most of the children at the Village had lost their parents and having a sponsor is very meaningful to them. The school is run completely on donations and contributions from individuals and various organizations around the world, but it is not eligible for refugee relief because Tibet is not recognized as an independent country. Much of their funding comes from SOS-Kinderdorf in Vienna, from Germany, Great Britain, many European countries, North and South America as well as India.

When we arrived at the "Baby Home," several women, referred to as "mother," with babes in arms or babies clinging to the long Tibetan skirts and aprons they wore, invited us into the outdoor play area. The babies love having visitors. I was given permission to video the children.

What happened next unfolded slowly. The "mothers" and I tried to get all the children to line up together to have their picture taken. There was some pushing and shoving to be in front and someone began to cry. It was hard to tell the girls from the boys—most of the children had on pants and hand-knitted sweaters. As was to be expected, the babies wouldn't stand still for very long—they were much more intrigued by the camera around my neck.

I sat down on the ground in front of them, and several of the children came over to investigate. They got very excited and animated when they saw their friends' faces on the video screen. They didn't understand how this happened and began to crawl all over me to get their little hands on the camera itself. The kids were squealing, I was cooing and laughing, as I handed the camera to Mrs. Lungrig, who continued to shoot this somewhat awkward, but funny mob scene. It was a little like an army of ants crawling over a morsel of food. Babies were in my lap, leaning against my shoulders, fondling the jewelry around my neck, playing with my earrings, touching my face and stroking my hair, which was in a long ponytail. It felt good.

"What's your name, little one?" I asked a moon-faced girl with big, dark eyes.

"Her name is Rinchen Lhamo," Mrs. Lungrig replied, "It means Precious Goddess."

"You are precious," I whispered in her ear, "I hope you have a happy life."

I sat on the ground playing with the children for a few more minutes, then began to pull myself out from under the blanket of babies that covered me. All the children crowded at the fence in the play area when we left. The "mothers" told them to say good-bye to the visitor, which we could hear them saying over and over again as Mrs. Lungrig and I walked down the narrow terraced path back to the office.

I hadn't thought about sponsoring a child before I came to the Tibetan Children's Village, but that precious little goddess had stolen my heart. I wanted her, but Mrs. Lungrig said Rinchen Lhamo already had a sponsor.

"Most people want a baby, but there are so many older children who have no one that desperately need a sponsor. Wouldn't you consider an older child?" she asked.

Slightly disappointed, I said, "Yes, of course, I understand, but it will have to be a girl."

Mrs. Lungrig looked through several folders on her desk. She pulled out two documents and handed them to me. "Here are histories on two girls; both are thirteen years old," she said.

I began to read the first report when, to my surprise, I noticed the girl's name.

"This girl is named Namgyal Youdon. I can't believe it...I'm here in India on a pilgrimage with a monk from Namgyal Monastery, and the first girl I see is named Namgyal. It must be a karmic connection," I said.

The file stated that her mother died in Tibet when Namgyal was an infant. Her father, Dr. Namgang, was a doctor of Tibetan medicine, still living in Lhasa at that time. She had two brothers, one in India, and one in Tibet. Her father wanted his daughter to have the opportunity of a Tibetan education which she could never receive in Tibet under the regime of the Chinese Communists. She had been brought to India under very dangerous conditions across the Himalayas by a friend of her father's.

I thought to myself, "She's a motherless child and I'm a childless mother. I've always wanted a daughter, and now I have a teenager."

I signed the papers committing myself to be responsible as a foster parent for the welfare of this child throughout her academic life at TCV.

"Can I meet her? Now?" I asked. Mrs. Lungrig replied, approvingly, "Yes, yes. Classes are almost over for today. We'll go down and take her out early."

The late afternoon sunlight reflected a warm golden glow off the school buildings. Several older children watched as I filmed Mrs. Lungrig entering one of the classrooms. She reappeared moments later with a young girl in tow who had short-cropped dark hair. The girl was wearing trousers and a blue and white checked shirt under a big knit sweater—the TCV uniform.

Mrs. Lungrig made the introduction, explaining to

Namgyal that I was from America and would be her sponsor. The girl was painfully shy, her eyes furtively looking up and down to get a glimpse of her new "mother."

"Namgyal, could we sit and talk for a few minutes?"

She nodded. I handed the video camera once again to Mrs. Lungrig. Namgyal and I walked a few yards to a low retaining wall next to the playground. We sat on the wall, turning our bodies around to face each other. I did most of the talking, Namgyal nodding sweetly. Mrs. Lungrig filmed the first meeting between mother and daughter.

I realized she might not be fluent enough to speak in English and motioned to Mrs. Lungrig for help with translation. She knelt next to us with Namgyal still in the video frame. They spoke in Tibetan.

"She says English is the most difficult subject she studies."

I said to Namgyal, "I'll write to you when I return to the United States. Will you be able to write to me?"

As Mrs. Lungrig translated my question, Namgyal again nodded yes.

"Good, then you can practice your English when you answer my letters."

She laughed a little. Our brief interview was almost over. I asked her about her father who had recently visited her at TCV. He had visited her twice in the four years she had been there. We spoke a few moments longer, about trivial things, like whether she liked American music, which she didn't, until the afternoon recess bell began to ring and the playground filled with children. Many of them came over to see what was going on with Namgyal, and to check out the video camera.

"I'm very happy to meet you, Namgyal, and I look forward to getting to know you," I said.

Namgyal addressed Mrs. Lungrig in Tibetan. "She says she is very lucky to have a sponsor like you."

We said goodbye. Namgyal and three of her girlfriends walked away toward the dormitories. Mrs. Lungrig relinquished the video camera which I kept focused on the girls. Suddenly, Namgyal stopped, turned back toward us and waved, her sweet, round face covered from ear to ear with a big, wide grin.

I thought my heart would jump out of my body from the joy that I felt. For as long as I could remember, I had wanted to have children. I had expected to grow up, marry well, have four children, two boys and two girls, a dog, and a cat. I had already picked out names for the girls before I entered puberty—Paige and Tracy. Now I had myself a daughter. One who would call me "mother."

Waving goodbye to the guard at the TCV gate, I walked, almost on a cloud, back toward town. The gentle sloping road meandered past a small lake with cattle grazing nearby and a cluster of Indian homes and storefronts. I walked through the old British military outpost at McLeod Ganj now occupied by the Indian army to St. James In The Wilderness Church and Cemetery, another vestige of the glory days of the British Empire. I stopped at the church and walked through the cemetery, pausing here and there to read the headstones of proper English men and women whose remains lay buried in the foreign soil.

A poem by Pablo Neruda crossed my mind:

> *How much does a man live, after all?*
> *Does he live a thousand days, or one only?*
> *For a week, or for several centuries?*
> *How long does a man spend dying?*
> *What does it mean to say "forever"?*

It was a sobering reminder of impermanence, but my lifelong dream of being a mother had come true, and thoughts of death lingered not on my mind.

That night at the Tibet Hotel restaurant, over a meal of *tragpa* (roasted chicken), *shokot khatsq* (curried potatoes) and *kantse* (Tibetan salad), I told Losang about finding Namgyal. After dinner I showed him the video. It had been a very good day.

Within six weeks of returning home, the President of the United States changed his mind about most favored nations status for China. He gave it to them without even the slightest attempt to link human rights violations to the conditions of the trade agreement. Big business had won again. The effects on Tibet were swift and severe. Street beatings began with a flurry; arrests began in earnest. The strong arm of totalitarianism reached out and grabbed the throat of any voice raised in protest and choked the very breath out of the resistance. The Chinese gloated over their victory, with loudspeakers in the streets of Lhasa telling the Tibetan people they had been betrayed by their American friends. A new reign of terror had begun.

As the months passed, my relationship with Namgyal began to grow and blossom. She practiced her English in the letters I received addressing me as "My Dearest Mother Jane," and signed, "With love from your loving daughter, Namgyal." She wrote mostly about her schooling, and how hard she was studying as she had so much catching up to do academically. The Chinese education she received in Tibet was terribly lacking. She got her lowest marks in Hindi which she was studying along with English and Tibetan language, math and science.

Her letters were conversational, as though she was telling me about her day after coming home from school. They were decorated with pretty pictures, drawn with colored pencils, of stars and moons, hearts and flowers, mountains and rivers, and the rising sun. I wrote her stories about my black and white cat, Keyboard, and sent her pictures knowing she couldn't have a pet at school. She always included a little message to Keyboard in her letters.

One letter contained her school photograph. She was dressed in the TCV uniform of blue pants, a blue and white checked shirt with a cardigan sweater. We began to get to know each other. I asked the school placement secretary if I could send her gifts and received a reply that Namgyal needed a new pair of shoes. Tucked in her next letter was a drawing of her two small feet on a piece of paper. The thought of her drawing her feet on that paper melted my heart. I cut them out with scissors, like a set of paper dolls, and headed straight for the mall.

In the shoe department at Macy's, I found the perfect pair of shoes for Namgyal: Easy Spirit Mary Jane's. The salesperson thought it was a little strange trying on shoes with paper feet, but we found just the right size. I liked them so much, I got a pair for myself as well. Mother-Daughter shoes. I wrapped Namgyal's for shipping, put them in the next post to India, and very shortly received her response. She now had a pair of shoes that fit. It was, alas, the last letter I would receive from her.

In the bright light of the December full moon, I sat on the front porch steps of my old country Victorian house, my arms wrapped around my knees, not to warm myself from the cold, but to contain the trembling of my spirit. In my hand was a letter from Namgyal's school which arrived, coincidentally, almost nine months to the day from when we met. Its contents shook me to the very core of my being.

We deeply regret to inform you that Namgyal Youdon has been recently withdrawn from our school by her father following a directive issued by the Chinese authorities to families in Tibet to bring back their children studying in India. Failure to do this would lead to the parents losing their jobs, homes and food ration cards, and possible imprisonment. As the families, especially the parents, have many members to support, and fearing the consequences, they withdrew their children with a heavy heart. We are very concerned about this turn of events and fear for the children's future...

With tears that felt like molten lava streaming down my checks, I looked up at the full moon and saw in it her face. I knew that same moon was shining over the roof of the world and with trembling voice called out to her.

"Namgyal, you will be forever in my heart and always in my prayers which I send to you on moonbeams. I hope you can hear me. I will never forget you. I will try to find you."

I heard the murmur of my breaking heart.

Days ran into nights in a river of tears as grief flowed through me. I made no effort to bury the pain I felt. The floodgates of mourning burst open, for the child I had lost in miscarriage and never mourned, for the separation from Namgyal, and on the deepest emotional level, for what seemed to be the finale to my last chance of being a mother. Music was my only source of solace, the place where I could go for comfort. I listened to "ripple/wind over water" from Ottmar Liebert's CD *Opium* over and over again.

It took days to get through by phone to India after having received no response to a dozen faxes I had sent pleading for information about Namgyal's fate. My mind was spinning desperately out of control. Finally, calling from Santa Fe on New Year's Eve, I managed to get an open telephone line, and was put through immediately to the director of the school. His words were not encouraging except he thought she might not fare too harshly because her father was a doctor of Tibetan medicine and the Chinese needed his services. I managed to convince him to give me her father's address in Lhasa and was surprised to learn his medical office was on the Barkhor, the Tibetan market in the center of old Lhasa. I might have walked passed it when I went on to Tibet after meeting Namgyal in Dharamsala.

The head of the Tibetan Children's Village implored me not to write inflammatory letters to Namgyal. It would surely result in trouble for her and her family which, of course, I understood.

I tormented myself with the knowledge of where she might be and what might happen to her. Would she be "brainwashed," or "reeducated" as the Chinese call it.

Would she be singled out for ridicule because she had been in India and close to the Dalai Lama? I began composing letters to her. They were short and sweet. I wrote things like, "I know you must be happy to see you father and brother again," or "You are probably settled at your new school by now, and I hope you will study hard." I sent a stuffed animal, a black and white cat like Keyboard, that was "made in China," thinking it might get through the omnipotent eye of the authorities who would surely read her mail (any mail from the U.S.) and open her packages. Still, I received no response.

Three years later, Losang and I embarked on a journey to the roof of the world. Losang had left the Dalai Lama's monastery and was living and working in the United States, having set up several Tibetan Buddhist Centers around the country and teaching the sacred arts of Tibet. Losang had recently become a U.S. citizen and he had served as the "religious advisor" on Martin Scorsese's film, *Kundun*, a story about the life of the Dalai Lama. Losang also had a small acting part in the movie, playing the role of the personal attendant to the Dalai Lama, a position he had held in real life during his years as a monk at Namgyal Monastery.

Our trip to Tibet was sponsored by Myths and Mountains Inc., an educational travel company. Losang was hired as a teacher. We were accompanied by two other people on the trip—Mark Parnes, an attorney from San Francisco who had quit his job at a law firm, sold his house, and embarked on a year long pilgrimage in Asia; and Ruth Lekan from Chicago, a retired industrial interior designer. It was a Buddhist tour to visit monasteries and sacred sites, however, Losang and I were on a secret mission.

I was going to look for Namgyal in Lhasa, and Losang hoped to find his two elder brothers who had been imprisoned for trying to save the sacred objects in their village temple when the Chinese invaded Tibet in 1959. A third brother had died in prison, but the two elder brothers had been released after twelve years of brutal incarceration. One brother had lost an eye from beatings and torture he received while in prison. Losang had not seen or spoken to his brothers in thirty-eight years, but heard from several monks that they still lived in the house he left at the age of seven.

It was a dangerous mission, but Losang was successful in locating his family. He spent twenty-four hours with them, sleeping only briefly on the bed in the room where he had slept every night of his life until he fled Tibet with his mother, father and younger sister. It was a bittersweet reunion. His family had suffered terribly during the intervening years.

But, I did not find Namgyal. The building where her father had practiced Tibetan medicine had been torn down by the Chinese under the pretense that the building was unsafe. It was actually part of a campaign to destroy all vestiges of traditional Tibetan architecture and replace it with garish, prefabricated Chinese style buildings.

People in the neighborhood near her father's old office said they remembered the family, but hadn't seen or heard of them in over a year and a half. No one knew where they had gone. A Tibetan friend went to the local police, who know everything, under the pretext of having a medical problem that only Dr. Namgang could treat. Even the police knew nothing of her family. It was as though they had vanished from the face of the earth. My heart ached with sadness. I was disappointed. I had thought that I would find her.

I remembered the Buddha's words:

> *Birth ends in death;*
> *Youth ends in old age.*
> *Meetings end in separation.*
> *Wealth ends in loss.*
> *In cyclic existence everything*
> *Is transient—impermanent...*

When I returned to the U.S., I finished writing the manuscript of *Precious Jewels of Tibet* that I had started when Namgyal was forced to leave India. Shortly after *Precious Jewels* was published, I began a book tour on the West Coast from Seattle to Los Angeles and in the Southwest to Santa Fe and Tucson. During the New Mexico leg of the tour, Losang flew in from Philadelphia to introduce me at an author appearance and book signing at "The Ark" in Santa Fe that had been organized by my publishers who are based there.

Santa Fe is my second home. During the past quarter of a century, I've spent most holidays and vacations there, and have a wide circle of friends in the film and art community, many of whom came to the event to celebrate the publication of my first book.

Earlier on the day of the book signing, my dear friend, Judy Margolis, the owner of Origins, one of my favorite clothing stores in Santa Fe, hosted a luncheon in my honor at the India Palace Restaurant that was attended by Losang and some of Judy's women friends she wanted me to meet. I woke up that morning with a sore throat and the warning signs of an oncoming cold. The last thing I wanted to do was eat curry and sit around with a lot of people I didn't know. Showing up half an hour late, I made my apologies and was seated at the head of the table at the opposite end from Losang, who was graciously entertaining the ladies.

Seated to my left was Peggy Hitchcock, a woman I knew by reputation for her good work on behalf of Tibet. She had organized the Arizona Teachings given by the Dalai Lama that I attended the year before my first journey to the roof of the world began. The moment I sat down at the table, we began an intimate conversation.

During lunch, we talked about Peggy's two daughters, and I told her the story of my Tibetan daughter, Namgyal. She hadn't read *Precious Jewels*, but was planning to get a copy that night at the book signing. When I told Peggy that my search to find Namgyal in Tibet the previous summer had failed, tears welled up in her eyes.

She touched my arm and said, "I know two women doctors from Tibet who are here in the U.S. Lhasa is a small town, and they're bound to know Namgyal's father. I'll try to help you find your daughter."

Having traveled halfway around the world, with good political connections and friends in high places who had tried in vain for three years to help locate Namgyal, I felt I had done everything possible to find her. I was touched by Peggy's empathy but didn't give it much credence.

Through the practice of Tibetan Buddhism, I had come to realize it wasn't meant to be, and in facing the loss of this child, I had learned one of life's greatest lessons: the true nature of reality—impermanence. Everything in life is constantly changing, and the only thing we have is the present moment. The past is history, and the future is unknown. From a Buddhist perspective, grasping and clinging are the primary causes of suffering, and in writing *Precious Jewels of Tibet*, I had been able to let go of my longing to be a mother. It had been a huge catharsis in my life.

The book signing event was a great success. I was all aglow from the warm response of the audience to my talk (as well as a low grade fever), and a lot of books were sold. As Peggy was leaving for the airport, with a copy of *Precious Jewels* in hand, to catch a late flight back to her home in Tucson, she again declared her intention to help find my daughter, but I was caught up in the excitement of the moment and didn't give it a second thought.

Much too early the following morning, the phone rang in my room at the El Rey Inn. It was Judy. We went over the magical moments of the night before, and she mentioned she had some herbal medicine for my cold which had by this time come on with a vengeance.

"I'm sorry I can't bring it to you, but throw on a bathrobe, drive downtown and just double park in front of the store. The pills will be waiting for you at the counter," she said.

I really didn't want to get out of my sickbed to pick up some herbal remedy. What I needed were good old-fashioned American antibiotics, but something told me to go. I got dressed, parked the car in a nearby lot, and went inside the store. Judy greeted me with a glass of water and the pills, and I sat down in the lounge to take my medicine. Less than five minutes after I arrived, one of the salespersons rushed over to where we were sitting, saying Judy had an urgent call. She hurried to the nearest telephone, and I overheard Judy saying, "Jane is here, she's here right now," as she motioned for me to come to the phone. It was Peggy Hitchcock.

"Jane dear," Peggy said, "I talked to the Tibetan women, and not only do they know your daughter's father, they are her aunt and cousin."

I couldn't believe my ears!!! Peggy went on to say the younger woman, Dr. Dickey Nyerongsha, who had been traveling around the U.S. for six years consulting on Tibetan medicine, wanted to talk with me. Peggy had a telephone number in San Diego where Dickey was working for the next few days. My head was reeling.

All I could say in response was, "Thank you, Peggy, thank you from the bottom of my heart. Can it really be true?"

With telephone number in hand, I raced back to the hotel to call Dickey. When I finally reached her later that afternoon, I kept asking question after question. "Was this the Namgyal Youdon who had been at the Tibetan Children's Village in Dharamsala who had been forced to return to Tibet by an edict from the Chinese Communist government in Lhasa? Is she the Namgyal who had an older brother at TCV when she was there? Would she be about fifteen or sixteen years old now? Did her mother die when Namgyal was a baby?"

Dickey responded, "Yes, it is our Namgyal. She came to live with us when her mother died."

Dickey asked if I had a picture of Namgyal. Namgyal had sent me a school photo from TCV, but it was at home in California. Then I remembered the photograph in *Precious Jewels* of Namgyal and me together the time we first met in Dharamsala. It was blurry because it had been taken from the video, and because I hadn't wanted the Chinese to recognize her if they ever got hold of the book. I told Dickey I'd FedEx a copy to her overnight.

The next day, which happened to be my own mother's eighty-seventh birthday, and just two days after meeting Peggy Hitchcock, Dickey phoned my hotel. She had received the book, and before reading my letter telling her the photograph of Namgyal was on Page 78, Dr. Tinley, Dickey's mother, opened the book to exactly that page and began to cry when she saw the picture. Dickey said, "It is our Namgyal who we raised after her mother died when Namgyal was only nine months old."

After all my searching for Namgyal, it turned out some of her family lived in Berkeley, only a few miles away from my home in Marin County. On Labor Day, I went over to Dickey's apartment and met Namgyal's aunt and cousin for the first time. Shortly after arriving, Dickey picked up a cellular phone, dialed a long series of numbers and, handing the phone to me said, "She's been waiting for your call..."

And in that exquisite moment, through the divine grace of the universe, I was reunited with my Tibetan daughter.

"Namgyal, this is your mom, Jane. I'm so happy to talk with you again." For a moment, I could only hear her softly crying, but finally she spoke. "I'm happy, too, Mom."

We talked for a few minutes, mostly my asking questions about school, her health, and her family. Finally, I asked if her father was there with her, could I speak to him. She immediately called him to the phone. I had been concerned that Namgyal might not have told him about me, and if she had whether or not he would want me to be involved in her life in Tibet.

Namgyal had told him everything. With Dickey translating since her father didn't speak English, I said, "Dr.

Namgang, I would like to continue to be Namgyal's foster mother as I had been when she was at TCV, and I'd like to financially support her education, and help with her daily needs of clothing, food and housing."

Dickey said, "He wants to thank you and says he thinks Namgyal's mother would be happy that she has found a mother like you."

And thus began my renewed relationship with Namgyal Youdon. Over the next five years we forged a bond as deep as any mother-daughter relationship I have known, and we focused primarily on getting the Chinese to issue Namgyal a passport so that she could come to the U.S. which she wanted more than anything in the world. She now had a mother of her own, and I had the daughter I had always wanted. I told her we would never be separated again in this lifetime.

What follows is an "Email Diary" about my relationship with Namgyal beginning at the time she first got internet access in Tibet. It is based on emails I sent out immediately after she died, replies I received from my dear friends, emails from her brothers, Tenzin Tsering in Lhasa, and Tsetan Khensur in Dharmsala, before and after Namgyal's death, and emails that she and I exchanged during the last two years of her life.

For months after Namgyal died, I was unable to talk openly about the sorrow I held in my heart, but I found I could express the depths of my emotions by writing about my experiences. It created a safe place, a sanctuary, a container to hold the pain.

Who could ever have imagined that through the relatively impersonal medium of email I would be able to come to the end of mourning, celebrating the gifts of grief I had received by loving and losing Namgyal Youdon.

CHAPTER ONE

My Daughter

YAHOO! Greetings

Title: Always On My Mind
Brought to you by Bamundo.com   Wednesday 04-17-02 8:30 PM

To: janebay

You're always on my mind. i reaaly miss you a lot. i want to see you
soonn as possible even in my dreams appear you lot.
yours'loving daughter
namgyal

From: Jane Bay
Sent: Wednesday, April 17, 2002 8:42 PM
To: Namgyal Youdon
Subject: Re: I miss you – (email greeting card)

Dearest Namgyal,

Thank you so much for the wonderful email greeting card. It was a very exciting surprise. I am so happy that you now have email access, and I look forward to hearing from you again soon.

You are always on my mind, too, my dear daughter. I have a picture of you on my desk at the office so you are with me every day while I'm working. I've also had the photographs framed that Sandra Lovelace took of you and your family when she was in Tibet with your cousin Dickey during Losar.

I am counting the days, weeks and months until I come to Tibet to see you next year.

Also, I got the gifts and beautiful bags you sent for my family. Dickey gave me the Hi-8 tapes she shot when she was in Lhasa, and I'm having VHS copies made of them. One set for her and one for me, so I will get to see you on video very soon.

I got a telephone calling card and will call you at your auntie's house on Sunday afternoon, May 5. If you can't be there that day, please send an email advising a better day and time to call you.

Sending you all my love, your mom,
Jane

From: Namgyal Youdon
Sent: Wednesday, April 25, 2002 7:34 PM
To: Jane Bay
Subject: Happy Mother's Day

Dear Mom,

I wish you Happy Mother's Day. I miss you so much.

Yours' loving daughter,
Namgyal

From: Namgyal Youdon
Sent: Friday, April 26, 2002 3:56 AM
To: Jane Bay
Subject: hello

Dear Mom,

I'm so sorry today open my net. I knew you sent me email, but my computer got some trouble. I haven't seen what you write so please send me email again. Last time sent some mother's day card in net, did you get it?

Yours' loving daughter,
Namgyal

From: Jane Bay
Sent: Friday, April 26, 2002 10:11 AM
To: Namygal Youdon
Subject: Re: hello

Dear Namgyal,

I did get your Mother's Day card. It was adorable. I like the mother bear and the child bear, like you and me. I showed it to some of my friends at my office.

I am very happy that we can email each other. I'll call you on Sunday, May 5 at 12PM (noon) at your auntie's house. I'm very busy at work now because the new movie (*Star Wars:* Episode II) is opening in theatres in a few weeks. It's a very good movie and I'll send it to you when it comes out on video in December.

You are always in my heart and prayers.

I love you, your mom,
Jane

From: Namygal Youdon
Sent: Friday, April 26, 2002 5:34 PM
To: Jane Bay
Subject: Re: hello

Dear Mom

I'm so glad to receive your reply. Yesterday I was so worried did my email get to you. On this week we had basketball match, our class won, Mom. I'm also a player. On April 30 we go to last match. If we won we are the first class.

I wish you good luck on your job and wish you happy forever.

Yours' loving daughter,
Namgyal

From: Jane Bay
Sent: Friday, April 26, 2002 6:37 PM
To: Namgyal Youdon
Subject: Re: hello

Dearest Namgyal,

This is so cool.... I love getting email from you all the way from Tibet. I'm happy to hear you are playing basketball. I think sports are fun and good exercise, too.

With all my love, your mom,
Jane

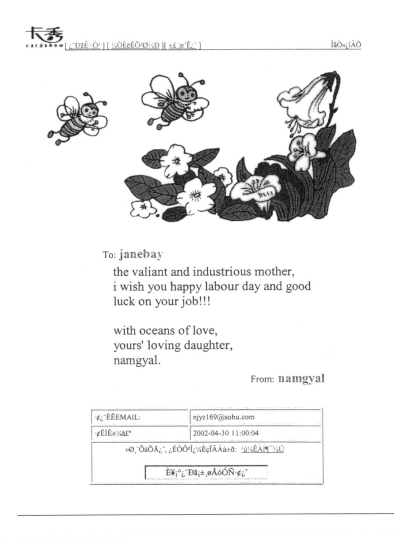

To: **janebay**

the valiant and industrious mother,
i wish you happy labour day and good
luck on your job!!!

with oceans of love,
yours' loving daughter,
namgyal.

From: **namgyal**

·¢¿¨ÈÊEMAIL:	njyz169@sohu.com
·¢ÊÍÉ±¼ä£°	2002-04-30 11:00:04
»Ø¸ÔàÕÅ¿¨, ¿ÉÒÒ²Î¿¼ÈçÏÂÀà±õ: ¡ú¼ÊÀí¶¯¼Ú
È¥¡°¿¨Ðã¡±øÅóÓÑ·¿¨¨

To: janebay

dearest mom,
i wish you happy birthday and have a
nice vacation!!!!

with oceans of love,
yours' loving daughter,
namgyal.

From: namgyal

·¢¿¨ÈÈEMAIL:	njyz169@sohu.com
¢ÊÍÊ±¼ä£°	2002-05-20 18:52:43
»Ø¸ÕåÕÅ¿¨¨, ¿ÉÒÔ²Í¿¼ÈçÏÂÀà±·ð: .ÐÐ»	
È¥¡°¿¨Ðã¡± øÅóÓÑ·¢¿¨¨	

From: Jane Bay
Sent: Monday, May 20, 2002 12:55 PM
To: Namgyal Youdon
Subject: Thank you

Dearest Namgyal,

Thank you for the beautiful birthday card. I had a wonderful birthday.
I celebrated with my friend Shana Chrystie who works at Geographic
Expeditions, the travel company that arranged my first trip to Tibet.
She is organizing my trip to see you next year. I also went to a concert

of guitar music by my friend Ottmar Liebert. I'll send you a CD of his music when Dickey comes to Tibet in July.

I'm leaving on May 25 to go to Santa Fe for a much needed vacation. The last three months have been the busiest work cycle in my 25 years working with George Lucas, and I really need a rest. The *Star Wars* movie *Attack of the Clones* opened last week, and it was very successful, so all the hard work paid off.

I'll send you special prayers from Santa Fe next week on the full moon.

All my love to you, my darling daughter, your mom,
Jane

From: Jane Bay
Sent: Friday, June 21, 2002 9:47 AM
To: Namgyal Youdon
Subject: Greetings from your mom

Dearest Namgyal,

I haven't heard from you lately and hope you are well and happy in school. My work has slowed down, and I am enjoying the summer at Skywalker Ranch. I take a walk for about a half an hour every day around the Ranch. There are many wild animals here. The deer have recently had babies so there are a lot of baby deer with white spots (like Bambi), as well as rabbits, raccoons, possums, ducks and birds. There are bobcats, too, but they don't appear very often, staying mostly in the hills surrounding the Ranch. Hope to hear from you soon.

With all my love, your mom,
Jane

From: Namgyal Youdon
Sent: Monday, June 24, 2002 6:19 AM
To: Jane Bay
Subject: Re: Greetings from your mom

Dearest Mom,

Today I'm so glad to got your email. Few days ago I received Kelly's email and I also replied her. About two weeks later is our final examination. In September, I'll be in second year. Then we can learn the Tibetan medicine. In our first year we hadn't learn medicine, we just learnt the basis of Tibetan language.

Last, I wish you happy forever!!!

With thousands of blessings, yours' loving daughter,
Namgyal

From: Jane Bay
Sent: Tuesday, August 13, 2002 4:33 PM
To: Namgyal Youdon
Subject: Hello

Dearest Namgyal,

It was wonderful to talk to you yesterday. I am so proud of you for getting high scores on your exams. You are such a good student, and I know your education will be a very valuable asset to you in the future.

I am sorry to hear that your father's health is not good. Is he able to continue working, or is he at home? Please tell him that I will say prayers for his health to improve. My health is improving every day, and I think I'm done with all the medical treatments I've needed during the past year. I want to be in very good health when I come to visit you next year.

It has been a very busy summer at work, but my schedule is finally slowing down, and the rest of this year will not be too difficult. George Lucas is hosting a party on August 23 to celebrate my 25th anniversary of working for him. It's hard to believe so much time has passed, but I really enjoy my work and look forward to many more years of service. Maybe in about 10 years I'll retire, which means I will no longer have a job, but will be able to do other work I want to do for myself. I plan to live in Santa Fe, New Mexico when I retire, and there is a room in my house there for you, too.

I'm going to see Anne Millikin when I'm in Santa Fe and will give her something to bring to you when she comes to Lhasa in September. I'll be in New Mexico for a week, then return to California on September 9.

Let me know when I can call you again, and we'll have another visit on the phone before you go back to school. Know that you are always in my thoughts and prayers,

With oceans of love from your mom,
Jane

From: Jane Bay
Sent: Sunday, August 18, 2002 10:50 PM
To: Namgyal Youdon
Subject: Your letter and gifts

Dearest Namgyal,

Thank you so very much for your letter, and for the beautiful bracelets and necklace you sent. Dickey took a picture of me wearing them, and I'll send you a copy. I love the picture of you with the snowman in front of the Potala Palace.

When Dickey and I had dinner together Friday night, it was the first time I had been able to see her because of recent gall bladder surgery, but I want you to know that I am completely recovered now and am in very good health.

We looked at the video from her visit to Lhasa with Sandra and Walt for Losar this year. It made me want to come to see you for Losar next year. Would you like that? I thought it would be better to come to see you when you have your school break, so we can spend the entire two weeks together when I'm there. I'll stay at the Kyichu Hotel, near Dickey's family home, and you can stay with me at the hotel if you want.

Dickey and I talked about you and your family, and I wanted to tell you about some of the things we discussed so you can start thinking about what you want to do in the future.

I gave Dickey money through the Nyerongsha Institute to help your father get an apartment near Dickey's mother's house, and I am sending your tuition ($500) for school through the Nyerongsha Institute as well. When Anne Millikin comes to Lhasa in September, I will send some spending money for you, too.

When we talked last week on the phone, I was very happy to hear that you may be able to get a passport. I hope you will get it soon and that it will be valid for five years. I want you to start thinking about a "Five Year Plan" in relation to your schooling and your coming to the U.S., and what kind of work you want to do, whether it is here or in Tibet or both places. Please think about the following ideas, talk with your father about them, and to Dickey, and then you and I will make our "Five Year Plan."

The first thing I want you to consider is how important it is for you to finish your college studies in Lhasa. Getting a degree from Tibetan Medical College will be a great asset and a benefit to you whatever you decide to do. I also think it is very important for you to be near your father at this time when his health is not so good.

Secondly, I think once you get a passport, we should make a plan for you to come to visit me in the U.S. during a school break, even if it is just for two weeks. What I'd like to propose is that I come to Lhasa to see you for Losar in 2003, and you come to the U.S. during your summer break in August 2003. Then the next year, 2004, and every year until you graduate from Tibetan Medical College, I will either come back to Lhasa, or you can come to the U.S. to visit me.

As soon as you finish your schooling, then you will be able to decide whether you want to work with Dickey doing Tibetan medical consultations here in the U.S., or with the Nyerongsha Institute that she has established to help Tibetans in Tibet. In any case, once you have a degree, you will be in a position to make good decisions about your own future.

You are the most precious person in my life, Namgyal, and what I want more than anything is for you to be happy. I love you so very much! I am looking forward to being with you, and I want you to know that you can live with me whenever you want, and for as long as you want. You will always have a room in my house that is just for you, whenever you want to be there.

Please think about these ideas and let me know how you feel and what you think you want, and then we will make our plans for the future, together.

Good luck when you go back to school in September. It will probably be more challenging as you begin to actually study Tibetan medicine. It was very interesting what your teacher said about learning the Tibetan language first. I am so proud of you, Namgyal.

If you can, please send me an email to let me know you got this letter.

With oceans of love, from your loving mom,
Jane

Namgyal made snowman in front of Potala Palace – Lhasa, Tibet
Photographer: Kelsang Dolma

From: Namgyal Youdon
Sent: Monday, August 19, 2002 5:24 AM
To: Jane Bay
Subject: Coming to visit me

Dearest Mom,

I'm so glad to hear that you'll come to visit me on Losar 2003. I have school break at this time then we can stay together for two weeks. It's so wonderful, Mom. At anytime I get the passport, I want to come U.S.A. and I want to live with you forever. I didn't want to live in Tibet.

Whatever I finished my Tibetan medicine school, I like to study in U.S. If you want to know what I want to work in future, you can plan all. I haven't any suggestions. Most of the Tibetan parents will plan their child's future. If I can get the passport before my graduate, I hope I can do another things, if I can get the passport after my graduate I want to work on Tibetan medicine. Mom, my most desire is come U.S.

soon and I need the foreign education. Whenever I get the passport I'll give you email.

Mom, thank you so so so so so much you do all for me. I shall never forget my foster mother's loving kindness as long as I live. You are the same as my own mother.

I love you forever with thousands of love, yours' loving daughter,
Namgyal

From: Jane Bay
Sent: Monday, August 19, 2002 9:30 AM
To: Namgyal Youdon
Subject: Re: Coming to visit me

I'm so glad you got my letter. For now, it's important for you to focus all your attention on your studies at Mentseekhang (Tibetan Medical College in Lhasa). There are very few jobs for Tibetans in the U.S., but if you have a degree from medical school in Tibet, you would have no problem getting a job here. I know it seems like a long way in the future, but it will go by quicker than you think, especially if you come to the U.S. to visit during your school breaks before you graduate.

When I come for Losar 2003, we'll work out all the details for you to come to the U.S. I love you so very much, and I am so happy that I will be able to see you again.

With love from your mom,
Jane

From: Tenzin Tsering
Sent: Monday, August 19, 2002 6:47 PM
To: Jane Bay
Cc: Namgyal Youdon
Re: Family photos

Dear Mom,

How are you these days? I hope you are in sound health. Today I am attaching some photos of my family. See you soon as possible. Take care your health.

Yours' lovingly,
Tenzin

From: Jane Bay
Sent: Tuesday, August 20, 2002 1:33 PM
To: Tenzin Tsering
Subject: Re: Family photos

Dearest Tenzin,

Thank you so much for sending the beautiful photos of your family. I am so happy to see them. Are both the children your children? Is the older woman your mother-in-law? Please send me the names of everyone in the pictures. Did Namgyal tell you that I'm coming to Lhasa to see her for Losar in 2003? I look forward to meeting you and your family in person at that time.

With much love,
Jane

From: Tenzin Tsering
Sent: Tuesday, August 20, 2002 8:22 PM
To: Jane Bay
Cc: Namgyal Youdon
Subject: thank you so much

Dear Mom,

I received your email this morning and I am so sorry that I didn't mention their name. Both daughters are not mine. One which is elder holding by my wife's mother is child of my wife's sister. One is hold by myself and my wife. The elder daughter is called Tenzin Saldon, mine one is Tenzin Monkyi. Wife name is Sonam Lhakyi, mother-in-law's name is Sonam Chopel.

Today on behalf of brother and myself I really appreciate for your kindness, taking really care and love to my sister Namgyal as same like our mother. We all missed our mom when all were child. I really miss my mom very much, but any where it seems like these time we got a mom. We all are so proud of that.

I thought that you will come in next year maybe. See you on Losar. By the way right now I am working in TIBET POVERTY ALLEVIATION FUNDS based in Boston. Our president is Arthur Holcombe. If you are interesting in my job and if you are not so busy, you can visit our website at www.tpaf.org. I have interesting job in TPAF-NGO microfinance project both in Lhoka and Nakchu. Now I full stop here.

Yours' lovingly,
Tenzin Tsering

From: Jane Bay
Sent: Wednesday, August 21, 2002 10:01 AM
To: Tenzin Tsering
Cc: Namgyal Youdon
Subject: Re: thank you so much

Dear Tenzin,

Thank you for the names of your family. Your wife and baby are very beautiful. I am looking forward to meeting everyone when I come to see Namgyal for Losar.

I have been married twice, but was never able to have children, so I'm happy to have Namgyal as my daughter and to be part of your family, too. It will be wonderful to get to know you all.

My job is very busy right now, but I will take a look at your website when I return from Santa Fe in September. I will be there for a few weeks.

I send all the best good wishes to you. With much love,
Jane

Last year around Thanksgiving when talking to Namgyal on the phone, she said, "Mom, you're going to be a grandmother!" I said, "What?" thinking she had gone and gotten herself knocked up. She said, "Tenzin's wife is pregnant. The baby will be born in December." (She was born on Christmas Day). I realized that because Namgyal considered me her mother, I was her brother's mother as well, and I felt an enormous pride in being accepted into Namgyal's family.

Lhakyi and Tenzin Monkyi—Photographer: Tenzin Tsering

From: Jane Bay
Sent: Wednesday, August 28, 2002 2:26 PM
To: Namgyal Youdon
Subject: Got your greeting card

Dearest Namgyal,

Thank you for the sweet greeting card. I'm glad you got the money. I hope Dr. Tinley told you that $100 was for your father to get a new apartment closer to her house, and the $500 was for your school fees. I'm worried about your father living so far away from Dickey's mother and hope he will be able to find a new place to live soon.

I had lunch yesterday with Dr. Nancy Harris, who has a medical clinic in Lhasa. She created the Tibet Child Nutrition Project and the Terma Foundation that is involved in training Tibetans in western medicine, health care, and nutrition. Dr. Nancy will be returning to Lhasa in October, and I have asked her to contact you at your school. I'd like for you to meet her, and maybe you would be interested in working with her while you're going to Tibetan Medical College in Lhasa as a way to learn about western medicine, too. If not, I thought you would like to meet her anyway because she is one of my best friends. She has been working in Tibet for almost twelve years and only comes to the U.S. a few months of the year to work in an emergency room at a hospital in Palo Alto to earn enough money to fund her projects in Tibet, so I don't get to see her very often.

I'm going to Santa Fe on Saturday, August 31, for a few weeks and will see Ann Millikin there before she comes to Tibet. I have a small gift for you that she'll bring to you in September.

You're probably back in school now, so I wish you good luck in your studies this year and know that you are always in my thoughts and prayers.

Oceans of love to you, my dearest daughter, your loving mother,
Jane

From: Namgyal Youdon
Sent: Saturday, December 7, 2002 6:49 AM
To: Jane Bay
Subject: good news!

Dearest Mom,

I hope you are sound health. I am very well. Today I want tell you good news. I got the Chinese passport. Next week, me and my auntie are going to the U.S. Embassy in Chengdu (China) for the visa. So, I need your help. It would be best you give a phone call or do something else to the U.S. Embassy in Chengdu.

Mom, please don't tell this news to sis Dickey. It's so important. The passport was another man helped me since bro Tsedor hasn't done anything. They waste my four years time. When my English become very good I tell you the detailed things. If you got my email, please tell me your opinions on email reply.

With oceans of love, loving daughter,
Namgyal

From: Jane Bay
Sent: Monday, December 9, 2002 11:37 AM
To: Namgyal Youdon
Subject: Re: good news

Dearest Namgyal,

This is wonderful news. As soon as you get your passport, let me know by email what you want me to do. Maybe you should wait to get your visa from the U.S. Embassy in Chengdu when I come to see you in Tibet.

At that time, we can talk about your first visit to the U.S. in August 2003 during your summer break from school. It is very important that you finish your education at the Tibetan Medical College in Lhasa.

I am eagerly looking forward to seeing you for Tibetan New Year's, and we can plan your future when I get to Lhasa on March 1, 2003.

Oceans of love to you, my dearest daughter, from your mom,
Jane

From: Namgyal Youdon
Sent: Friday, December 13, 2002 1:46 AM
To: Jane Bay
Subject: I need your help

Dearest Mom,

Now I'm already in Chengdu. Today we went to the U.S. Embassy for the visa, but they said it is difficult, so need your help. Please give a phone call to the Embassy. Can you also give me email soon.

With oceans of love, yours' loving daughter,
Namgyal

From: Jane Bay
Sent: Friday, December 13, 2002 11:11 AM
To: Namgyal Youdon
Subject: Information

Dearest Namgyal,

There are many things that need to happen now that you have a passport before the U.S. Embassy will issue you a visa. You will not be able to get a visa until we go through a lot of paperwork to submit an application, and you need a specific reason for coming to the U.S.

I will have to talk to Dickey about this because I need an immigration attorney to help me with the paperwork. She has a good attorney that

I can use. I know how anxious you are to come to see me, but I really think we must wait until I come to Tibet in March to make the final arrangements for you to come.

What I propose is for you to apply for a "Visitor's Visa" to come see your cousin Dickey next summer while you are on school break in August 2003. I'll explain all this to you when I see you in Tibet. We need to make sure that you apply for a reason that you will get approved because we don't want you to get turned down. It would make it more difficult to get a visa in the future if you have been denied.

The option that I think would be the best is to get a "Visitor's Visa" indicating that you will be returning to Tibet to continue your education. That way, every time you have a break from school, for New Year's, and summer break in August, you can come back to the U.S. Once you finish school, we will apply for a "Green Card" for you to stay here, and you can work with Dickey on Tibetan medicine consultations through the Nyerongsha Institute. This way, you will be able to go back and forth between Tibet and the U.S.

Please remember, I will be seeing you in Lhasa in just eleven weeks. In the meantime, I need to talk to Dickey and her attorney to start the application paperwork for your visa.

I love you very much, Namgyal, and want only the best for your future. Please be patient a little longer so that the outcome is most favorable.

With oceans of love from your mom,
Jane

Yahoo! Greetings

Title: Blooming Joys
Brought to you by Yahoo!   Monday, January 6, 2003 11:38 AM

To: jane

dearest mom,
i wish you happy and best wishes in the new year!

with lots of love
loving daughter,

- namgyal

From: Namgyal Youdon
Sent: Tuesday, January 14, 2003 11:47 AM
To: Jane Bay
Subject: Hello!

Dearest Mom,

I came back to Lhasa yesterday. When you have free time give me a call. Please tell me the day and time in email.

Yours' loving daughter,
Namgyal

From: Jane Bay
Sent: Tuesday, January 14, 2003 12:47 PM
To: Namgyal Youdon
Subject: Re: Hello!

Dearest Namgyal,

I'm glad you are back in Lhasa. I'll call you at your auntie's house on Sunday, January 19, at 11:00 AM your time in Tibet.

All my love, your mom,
Jane

From: Jane Bay
Sent: Friday, February 21, 2003 5:30 PM
To: Namgyal Youdon
Subject: Coming to see you soon!

Dearest Namgyal,

Finally, after all these years of anticipation, I will be coming to see you in one week. I arrive on Saturday, March 1, and will be staying at the Kyichu Hotel.

I should arrive at the hotel around 5:30 PM and would like for you to meet me there. If you're not there, I will call your auntie's house as soon as I arrive at the hotel. Let me know if there is another phone number where I can reach you in Lhasa.

This is going to be a dream come true. I am counting the days, hours, and minutes until I can see you.

All my love, your mom,
Jane

From: Namgyal Youdon
Sent: Friday, February 21, 2003 11:07 PM
To: Jane Bay
Subject: Re: Coming to see you soon!

Dearest Mom,

It's really a dream! I'm always counting the days and waiting the date of your coming. I will wait you at the Kyichu Gate on March 1 at 5:30 PM. See you soon Mom!!!!!!!!!!

Yours' loving daughter,
Namgyal

From: Jane Bay
Sent: Sunday, March 2, 2003 11:41 PM
To: Anne Merrifield
Subject: Greetings from Tibet

Dear Anne,

Tashi Delek!!! and Happy Tibetan New Year.

I'm here and very happy. Meeting Namgyal again is indescribably delicious. She's wonderful and is staying with me every moment, we're even sleeping in the same room together. Mother and daughter have bonded beautifully.

On the first day I had terrible altitude sickness, with much throwing up, but Namgyal's Auntie Drakpa made a special tea that cured my upset stomach, and after a restful day yesterday, I am embracing the first day of Tibetan New Year (Losar) with great enthusiasm.

This morning we went to the Jokhang Temple, then to Namgyal's father's house where I met him for the first time. It was really wonderful. Next, we went over to Auntie Drakpa's (where Namgyal is living) for the traditional New Year's meal of pork, boiled radish, a leafy green vegetable, carrots, and something that looked like pickled watermelon rind. It was the best Tibetan food I've ever eaten.

Tonight there's a Tibetan New Year's party at the Kyichu Hotel for all the guests, including the U.S. Consul General to Chengdu, China, who I met yesterday at the hotel. Needless to say, I am having the time of my life.

You can email me here at Namgyal's address anytime. I'd love to hear from you, and if there is any news about Chris, please definitely let me know.

Much love to you, and George, too.
Jane

As soon as I arrived in Lhasa, there was an easiness between us as though we had only been separated for a short period of time, and we picked up our conversation where we left off as a continuation of a relationship, not the beginning of one.

How could I have known her so well from such brief encounters? I think it's partly because we have known each other in many previous lifetimes, and that karmic connection will continue in future lives as well. But also, from the very first moment we met in Dharamsala, we were totally present with each other. It was like the kind of feeling you have when you first fall in love with someone. You let them come into your heart, and have nothing to hide or fear. We knew each other at the level of the soul.

The second night we were together as we were getting ready to go to sleep, Namgyal turned down the covers on my bed. I told her how sweet that was and she said, "Mom, that's what Tibetan children do for their parents." Then she asked if I wanted a massage, and I lay on the bed on my stomach as she began to massage my neck and back. It was such an intimate gesture, and I was a little surprised by it, but her hands were strong and confident as she rubbed my body from head to toe.

"Namgyal, this is great, how did you learn to do massage?"

She told me that massage is taught at Mentseekhang, and she knew she was good at it, so if she didn't become a Tibetan doctor she could always be a massage therapist. She was making a joke, and we both laughed.

I had brought gifts for all Namgyal's relatives that I had given to them at the Kyichu Hotel the afternoon I arrived. Every day during the first week, we went to lunch at the home of one of Namgyal's aunties. These women were actually Namgyal's mother's first cousins but were around the same age as her mother. They had children who were a few years younger than Namgyal so she called them auntie, and their husbands, uncle, and the children, cousin. Auntie Drakpa was the only auntie who was actually Namgyal's mother's younger sister. And Uncle Losoel was her mother's half brother.

By Tibetan standards, Namgyal's family was well-to-do. They all had professional jobs. Some were teachers, some were doctors, one worked in a bank, and an uncle was the principal of the high school that Namgyal attended when she returned from India. Auntie Drakpa was an editor at the recently authorized *Tibet Daily News*, the only Tibetan language newspaper in Tibet. Her job was translating the Chinese news stories into Tibetan.

No one other than Namgyal, and her eldest brother, Tenzin Tsering, spoke English, but somehow with her translating what I said, I got to know them all, including the auntie's eighty-two-year-old grandmother, Dhechen Wangmo. We spent a lot of time with Tenzin Tsering, his wife Lhakyi, and their baby, Tenzin Monkyi. I fell in love with everyone.

I took tons of pictures and, in the afternoon, Namgyal would take the rolls of film to be developed at a photo lab near the Barkhor, the Tibetan market/bazaar that circles the Jokhang Temple in the center of the old part of town. And we'd do some shopping at the various stalls, but only at the Tibetan ones (the Chinese have taken over at least half of them). I'd tell Namgyal what item I wanted to buy, and she'd negotiate the price. However, after a few visits, the shop owners recognized us, and one of them told Namgyal he'd give her a percentage if she'd get me to pay a higher price. She was so incensed, she walked away from the stall, telling me what he said and that we weren't going to buy anything from him ever again.

Every night, we'd have dinner in our room at the Kyichu Hotel and spend the evening talking (she told me the story of her life), looking at the photographs from the day, and on a few occasions we'd watch a DVD of an American film. My friend Wangdu had recently been to Chengdu, China, on vacation with his eleven-year-old son, and he brought back a dozen films on DVD that had been pirated from movie "screeners" that are sent out annually by the Academy of Motion Picture Arts & Sciences for Oscar consideration. He paid about a dollar for each one.

One of the films Wangdu loaned us was *Catch Me If You Can* directed by Steven Spielberg and starring Leonardo DiCaprio. The Kyichu Hotel had a DVD player that they set up in our room, and as Namgyal started to load the movie she said, "Mom, this film was produced and written by George Lucas." When I looked at the packaging for the DVD, I realized that the Chinese had put the movie credits for *Raiders of the Lost Ark* on the *Catch Me If You Can* DVD box.

Namgyal liked the movie, and she liked Leo, too, but she told me that her favorites are Disney movies. "How do you know about Disney films?" I inquired. She said she used to watch them on video all the time in India when she was at TCV (Tibetan Children's Village). She wanted to go to Disneyland when she came to the U.S. Sometime after I returned to California, I noticed in a photograph taken at Namgyal's father's apartment that images of Minnie and Mickey Mouse and other Disney characters were printed on the fabric of the new curtains Namgyal had hung before my arrival.

One day we went to Dickey's mother's house where her brother Tsedor and sister-in-law Lhakpa were having a karaoke party and served American beer, nuts, and several Tibetan snacks. Their friends were all in their late thirties/early forties, and were smartly dressed in western clothes. I was so surprised when Namgyal took a turn with the microphone and belted out several pop American songs. The words were in either English or Chinese.

"Mom, this is how I practiced speaking English. Don't you think I speak better now?"

She even got me to sing a few songs, too; Elvis Presley's "Love Me Tender," the Beatles "Yesterday," and John Denver's "Take Me Home Country Roads." It was so much fun.

Namgyal's English had improved greatly, so much so that she was teaching basic English to eight to twelve year old children on the weekends.

During the second week, we visited monasteries and nunneries around the Lhasa Valley and had a picnic at Yamdrok Tso (lake). Neither Auntie Drakpa nor Namgyal had ever been to Yamdrok Tso, and I wanted to go back to the sacred turquoise lake that holds so many memories from my previous trips to Tibet. I hired a car and driver and Auntie Drakpa prepared a picnic lunch of fried chicken (as good as my Southern mother's recipe), hard-boiled eggs, cooked carrots, and sliced cucumbers. And, of course, the ubiquitous thermos of Tibetan butter tea, and a couple of cans of Coca-Cola for me.

The road to Yamdrok Tso is treacherous. It's a white-knuckle ride up narrow dirt roads strewn with rocks and boulders, winding around mountain after mountain all the way from Lhasa until reaching the top of the Kamba La Pass at 15,724 feet. From there, only a few hundred feet below, is Yamdrok Tso, the breathtaking body of deep blue-green water in the shape of a scorpion.

We stopped at the Kamba-La Pass where travelers and pilgrims for hundreds of years have put up prayer flags that flutter in the winds and where mani shrines (stones stacked on top of each other) have been built and where incense burners have been made for those who cross the Pass to offer prayers. Auntie Drakpa had brought a bag of loose incense leaves (not sticks), some ghee (clarified butter) and matches to make an incense offering. We each placed a few stones on the existing shrine.

Then it was time for a photo op. Auntie Drakpa took a

picture of Namgyal and me standing together at the very spot where the photo on the cover of *Precious Jewels of Tibet* had been taken. The only difference was that now it was late winter, the sky was overcast, and it was unseasonably cold. When we got down to the lake, we found that what had looked like foam on the shore was actually ice crystals. We had our picnic in the Landcruiser, listening to our driver's cassette of Tibetan music, before we began the two and a half hour drive back to Lhasa.

Namgyal had brought some of her personal things, including her photo album, from Auntie Drakpa's house over to the Kyichu Hotel. One night she showed me all the pictures in the album and told stories about the people and places in them. There were mostly photos of her current friends at Tibetan Medical College. She pointed out her best girlfriend, Kelsang Dolma, when they had made snowmen in the park in front of the Potala Palace the previous winter. When we came across a picture of Namgyal and a very handsome young man with his arm around her shoulder, I asked if he was her boyfriend, and she replied he was just a good friend. She went on to say that she was very popular at school and had lots of good friends who are boys as well as girls.

"But do you have a boyfriend?" I prodded.

"Yes, Mom, but you can't tell anyone, not anyone, because we're not allowed to have boyfriends at school. I'd get expelled if anyone found out."

I assured her I wouldn't tell a soul, and she showed me a photo of Sonan Dundul, who was a fourth year student at Mentseekhang. It was a picture of him as he jumped in the air with his arms and legs spread-eagle. She hadn't seen him for several months since school closed for the winter, but they had been emailing each other. He would return to Lhasa while I was there, but Namgyal was too shy to introduce us.

The day before I left Lhasa, I went with Namgyal and Kelsang Dolma to register for the spring semester of their second year at the Tibetan Medical College. As we walked around the campus, Namgyal pointed out the dorm where she lived her first year, the faculty quarters, and classroom buildings. We entered one of the buildings and walked up three flights of stairs to her homeroom that looked like a typical classroom you'd find in an American school, with one jarring exception. Written on the blackboard in colored chalk was a "Loyalty Oath" to the People's Republic of China praising the Communist Party that the students were required to recite every morning before class. It was a sobering reminder of the repressive Chinese occupation of Tibet.

That night in the restaurant at the Kyichu Hotel, I threw a party for all of Namgyal's aunts, uncles, nieces and nephews, and of course, her brother and his family. I also invited Wangdu, who came with his son. My only regret was that Namgyal's father was not well enough to attend. We had gone to visit him that afternoon, and he placed a khata (white blessing scarf) around my neck, thanking me again for taking care of his daughter. He had an oxygen tube in his nostrils, and I knew in my heart that I would not see him again. His apartment butts up against an exterior wall of the Jokhang Temple, and right outside his front door is a view of the roof of the Jokhang. I was dismayed to see a Chinese flag blowing in the wind alongside prayer flags at every corner of the building.

The restaurant prepared a feast of Tibetan and Nepali food, provided us with Budweiser beer, Sprite and Coca-Cola, and Tibetan tea. It was a wonderful dinner with toasts to Namgyal and me. We had put together small photo albums of each family, taken when we visited their homes for lunch, and we gave them out as party favors at the dinner. One of the nephews, Kaltsun, asked me to autograph a photo taken of him pouring Coca-Cola into a champagne glass for me at his family's luncheon. I inscribed it to him saying, "I look forward to seeing you grow up, but you're already a gentleman." I don't know if he understood it or not, but everyone laughed when Namgyal told them what I had written.

After dinner, we went upstairs to the sitting room

adjoining our bedroom. On behalf of the family, Tenzin Tsering made a little speech (in English) that brought tears to my eyes. I looked around the room and several of the relatives were also crying, particularly Auntie Tseyang, one of the aunties of whom I had become especially fond. Tenzin translated my reply in which I thanked them for welcoming me into their family.

One by one, they placed khatas around my neck and presented "going away" gifts, all of which were unique and special. But I was overwhelmed when Auntie Tseyang's husband gave me a large, old prayer wheel that I immediately recognized as the one Grandmother Dhechen Wangmo was using when I met her at their home for lunch.

For a few moments I was speechless and could hardly comprehend the significance of being honored with such a gift. I was told she wanted me to have it.

Finally, I said, "Please tell Grandmother that I will keep her prayer wheel until Namgyal has a daughter. Then, I will give it to my grandchild when she's old enough to understand and I will tell her all about her great-grandmother, Dhechen Wangmo, in Tibet who gave her prayer wheel to me."

Namgyal and I didn't get to bed until almost midnight. Wangdu was coming at four o'clock in the morning to take me to the Gongkor Airport and little sleep was to be had that night. It had been an amazingly intense, exhilarating two weeks, yet even though we were already planning her trip to the U.S. during summer break from Tibetan Medical College, Namgyal and I both became somewhat subdued.

It was still dark when Wangdu knocked on our door the next morning. A porter took my heavy bags, all four of them, to the Landcruiser waiting outside the hotel while I checked out and paid the bill. There was no time for a long goodbye, but before I got in the car, Namgyal placed a khata around my neck. She didn't say a word, but the expression on her face and the look in her eyes said volumes.

"Don't be sad, my darling, I'll see you again very soon."

Namgyal and Jane in manager's apartment at Kyichu Hotel

Tenzin Tsering, Dr. Namgang, Jane and Namgyal

Namgyal, Jane and Auntie Drakpa   *Namgyal in New Years dress*

Jane feeding yak yogurt to Tenzin Monkyi with Namgyal

Dickey's brother, Tsedor, and his wife Lhakpa

Jane and Namgyal toasting

Kaltsun pouring Coca-Cola into champagne glass

Jane with Auntie Sonam, daughter Tsedon, husband Lhoka and Grandmother Dhechen Wangmo

From: Jane Bay
Sent: Monday, March 17, 2003 3:56 PM
To: Namgyal Youdon
Subject: Back in the USA

Dearest Namgyal,

Wanted you to know I arrived safely this morning after a very gruelling flight. I'm so tired I can hardly keep my eyes open, so this will be a short and sweet message.

Getting to know you again was one of the most wonderful experiences of my life. You are a beautiful human being, and I am so thankful that we have been reunited.

Hope school has gotten off to a good start and that you have reconnected with all your friends. More from me later, I must get some rest now.

All my love, your mom,
Jane

From: Namgyal Youdon
Sent: March 18, 2003 3:58 PM
To: Jane Bay
Subject: So happy!

Dearest Mom,

In those few days I had with you I got a chance to tell you all about my sad and happy things just like my best friend and my real mom. Thank you so much my dearest mom.

Know I am beginning my studies again. Yesterday my boyfriend (Dundul) and I had a very nice day!!!

With oceans of love, yours' loving daughter,
Namgyal

From: Namgyal Youdon
Sent: Thursday, March 20, 2003 1:14 AM
To: Jane Bay
Subject: How are you!

Dearest Mom,

How are you? Are you so busy? I'm also so busy. Dundul and I haven't seen each other for three months so at these moments we are always together now. Yesterday we went to Drepung monastary. I teach him English and he helps me on Tibetan medicine.

I miss you so much Mom! My dad is becoming so well and maybe after something months he can go back to work at clinic.

Oceans of love, loving daughter,
Namgyal

From: Namgyal Youdon
Sent: Monday, March 24, 2003 1:22 AM
To: Jane Bay
Subject: I'm so unhappy!

Dearest Mom,

I got some love trouble! I'm so unhappy! One of my friends also loves Dundul so much. I didn't want to lose my friend and also didn't want to lose Dundul. Mom, I love him soooooooo....much! What can I do now?????

Loving daughter,
Namgyal

Dearest Namgyal,

I'm so sorry to hear about your love trouble. The best thing to do in this situation is to talk to Dundul about it. Be open and honest about your feelings. Find out what his feelings are for you. If he also has feelings for your friend, then he will have to choose between you and your friend who he wants as a girlfriend.

It may be painful to hear his answer, but it's better to make a clean break if he has love for another girl. If he chooses the other girl, try to give them your best wishes for their happiness, and hopefully, you can stay friends with them even though your heart may be broken.

It is important to face the situation and work for an honorable outcome. Holding on to love that is lost is a very unhappy situation, and the pain will not diminish until you let go. It won't feel like it, but you will find love again if Dundul goes with the other girl.

Be brave and courageous with your heart, my darling daughter. Please let me know what happens, and know that I love you and hope and pray for your happiness in this matter.

All my love, your mom,
Jane

Dearest Mom,

I'm so glad to tell you that Dundul just loves me! He said he loves me sooooo.... much too. But I'm so sorry to my friend. Have a nice day!

Yours' loving daughter,
Namgyal

From: Jane Bay
Sent: Tuesday, March 25, 2003 10:43 AM
To: Namgyal Youdon
Subject: Re: I'm so happy

Dearest Namgyal,

I'm very happy for you!!! Hopefully, your friend will accept Dundul's choice and you will be able to continue your friendship with her, but at this time, it would be better not to spend too much time with her.

I'll call you this coming Sunday, March 30, around 12 noon in Lhasa. I'm having dinner with Dickey tomorrow night, and we're going to talk about an "internship project" for you with the Nyerongsha Institute of Tibetan Medicine and Culture. Hopefully, we'll have a meeting with the immigration attorney within the next two weeks to start the application process. Please let me know just as soon as you can the dates of your summer break this year.

I miss you so much and think about our wonderful visit every day. Please give my love to all your aunties, especially Auntie Drakpa, your uncles and cousins. I can never repay their kindness from when I was in Lhasa visiting you.

With oceans of love from your mom,
Jane

From: Namgyal Youdon
Sent: Sunday, March 30, 2003 11:16 PM
To: Jane Bay
Subject: So sorry!

Dearest Mom,

I am so sorry that I haven't open my email for long time! My auntie told me that you gave me call, but on that day I had examination because, at the time of exam I went to Chengdu. I am so well! I miss you so much! Take care yourself!

Oceans of love, loving daughter,
Namgyal

___

From: Jane Bay
Sent: Monday, March 31, 2003 1:55 PM
To: Namgyal Youdon
Subject: Re: So sorry!

Dear Namgyal,

I understand and thought that might have happened. Next time I will wait for you to reply to my email to confirm that you will be home before I call. It's not a problem. Let me know how you did on your exam when you get the results. Hope it wasn't too difficult.

My friend Chris Michie died last Thursday, March 27. It was a quiet and peaceful death. His wife, Deborah, and their twenty-two-year-old daughter, Claire, are having a wake for him on Sunday, April 6 and I am helping them with the party. It will be a celebration of Chris' life. We will have good food and drink with all his friends.

I'm finally over that cold I got in Lhasa, and I'm beginning to feel rested. I will take care, and you take care of yourself, too.

All my love, your mom,
Jane

From: namgyal youdon
Sent: Saturday, May 17, 2003 11:19 PM
To: Jane Bay

MOM,

HAPPY BIRTHDAY TO YOU !

lovesss namgyal.

漫画签名:

做自己的卡通签名，去搜狐漫画宝

注册搜狐短信收藏家，肯德基优惠券等你拿
搜狐新闻中心，报道前线不断线
搜狐短信美伊战报，快如闪电！ 写短信XW，发到6666（移动用户）或9666（联通用户）

From: Namgyal Youdon
Sent: Sunday, May 18, 2003 9:50 AM
To: Jane Bay
Subject: Happy Birthday (Singing-Animated email greeting card)

Dearest Mom,

I wish you Happy Birthday! Happy Forever!

HAPPY BIRTHDAY TO YOU,
HAPPY BIRTHDAY TO YOU,
HAPPY BIRTHDAY DEAR MOMMY,
HAPPY BIRTHDAY TO YOU!

Yours' loving daughter,
Namgyal

Dearest Namgyal,

Thank you, darling, for the sweet birthday messages. I had a wonderful birthday yesterday. I slept late, got up and played with my new cat, planted new flowers in the garden for summer which has finally arrived in California, and then went to the ballet and out to dinner with my friend, Shana Chrystie. It was a happy birthday.

I am on a medically monitored diet, and have lost 15 pounds since I returned from Tibet. I am doing light yoga every morning, and I feel great.

About a month ago I got a new cat. I think I told you Keyboard died, and I've wanted to get another cat for a long time, but I didn't want to get one when I was traveling so often. When I came back from seeing you, I thought it was a perfect time because I'll be home most of the summer, except for two weeks in August when I'll be in Santa Fe. Shana will stay at my house here for those two weeks, and Marmalade really likes her so he won't miss me too much. His official name is "Mr. White Bread N. Marmalade" because he has white and orange fur. Orange is the color of the jam/preserves made from orange rind that is called marmalade, so I just call him Marmalade for short. He is the sweetest boy cat I've ever known. I got him from the Marin Humane Society, a shelter for stray animals, and he is two years old. I'll try to send you a picture of him via email.

Do you know when your summer break is scheduled? Please let me know as soon as possible so Dickey and I can start the paperwork. I would really like for you to come in August, even if it is for just a week or ten days, so let's try to work on that, and a longer visit during your winter break. We'll try to get a multiple visa entry for you that is good for six months, I think.

When you have time, tell me all about school and how things are going with your friend. How did you do on your winter exam?

You are always in my heart and prayers,
With oceans of love from your mom,
Jane

From: Jane Bay
Sent: Wednesday, May 28, 2003 6:16 PM
To: Namgyal Youdon
Subject: How are you doing in school?

Dearest Namgyal,

I have news about applying for your visa to visit the U.S. this summer. Please let me know the dates of your summer break from medical school as soon as possible.

I will make an appointment for you for a visa interview at the U.S. Consulate in Chengdu as soon as we get all the necessary information and letters prepared. Auntie Drakpa should take you to Chengdu for the appointment. You will be applying for a B-2 Visitor Visa, not through the Nyerongsha Institute as I mentioned before.

I will write a letter to sponsor your visit, and Dickey will write a letter to request that you be permitted to come to the U.S. with her in August 2003 for a brief visit during your summer break from medical school. We will need to give the date you will return to Tibet to continue your education.

We will need a letter from your father or Dr. Tinley stating that they are your relatives and that you are expected to return to Tibet. You must also provide documentation of your family's financial situation. They need to know that your family is financially able to take care of you in Tibet.

You will also need a letter of recommendation from Auntie Drakpa (in Chinese) saying she works for the *Tibet Daily Newspaper*, and that you live with her during the week while you're going to Tibetan Medical College, and with your father on the weekends. The important information is that you will be returning to China in September to continue your education at the Tibetan Medical College in Lhasa.

You and Auntie Drakpa will take these letters, your passport, and your birth certificate to the U.S. Consulate in Chengdu for your appointment. I will fax my invitation/sponsorship letter and Dickey's letter to the consular officer in Chengdu that I have been referred to by a woman I met at the New Year's party at the Kyichu Hotel.

Please let me know as soon as possible if you want to proceed with applying for a visa to visit the U.S. this summer.

All my love to you and your family, your mom,
Jane

From: Jane Bay
Sent: Sunday, June 8, 2003 12:25 PM
To: Tenzin Tsering
Subject: Message for Namgyal

Dear Tenzin,

Please tell Namgyal to check her emails. I have urgent information about her visa application. Have not received a reply to either email address. Need to communicate with her as soon as possible. Thanks for your help.

Sending you and your family oceans of love.
Jane

From: Tenzin Tsering
Sent: Wednesday, June 11, 2003 2:47 AM
To: Jane Bay
Subject: Re: Message for Namgyal

Dear Mom,

I am very sorry to reply you as I just open my email today due to very unfortunate and sad situation that our father has passed away this Monday, June 9.

So we are so busy and I think Namgyal can't visit you this summer in States. Tomorrow is the day for the sky burial at 5:00 AM. We try our best to brought our father to the Emergency Center but no chance to save. We try to call you but no connection was success. But be calm and do the best to worship and prayer whatever necessary be done for our father. H.H. Bless. Call back to us soon as possible.

Yours' child,
Tenzin

"All great beings of the past have died;
Buddhas and Bodhisattvas, saints and kings alike.
The righteous as well as the sinful, all must one day
    face death.
How can you be any different?"
    —Konchok Dronme
    "Conversations With An Old Man"

From the late 1700s through the early 1900s, the British sent military expeditions into Tibet in the interest of expanding the Empire and controlling Tibet as a buffer zone between India and China. Reports sent back to England describe the Tibetan people as primitive, especially in regard to the treatment of the recently deceased.

Having no understanding of Tibetan Buddhism and culture, the English found the practice of sky burial particularly barbaric.

Yet from a Tibetan point of view, it is a natural process in the cycle of life, death, and rebirth. Also, since the Tibetan plateau is pretty much solid rock, the ability to dig a grave is simply not an option. The deceased, wrapped in white cloth or prayer scarves, is carried on the back of a monk to the top of a steep slope or mountain to an "offering site." Tibetans believe that one should benefit other beings at every stage of one's life. Since our bodies are what we are most attached to, offering one's body carries the greatest merit.

Sky burial is actually not an accurate description, and in *Tibet: Reflections from the Wheel of Life*, Carroll Dunham and Ian Baker describe what takes place during a sky funeral:

> At the top of the ridge, on a platform of stones encircled by prayer flags, the tomden, or yogin-butcher, unwraps the body and slices it from head to toe, exposing the underlying flesh and bones. Drawn by the smoke from a juniper fire and the smell of fresh meat, huge vultures begin to gather on the surrounding rocks. The deceased person's friends and family add handfuls of purifying juniper needles to the smoldering incense burner; the fragrant smoke rises as an ephemeral link between the human world and the world of unseen spirits. The majestic vultures—thought by Tibetans to be manifestations of flesh-eating dakinis—glide down from the high ridges and surrounding rocks and dance restlessly around the tomden and the unveiled corpse.
>
> "Shey, shey" (eat, eat), shouts the tomden, stepping back off the stone platform with his flaying knife. The birds descend, enveloping the dead person's body in a frenzy of dark, shifting wings. Like

71

a Bodhisattva shaman, the tomden goes back in amid the vultures and begins to dismember the skeleton, throwing arm and leg bones to the ravenous birds. Then, with a stone mallet he pulverizes the remaining bones. Reciting mantras he takes the skull and crushes it with a large rock. He mixes the brain and powdered bones with tsampa flour and again invites the birds to feast. Soon there is nothing left; only the wisps of smoke from the juniper fire drifting across the bare stones. The birds of appetite fly heavily to the crest of the ridge to digest, then slowly, one by one or in pairs, they soar off into the heavens – black shapes fading against a pale, unending sky.

Offering ourselves unequivocally in death and in love we overcome the delusions of self-clinging that keep us spinning on the wheel of life. Free of the gravity of entrenched attachments and fixed beliefs we soar unencumbered in the cloudless sky of our intrinsic nature, reuniting with what the Bonpos (followers of the Bon religion, the indigenous faith of the Tibetan people) call the "Great Mother of Infinite Space" – the source of all creativity and manifestation of all birth and death.

Tibetans say that everyone should witness a sky funeral at least once. It brings home the transience and impermanence of life, urging us not to waste the precious opportunity afforded by a human life.

"When one realizes that life is the expression of death and death is the expression of life, that continuity cannot exist without discontinuity, then there is no longer any need to cling to one and fear the other."
—Chogyam Trungpa

From: Jane Bay
Sent: Wednesday, June 11, 2003 11:02 AM
To: Tenzin Tsering
Subject: Re: Message for Namgyal

Dearest Tenzin,

I am very sorry to hear this sad news. I will say prayers for your father for his passage through the Bardo, and will ask all my teachers and friends to pray for him, too.

Please tell Namgyal I pray for her and you and everyone in your family. I am so grateful that I had the opportunity to meet your father.

All my love to you and Namgyal, your mom,
Jane

From: Jane Bay
Sent: Wednesday, June 11, 2003 5:55 PM
To: Namgyal Youdon
Subject: With Deepest Sympathy

Dearest Namgyal,

I was so very sad to hear that your father had passed away. My heart aches for you, my beloved daughter, and I wish I were with you to hold you in my arms, and comfort you at this terrible moment in time. I am thankful that I was able to meet your father when I was in Tibet, and I was very fond of him. He welcomed me with a loving heart into your family, and I will be forever grateful that he accepted me as your mother. I am honored to have known him if ever so briefly.

When I got Tenzin's email about your father's sky burial, I calculated what time it would be here in California, and I walked down to the small lake at Skywalker Ranch to say prayers for him. I sat in a chair on the dock and as I was meditating, several fish jumped up out of the water and splashed around where I was sitting. There were many birds chirping, and it was a very calming and beautiful meditation.

I called several of my spiritual friends here in the U.S. and asked them to offer prayers for your father's transition through the Bardo. I will make an altar for him at my house tonight, and offer prayers for him every night through the forty-ninth day from his passing.

Tenzin gave me telephone numbers to try tonight. I hope to talk to you very soon.

All my love, my dearest daughter, from your mom,
Jane

Namgyal and her father—Photographer: Jane Bay

From: Jane Bay
Sent: Thursday, June 12, 2003 12:25 PM
To: Tsetan Khensur
Subject: Your Father

Dearest Tsetan Khensur,

I was so sad to hear from Tenzin Tsering and Namgyal Youdon that your father had passed away on Monday. Fortunately, I was able to meet him in Lhasa when I visited Namgyal for Tibetan New Year's in March. He welcomed me into your family, and I am grateful for his blessing to be Namgyal's mother. I am thankful to have met him, but I'm very sad that he is gone.

Your father's passing will be very difficult for Namgyal to accept. Tenzin Tsering said he will take care of her, but I know he is also suffering at this time.

Please accept my sincere condolences. Your father will be in my prayers during the forty-nine day transition in the Bardo.

With great love and compassion for you and your family, I remain,

Sincerely yours, your mom,
Jane

From: Jane Bay
Sent: Friday, June 13, 2003 10:31 AM
To: Dear Friends
Subject: Namgyal's Father

Dear Friends,

Some of you know that the father of my Tibetan daughter, Namgyal Youdon, passed away on Monday, June 9, in Lhasa, Tibet. I am so thankful that I went to Tibet when I did and was able to meet him. He welcomed me into his heart and family, and it was especially meaningful that he acknowledged me as Namgyal's mother.

I spoke to Namgyal earlier this week, and she is devastated by her father's death, as is her eldest brother, Tenzin Tsering, who is also in Tibet.

I wanted to share the beautiful email I received from Namgyal's brother, Tsetan Khensur, who has been studying in India for many years. He is currently in Dharamsala at Mentseekhang (the Tibetan Medical College) studying to be a doctor, following in the footsteps of his father, and grandfather before him.

Dear Jane,

You might have heard the bad news of my dad's passing away and I always consider it as the worst thing that I have to face in my life. I was informed about it just after finishing the exam. If I was informed earlier, I think I could not have done well. What I am sorry the most is that I could not serve him and make sure there is nothing to worry about me at the moment of his last breath because every parent wants their children to be able to stand on their own feet with dignity. I feel unfortunate that I could not tell him not to worry about me.

At the most, I am very worried about my sis Namgyal as so far she could not stand on her own feet and she hasn't completed her studies yet so I am requesting you to help her and she needs your love and care especially at this very awful moment of her life.

With regards,
Tsetan

Please keep these precious children in your heart and prayers.

With love and gratitude,
Jane

Tsetan Khensur and Tibetan flag—Dharamsala, India

From: Nancy Harris
Sent: Friday, June 13, 2003 11:00 AM
To: Jane Bay
Subject: Re: Namgyal's Father

Dear Jane,

I'm so sorry to hear this, and also so glad that you were able to meet and acknowledge each other in this lifetime!

With fondest regards,
Nancy

From: Laurent Bouzereau
Sent: Friday, June 13, 2003 11:53 AM
To: Jane Bay
Subject: Namgyal's Father

My Dearest Jane,

I had no idea and Markus and I want to send you and Namgyal our deepest sympathy. How wonderful that you got to know him. We're on our way to France and there is this church I always go to on my trips. I will burn a candle in his name so that our prayers and celebration of this great man are heard from different continents.

We send you and your daughter all of our love,
Laurent and Markus

From: Jane Bay
Sent: Friday, June 13, 2003 11:57 AM
To: Laurent Bouzereau
Subject: Re: Namgyal's Father

Thank you so very much, Laurent. I am grateful to you and Markus for your prayers, especially coming from France which I love so dearly myself.

Love,
Jane

From: Tsetan Khensur
Sent: Sunday, June 15, 2003 7:39 AM
To: Jane Bay
Subject: Thank you very much

Dear Jane-la,

Thank you so much for your concern and I am so much released in knowing your kindness and geniune committment for helping my sis Namgyal. I am very grateful to you and hope I can do something for you in return for your concern.

I did every possible thing that I can do for my father's soul and visited every monastery in Dasa for prayers. I hope my prayers could pay a little bit in lieu of every hardship that he took for all three of us. Your help and concern for our family will be remembered forever.

With love and gratitude,
Your Tsetan

When I first talked to Tenzin Tsering and Namgyal after learning about their father's death, Namgyal was unable to speak. She cried throughout the entire phone call. I felt so helpless. I wanted to reach out and touch her, to comfort her and reassure her that she would be okay and that I would take care of her, but how could I, being halfway around the world. I urged Namgyal to talk to her boyfriend, Sonam Dundul, about her father's death, and to let him comfort her. She promised she would.

We spoke on the phone several other times in the following days, and by the end of the second week, her spirits had lifted. She was ready to go back to school.

During one conversation, I said, "Namgyal, I want to have a "mother/daughter" talk with you, and since I'm not in Lhasa to take care of you, we'll have to do it over the phone. It's about sex and money." I heard a little laugh on the other end of the line.

I explained that in the U.S., there are usually two thoughts about young men and women having sex. One thought is that they should wait until they get married to have sexual relations; the other is that if you have sex before marriage, it should be "safe sex," meaning the man would use a condom. I asked if she knew what that was, and she said she did. I told her it was her choice, and I didn't want to dictate what she did, but if she decided to have sex with Dundul, would she promise to have safe sex.

"Yes, Mom, but you don't have to worry about that."

I don't know if she meant she'd have safe sex or that she wouldn't have sex at all, but it was a very matter-of-fact response, and there was no awkwardness about the conversation whatsoever.

Dr. Namgang had been unable to work at the family Tibetan medical clinic during the last six months of his life, and his financial resources were depleted. I asked Namgyal to set up an account at the Bank of China in Lhasa. As soon as that was done, I would begin to wire transfer money to her account once a month to pay for her school, food and clothing, and, of course, her airline tickets to the U.S. in July. She was already living at Auntie Drakpa's apartment, and I felt confident that she would be well cared for, but I wanted to enable her to become self-sufficient and independent. She seemed relieved by our talk.

From: Namgyal Youdon
Sent: Tuesday, June 17, 2003 3:43 AM
To: Jane Bay
Subject: This is my new bank book

BANK NAME: BANK OF CHINA TIBET BRANCH
BANK ADDRESS: NO 28 LINKUO WEST ROAD LHASA
BANK SWIFT CODE NO: XXXXXXXXXXXX
NAME: NAMGYAL YOUDON ACCOUNT NO: XXXXXXXXX
ID NO: XXXXXXXXXXXXXX

From: Jane Bay
Sent: Tuesday, June 17, 2003 11:03 AM
To: Namgyal Youdon
Subject: Re: This is my new bank book

Dearest Namgyal,

Very good. I will wire transfer $500 U.S. dollars to your account this week. I will let you know the day the transfer is made.

Hope you are doing okay now that you are back in school. Please remember my advice about letting Dundul help you at this sad time in your life.

I have set up an altar for your father and put the picture of you and him on it. I'll keep the altar for the forty-nine days during his transition. You are always in my heart and prayers.

With oceans of love, your loving mom,
Jane

From: Jane Bay
Sent: Tuesday, June 17, 2003 11:40 AM
To: Namgyal Youdon
Subject: You will heal

Dearest Namgyal,

I heard a song by a musician named Stuart Davis and wanted to share it with you in hopes it will comfort you because of the loss of your father. If you would like to know more about him, his website is www.stuartdavis.com and you can also hear some of his music at that website.

Know that you are loved, my darling daughter, by your mom,
Jane

You Will Heal
Song written by Stuart Davis

Now believe me, you will heal
forever's not this hurting that you feel
you cannot see inside yourself what others do
but there's a stronger source of hope inside of you

And we all wish that we could take
away the human reasons for your ache
you may not see through all this dark how people care
but we're all pleading for your happiness in prayer

So know you're loved, and all this while
we are poorer from the absence of your smile
our deepest wish would guarantee
to see your heart as well as it may be

And when that heart comes out of hiding
and the suffering starts to ease
may your joy become contagious
so that others too may see

That the pain is not eternal, but the human spirit is
and no love's more real than one that heals
with the hope that it can give.

From: Jane Bay
Sent: Tuesday, July 1, 2003 2:52 PM
To: Namgyal Youdon
Subject: Need to talk with you

Dearest Namgyal,

I called at your father's number on Sunday, June 30, and a woman said you were not there. I need to talk to you about getting your visa to come to the U.S. for your visit in August.

All my love, your mom,
Jane

From: Namgyal Youdon
Sent: Thursday, July 3, 2003 5:40 PM
To: Jane Bay
Subject: Re: Need to talk with you

Dearest Mom,

I'm so sorry that I haven't sent you email. Our final examination will be starting from next week so I haven't got free time to send you email. Know I'm becoming better and I'm staying with Auntie Drakpa.

Mom, I just have twenty days summer vacation and it's from July 28 to August 17. So I must go back to school on August 17. Could you call me on July 12 at noon? I'll be at Auntie Drakpa's house.

With oceans of love, yours' loving daughter,
Namgyal

From: Jane Bay
Sent: Thursday, July 3, 2003 11:37 AM
To: Namgyal Youdon
Subject: Re: Need to talk with you

Dearest Namgyal,

Yes, I'll call you on Saturday, July 12, at 12 noon at Auntie Drakpa's house. If you still want to come to the U.S., we'll work it out for you to fly from Chengdu by yourself if you get a visa. It's not a problem for you to come for a short visit. I'll start making all the arrangements immediately.

Good luck on your final examinations.

All my love, your mom,
Jane

From: Jane Bay
Sent: Sunday, July 6, 2003 6:30 PM
To: Fu Ching
Subject: Namgyal Youdon

Dear Fu Ching,

I am faxing you the following documents to present to the U.S. Consulate regarding the visa application for Ms. Namgyal Youdon:

1. Invitation Letter from Jane Bay
2. Invitation Letter from Dr. Dickey Paldon Nyerongsha
3. Namgyal Youdon Passport and Identification Card
4. Namgyal Youdon Notarized Birth Certificate (3 pages)
5. Wire Transfer Confirmation: Namgyal Youdon's account at Bank of China/Lhasa Branch

Namgyal will bring her passport, I.D. card, and birth certificate when she comes to Chengdu on Monday, July 28. Please let me know if there is anything else you need for Namgyal's visa application.

Looking forward to hearing from you soon, and thank you again, Fu Ching, for all your help.

Warmest regards,
Jane

From: Jane Bay
Sent: Thursday, July 10, 2003 5:28 PM
To: Namgyal Youdon
Cc: Fu Ching
Subject: Your trip to the US

Dearest Namgyal,

I hope you are doing well on your final examinations at school and are getting ready to come to the U.S.

I have been working with Mr. Fu Ching to help get a visa for you. He has scheduled an interview for you with the appointment secretary, Ms. Yu Jun, at the U.S. Consulate in Chengdu on Monday, July 28, at 1:00 PM.

You will need to show her your Passport, I.D. card, and your birth certificate. Fu Ching will give you copies of the invitation letters from Dickey and me that you must also give to Ms. Yu Jun. If you have a registration notice or document showing that you will start school again on August 18, you should bring that for your interview as well.

Today I wire transferred another $500.00 U.S. dollars into your bank account at the Bank of China/Tibet Branch so you will have enough money on hand to pay some of your expenses for your flight. You will need to contact Wangdu at Wind Horse Travel in Lhasa to pay for your roundtrip tickets for Lhasa/Chengdu/Lhasa. I will email him the flights and he will issue you these tickets, but you need to pay him for them. I will pay Fu Ching for the international flights.

I'd like to get a ticket for Auntie Drakpa to go with you to Chengdu on Monday, July 28, so she can go with you to the U.S. Consulate for your interview. She should go with you to the airport on Tuesday, July 29, for your flight to Beijing/San Francisco, then she could return to Lhasa at her convenience. I'll ask Wangdu to issue her tickets, too, which you will also need to pay for before you leave Lhasa.

Will you be able to stay overnight in Chengdu with Auntie Drakpa's friends that you stayed with last December when you got your passport? If not, I'll ask Fu Ching to get you a hotel room. He will meet you at the airport, and take you and Auntie Drakpa to the U.S. Consulate for your visa interview.

Fu Ching will take you to the airport on Tuesday morning, July 29, for your flight to Beijing. He will also arrange for someone to meet you at the airport in Beijing and transfer you to the international terminal for the flight to San Francisco. Fu Ching will arrange the same services on your return flights in August. You will have to pay an airport tax in Chengdu and Beijing. Fu Ching will explain all this to you when you arrive in Chengdu. Following is your itinerary:

Monday, July 28 - Leave Lhasa on CH4402 at 10:25; arrive Chengdu 12:10.

Tuesday, July 29 - Leave Chengdu on 3U141 (Sichuan Airline) at 07:50; arrive Beijing 10:05. Leave Beijing at 12:45 on CH985; arrive in Shanghai/Pu Dong 14:45 (change planes). Leave Shanghai/Pu

Dong at 16:05 on CH985 (same flight number). Arrive San Francisco at 12:15 (same day) on Tuesday, July 29.

Thursday, August 14 - Leave San Francisco on CH986 at 14:20; arrive Beijing 17:05 on Friday, August 15.

Friday, August 15 - Leave Beijing at 19:35 on CH4106; arrive Chengdu at 22:00. You will have to stay overnight in Chengdu.

Saturday, August 16 – Leave Chengdu on CH4401 at 07:20; arrive Lhasa at 09:10.

I'm so excited about your coming to the U.S. even if it is a short visit.

All my love, your mom,
Jane

From: Jane Bay
Sent: Friday, July 18, 2003 11:35 AM
To: Namgyal Youdon
Subject: Call Wangdu to get tickets

Dearest Namgyal,

I received an email from Wangdu at Wind Horse. He needs to talk to you or Auntie Drakpa to get your airline tickets for Monday, July 28. Please call him on his cell phone as soon as possible.

I'll call you Saturday, July 26, at 12:00 PM Lhasa time to go over the final details about your trip.

Love you, darling, your mom,
Jane

The flower arrangement on the coffee table in my office at Skywalker Ranch that week was especially beautiful: garden roses the color of apricots, white freesias, and variegated mock orange. As our assistant, Anne, began her Friday routine of gathering up the vases to empty them before closing the office for the weekend, I thought how fortunate I was to be surrounded by the exquisite fragrance of fresh flowers in my workplace.

It was almost six o'clock when I noticed an email had arrived from Tenzin Tsering, Namgyal's brother in Lhasa.

From: Tenzin Tsering
Sent: Friday, July 18, 2003 5:42 PM
To: Jane Bay
Subject: Namgyal

Dear Mom,

Please relax your mind and I am going to tell you a very unbelievable sad situation. Actually Namgyal is preparing for coming to States as soon as possible. But unfortunately yesterday very early morning she is taking a shower before going to take examination. But no one believe that she would fall in the shower room and passed away. Also Auntie Drakpa cannot know that she has fallen in the shower because she is in the bed asleep. She found later when she suspected that Namgyal is not coming out from the shower. But that is her Karma.

Yours' child,
Tenzin and all family

I felt a wave of nausea sweep over me and I became completely disoriented. A current of electrical energy struck like a bolt of lightning, searing my central nervous system, propelling me into an altered state of consciousness outside my physical body. I could hear myself screaming,

"No, No, No – this can't be true!!!"

Instinctively, I hit Reply on the email.

From: Jane Bay
Sent: Friday, July 18, 2003 5:52 PM
To: Tenzin Tsering
Subject: Re: Namgyal

Tenzin,

PLEASE TELL ME THIS ISN'T TRUE

Jane

I hit Send and tried to reread the email, but my vision was blurred by the tears pouring from my eyes. Anne ran to my side, and after reading the message herself, simply put her arms around me. Crumpled over in pain, my body shaking, hardly able to breathe, I sobbed uncontrollably for some time.

I couldn't believe it. It was utterly incomprehensible!!! Namgyal dead, ten days before coming to the U.S. for the first time. How could this have happened?

Namgyal had been living at her Auntie Drakpa's house since her father died. I dialed her phone number, knowing Tenzin would be there. No one other than Tenzin in Namgyal's mother's family spoke English, but they all knew me from having visited Namgyal in Lhasa during the Tibetan New Year celebrations in March.

I grew intensely more agitated when the international phone lines were busy. It took about ten minutes to get through, but it felt like an interminable amount of time.

Thirty thousand miles away, a woman answered the phone, and very quickly I heard Tenzin's voice on the other end of the line. I couldn't stop crying.

"Don't be sad, Mom, Namgyal can hear you. Say prayers for her, this is her Karma."

That was impossible to accept. I wanted facts. I wanted to know exactly what had happened. Had she slipped and fallen, was the water still running in the shower? Was there blood, a bump on the head? What was the cause of death, did she suffer? I wondered if there had been any warning signs, but autopsies are not part of Tibetan medical practices. Namgyal was dead, and what was important to her family at that moment was helping her with prayers for a quick and peaceful journey through the Bardo, the stages between death and rebirth as defined in *The Tibetan Book of the Dead (Liberation Through Understanding In The Between)*.

Namgyal and I had talked five days before she died, to finalize the plans for her trip to the U.S. She was busy studying for final examinations in her second year at medical school. She had a bad cold. We joked about her taking amoxicillin, a prescription antibiotic drug that can be purchased over the counter in Tibet (China). Namgyal had bought amoxicillin for me when I came down with a sinus cold in Lhasa during New Years, after the Tibetan medicine pills prescribed by her Uncle Losoel hadn't worked.

Tenzin had few answers to my barrage of questions. Namgyal had fainted on the street one morning earlier in the week during her walk to school. Someone brought her back to Auntie Drakpa's house, but she seemed to be okay and later went to class. I didn't know what to make of it.

Her mother had died from a brain aneurysm when

Namgyal was only nine months old. Her mother was twenty-nine years old when she passed away. Namgyal was twenty-two. I remembered Namgyal telling me that her mother had headaches and a bad heart, and that she did, too. Namgyal was such a strong and vibrant girl it never occurred to me that she might be in any danger or vulnerable, even though she had a bad headache while I was in Lhasa. I mentioned that I suffered from chronic headaches as well, that I attributed it to stress. Maybe Namgyal died of a brain aneurysm, just like her mother. I will never know for certain.

Grabbing at every straw of information I could coax out of Tenzin, I found little comfort in his comments. I asked Tenzin to send Uncle Losoel out to buy the freshest, most beautiful flowers he could find, and place them on Namgyal's chest to cover her with an offering of flowers from me. Namgyal's body had been placed on her bed in Auntie Drakpa's house where she would be surrounded by family and friends, praying and lighting butter candles until the fourth day when she would be taken to the Jokhang Temple, the most sacred temple in Tibet. After one circumambulation around the temple, Namgyal would be carried to a monastery northeast of Lhasa for her sky burial. I could hardly bear the thought of it.

The Dalai Lama wrote in the foreward to Robert Thurman's translation of *The Tibetan Book of the Dead*:

> *We Tibetans have a reputation of being very spiritual, though we usually consider ourselves quite down-to-earth and practical. So we think of our systematic study and analysis of the human death process as a cautious and practical preparation for the inevitable. After all, there is not a single one of us who is not going to die, sooner or later. So how to prepare for death, how to undergo the death process with the least trauma, and what comes after death—these are matters of vital importance to every one of us. It would be impractical of us not to*

study these issues with the greatest of care and not to develop methods of dealing with death and the dying in a skillful, compassionate, and humane way.

I had been studying Tibetan Buddhism for over a dozen years, I knew what this was all about, but my mind was whirling in confusion and despair. I was Namgyal's American mother, and I had to find my own way of dealing with her death.

CHAPTER TWO

Prayers for Namgyal

The first phone call I made after talking to Tenzin Tsering was to Namgyal's cousin, Dr. Dickey Palden Nyerongsha, in Berkeley. Then I called my sister, Kitty Courcier, in Chico, and my meditation teacher, Yvonne Rand, as well as several other close friends. George Lucas, for whom I've worked since the original *Star Wars* movie was released in 1977, was in Australia shooting the last film in the saga, but I sent word to him through Sarita Patel, my friend and colleague on George's personal staff.

I could barely utter the words, but through my tears, managed to tell them the terrible news. Needless to say, everyone was shocked. Yvonne told me how to set up an altar for Namgyal, and she said to include pictures of Amitabha, the Buddha of the Western Realm, and Four-Armed Avalokiteshvara, the Bodhisattva of Compassion. The Dalai Lama is the living embodiment of the Bodhisattva of Compassion.

Yvonne said to make offerings at Namgyal's altar as often as possible during the first three days after Namgyal's death and she emphasized the importance of reciting the mantra of compassion, Om Mani Padme Hum. I called on Avalokiteshvara to hold my precious daughter, Namgyal Youdon, in the arms of compassion, and asked that she be delivered to Amitabha Buddha to protect and guide her safely through the Bardo.

Anne drove me home in my car and we were followed by one of the members of the Skywalker Fire Department staff who took Anne back to the Ranch. My friend, Deborah Michie, whose husband of thirty-five years had died shortly after I returned from Tibet in March, was waiting at the house, and she stayed through the evening until Kitty and her partner, David Samuels, arrived around midnight.

The day before, Thursday, July 17, around two-thirty in the afternoon, which would have been about the time Namgyal was dying in Tibet (sixteen hours ahead of California time), I happened to read some notes in my Filofax (used as a diary) that were written on the flight back to the U.S. shortly after having said goodbye to Namgyal in Lhasa. I showed them to Deborah.

Namgyal's History:
1. Mother died when she was nine months old. Death blamed on Tibetan medicine not appropriate to treat emergency situations (had bad heart and headaches).
2. Sent to India at age eight (Tibetan Children's Village).
3. Father involved with a married woman who had his child (boy) after Namgyal and brothers went to India.
4. "Obstacles" between father's family vs. mother's family.
5. Huge support system on mother's side: five aunties and uncles, many cousins.
6. Popular at school, four best girlfriends, one boyfriend, several "brothers."
7. Tomboy, wears jeans, T-shirts, sweaters, only wore dress on New Year's (Losar).
8. Young in years; old in life experience.

"It sounds like an obituary," she said.

The thought that I had been reading these notes as Namgyal was dying was agony.

By the time Kitty and David arrived, my mind was spinning out of control. I was filled with anger and self-pity. Why did this happen to me? It's not fair. What did I do to deserve this? Is it some kind of sick karmic joke? This isn't the way the story was supposed to end. We (Namgyal and I) were supposed to live happily ever after.

Finally, out of sheer exhaustion, I went to bed, but tossed and turned all night. Yet, Saturday morning, I got up early and focused my attention on setting up an altar for Namgyal in my bedroom (where I usually meditate), on the raised hearth of the fireplace. I placed *Celestial Gallery*, a large book of Romio Shrestha's magnificent paintings, as the centerpiece, and clipped the pages to pictures of Amitabha Buddha and Avaloketishvara with text written by Ian Baker.

Also on the altar, I added the statue of Green Tara that Uncle Losoel gave me at the going away party in Lhasa, and a handwritten postcard from Namgyal (for Mother's Day one year), that shows a photograph of a white yak, an auspicious symbol in Tibetan culture as is the white buffalo in Native American culture. Namgyal had given me a beautiful coral and turquoise necklace for my birthday in a plastic box she had lined with gold brocade satin fabric. I wore the necklace frequently while I was with her in Tibet for Losar. I put the open box containing the necklace on the altar as well, along with an incense holder, made by Tibetan nuns, in the shape of a lotus and painted red and gold, along with several small brass Tibetan butter lamps (filled with votive candles) that Namgyal and I bought when we went shopping at the Bharkor. And, a white cymbidium orchid in a blue and white ceramic flowerpot.

Last, but not least, I placed a copy of Robert Thurman's translation of *The Tibetan Book of the Dead* on Namgyal's altar.

Already on the fireplace mantle were photographs of Namgyal in her Losar dress, the photo of her with her father, Dr. Namgang, a pothos plant and several other decorative items.

Just as I was adding the finishing touches to Namgyal's

altar, Sarita Patel arrived with her husband, Tom Latinovich, and their baby, Nicholas. As soon as I saw her, I broke down again, unable to control the tears from the overwhelming grief. I collapsed into a big wingback chair in front of the altar, and Sarita and Nick sat on the floor. Tommy went outside to help my brother-in-law charge the battery in his car.

Sarita is an old soul. She was born in the U.S., but her parents came from a small village in India. She knows intuitively the true nature of reality, from both a Hindu and Buddhist perspective, and she was able to comfort me simply by her presence. Nick crawled around on the floor while we talked. Before she left, Sarita gave me a hand-written poem she had spontaneously composed before coming over that morning.

Your Daughter
Poem written by Sarita Patel

She was meant to be noticed by you.
She was meant to change you forever.

She had a purpose where time
was not relevant –
But where meaning and beauty
meant everything.

This angel, your daughter,
felt the meaning of life in ways
many cannot even begin to imagine –
And her journey included you.

Your journey continues
with the greatest gift
of having been chosen to know her.

Cry, grieve, celebrate –
Be grateful for her life.

Around noon, Dickey arrived with her friends Mary Ann Wong and Sandra Lovelace. We fell into an embrace and cried tears the size of raindrops. Finally, Dickey was able to tell me about her conversation the previous evening with her mother, Dr. Tinley, in Lhasa. No one on Namgyal's mother's side of the family had told Dr. Tinley yet, so Dickey had to break the news, which was a devastating shock to her mother.

Dickey, Mary Ann, and Sandra had brought gifts of incense, prayer flags, white blessing scarves, and Chinese food for lunch. We sat around the kitchen table, joined by Kitty and David, and told stories about our beloved Namgyal.

Dickey told a story about Namgyal when she was a little girl, around four years old. Namgyal had a big appetite, and ate like a little pig. Dickey and Namgyal had shared a bed from the time Namgyal's mother died when Namgyal and her brother, Tsetan Khensur, went to live at Dr. Tinley's house. None of the old Tibetan houses have central heating, and during the coldest winter months the indoor temperature could easily be close to freezing. Namgyal spent a lot of time in bed, bundled up in multiple layers of clothing, just to keep warm.

One morning, Namgyal woke up to the smell of meat and rice porridge being cooked on the wood burning stove, but it was too cold to get out of bed. Having a big appetite, and worried that she wouldn't get any breakfast, Namgyal stuck her head out from under the covers and shouted, "Save some for little pig."

We all just cracked up with laughter, and there was a great sigh of relief around the table.

Dr. Namgang, Tsetan Khensur, Namgyal, Dr. Tinley
(Dickey's mother) and Dickey—Lhasa, Tibet

Namgyal's sky burial was on the fourth day after her death. Tenzin Tsering carried her body, wrapped in white cloth, on his back for one circumambulation around the Jokhang, Tibet's most sacred temple. Then, three monks and six male friends and relatives took her body to a monastery northeast of Lhasa for the sky burial. For some reason that was never made clear, the men could not be her blood relatives, that is, Tenzin Tsering could not attend, but the husbands of her aunties could.

The sky burial occurred around two-thirty Sunday afternoon, California time. I decided to have a thirty-minute silent meditation in my bedroom, at her altar, at the same time, with my sister, brother-in-law, and dear friend Shana Chrystie.

I put several Navajo rugs on the floor for seating, lit candles and incense, and played a song on Baby Face's MTV Unplugged CD called "Gone Too Soon," before we began the meditation.

It was a sweltering July afternoon, and the heat generated by the flickering candles created a shimmering mirage effect in the room. I felt like I was on "acid" and I was having a very bad trip.

Kitty and David left shortly after the meditation to drive back to Chico. Shana and I took a pitcher of iced tea out to the wide front porch of my old Victorian country house. She sat in a high backed white antique wicker Bar Harbor chair and I lay down on the loveseat.

It was unusually, unbearably hot. It reminded me of the typical summer days of my childhood in the South when the air was thick and stickey as molasses, and I was rendered into a semi-conscious stupor by the humidity.

I couldn't have carried on a conversation if my life depended on it, but Shana had brought several books and she offered to read aloud. She read first an excerpt from Jack Kornfield's book, *The Art of Forgiveness, Lovingkindness, and Peace*, the chapter entitled A Meditation on Grief.

When after heavy rain the storm clouds
disburse, is it not that they've wept
themselves clear to the end?
    —Ghalib

Grief is one of the heart's natural responses to loss. When we grieve we allow ourselves to feel the truth of our pain, the measure of betrayal or tragedy in our life. By our willingness to mourn, we slowly acknowledge, integrate, and accept the truth of our losses. Sometimes the best way to let go is to grieve.

It takes courage to grieve, to honor the pain we carry. We can grieve in tears or in meditative silence, in prayer or in song. In touching the pain of recent and long-held griefs, we come face to face with our genuine human vulnerability, with helplessness and hopelessness. These are the storm clouds of the heart.

Most traditional societies offer ritual and communal support to help people move through grief and loss. We need to respect our tears. Without a wise way to grieve, we can only soldier on, armored and unfeeling, but our hearts cannot learn and grow from the sorrows of the past.

Shana also read the entire fourteenth chapter, The Love That Will Not Die, from Pema Chödron's book, *When Things Fall Apart: Heart Advice for Difficult Times.*

Several other friends stopped by late that afternoon bringing flowers and sympathy, but by sundown everyone had left, and I was alone with my grief.

From: Jane Bay
Sent: Sunday, July 20, 2003 10:54 PM
To: Dear Friends
Subject: Prayers for my daughter Namgyal

Dear Friends,

It is with the saddest heart that I tell you my precious daughter Namgyal Youdon died on July 18th in Lhasa. Apparently, she collapsed from possibly either heart failure or a brain aneurysm during her morning shower before going to school. My grief is indescribable, and it's difficult to accept that this is her Karma. It happened ten days before she was to come to the U.S. for the first time during her summer break from Tibetan Medical College.

I know in time my heart will heal, but today was her sky burial in Tibet and the thought of it was almost more than I could bear. I ask for your prayers for Namgyal, and her brothers, who so recently lost their beloved father, and please, say a prayer for me, too.

GONE TOO SOON
Song written by L. Grossman, A. Buz Kohan

Like a comet
Blazing 'cross the evening sky
Gone too soon

Like a rainbow
Fading in the twinkling of an eye
Gone too soon

Shining and sparkling
And splendidly bright
Here one day
Gone one night

Like the loss of sunlight
On a cloudy afternoon
Gone too soon

Like a castle
Built upon a sandy beach
Gone too soon

Like a perfect flower
That is just beyond your reach
Gone too soon

Born to amuse, to inspire, to delight
Here one day
Gone one night

Like a sunset
Dying with the rising of the moon
Gone too soon
Gone too soon

With love and gratitude,
Jane

From: Jane Bay
Sent: Sunday, July 20, 2003 11:00 PM
To: Fu Ching
Subject: Prayers for my daughter Namgyal

Dearest Fu Ching,

As you just learned by my previous email, my beloved Namgyal has died. I need your help and want to ask you to call Ms. Yu Jun at the U.S. Consulate in Chengdu and tell her this terrible news so she can cancel the appointment we had scheduled for Namgyal. In the near future, we can discuss what to do about your expenses, and arrange a refund on her airline ticket, but let's not worry about it now.

Thank you, Fu Ching, for your kindness and understanding. Please pray for all of us.

Yours truly,
Jane

From: Jacqui Louez
Sent: Sunday, July 20, 2003 11:08 PM
To: Jane Bay
Subject: Re: Prayers for my daughter Namgyal

Darling Jane,
I am sooo incredibly sorry to hear of your immense loss. I don't really know what to say other than that I am here for you in any possible way.

If there is ANYTHING I can do for you please let me know. It's incredibly unfair and unjust. I will pray for Namgyal and her family.

I am praying for you and sending you my deepest love, support and care.

I really am so sorry for your loss, Jane.
Jacqs
xoxoxoxoxoxoxoxxoxoxoxoxxo

From: Francis Ford Coppola
Sent: Sunday, July 20, 2003 11:12 PM
To: Jane Bay
Subject: Re: Prayers for my daughter Namgyal

Very sad Jane to hear of your loss. My condolences.

love,
f

From: Jane Bay
Sent: Sunday, July 20, 2003 11:14 PM
To: Francis Ford Coppola
Subject: Re: Prayers for my daughter Namgyal

Thank you, Francis. Please tell Ellie for me as I don't have her email.

From: Dennis Leonard
Sent: Monday, July 21, 2003 2:41 AM
To: Jane Bay
Subject: Re: Prayers for my daughter Namgyal

Jane Dearest,

I have no words, I know words cannot describe your pain, and loss....

Words have little meaning in the face of the eternal flame from which we all are born, and must return to, each of us at our own time.

I Love You

I pray for the safe and successful journey of the soul of Namgyal Youdon, across the great Bardo, I pray for her to find enlightenment and to experience the bliss and tranquility of the Clear Light, I pray for her to experience the absolute peace of the void....

I pray that should her soul have more work here, she arrive well placed for her new job in the thin veil we call reality....

Jane I pray for your heart, I pray for stillness of the torment of pain that you suffer.........I cry for you... My heart reaches out across the physical space that separates us... I will be strong for you... She moves on, done with this round, graduating early from this school of ours on earth...Advancement, evolution of the soul, and we shall stay behind til it is time.

Well My Love....No words really can tell.........But between the lines... Time stands still....and love flows......as a fire from my heart.... to you.

Dennis

From: Laurent Bouzereau
Sent: Monday, July 21, 2003 5:57 AM
To: Jane Bay
Subject: Re: Prayers for my daughter Namgyal

Oh my dearest Jane — I just cannot believe this sad news. I was just in France praying for her father and lighting candles as I had promised I would. Jane, you gave her so much love, I know she is above, protecting you forever. She has touched so many people thanks to you and through you, she will remain a light in all our hearts.

Markus and I are sending you love and sympathy.
Laurent

From: Jan Matthews-Hodges
Sent: Monday, July 21, 2003 6:17 AM
To: Jane Bay
Subject: Re: Prayers for my daughter Namgyal

Dear Jane,

I was just thinking about you and your daughter and her father last night, then to come in and read this. I wish there were something anyone could say or do, but as I know, it takes time. She was just too young. I will let Lucinda know. Please know we are thinking of you.

I hope that one day soon you, Kitty and Jim will return to your family in North Carolina.

Love,
Jan

My second cousin, Lucinda Matthews Coates, still lives in Benson, North Carolina, thirty-two miles southeast of Raleigh on the cotton and tobacco farm that our great, great grandfather bought in the early 1800s.

Jan is the daughter of Lucinda's brother, Mickey Matthews, who died prematurely young at the age of forty of malignant melanoma from a mole on his back. Lucinda's mother and my mother were first cousins and best friends, and our families spent most summer vacations together on the farm when I was growing up. Actually, our family never took vacations, we went "visit'n" to a relative's house not just in summer, but throughout the year for any reason or no reason at all.

In November the year before Namgyal died, Kitty, our brother Jim, and I had gone "visit'n" from North Carolina, to Georgia, to Florida tracing our family history as research for a book I'd started writing called *Growing Up Southern—Stories from the Attic of Childhood Memories*. Even though I was born and raised in Florida, with a mama from North Carolina, and a daddy who hailed from Georgia, I grew up thinking I was a Southern belle.

With Namgyal's death, *Growing Up Southern* was put on the shelf. It was the farthest thing on my mind, but it's a story to be told another day.

From: Harmon Houghton
Sent: Monday, July 21, 2003 6:27 AM
To: Jane Bay
Subject: Re: Prayers for my daughter Namgyal

Dear Jane,

We offer our condolences and prayers at this time for grieving for such an untimely loss. We shared your enthusiasm for finding Namgyal and we share your pain.

We wish that we could be there to hug you and shelter you. I hope you are still planning on coming to Santa Fe so we can be with you.

With lots of love,
Harmon & Marcia

From: Amy Ho Seto
Sent: Monday, July 21, 2003 6:54 AM
To: Jane Bay
Subject: Re: Prayers for my daughter Namgyal

Jane,

I am saddened for your loss. My father passed away two years ago. I can only say that time heals. But the loss never goes away. I know you have wonderful memories to reflect upon. Take care of yourself. Today is a new day!

Amy

From: Ottmar Liebert
Sent: Monday, July 21, 2003 7:42 AM
To: Jane Bay
Subject: Re: Prayers for my daughter Namgyal

I am sorry, Jane.

- ottmar

From: Leanne Sandoval
Sent: Monday, July 21, 2003 9:08 AM
To: Jane Bay
Subject: Re: Prayers for my daughter Namgyal

I am so sorry for your loss. I will of course pray for all of those touched, and burn my candles. But especially I will think of you and pray for you to be comforted. There is something, as you said, indescribable in grief of such an end to a life just started. I can only imagine that she has such a big heart she is continuing on with her work from above, free from the stress of our "global limitations."

Ironically, my husband's sister died the same way. She collapsed at her college graduation dance from an aneurysm at twenty-three. And her bags were packed at home for her first trip away to Europe. I will share the beautiful song with him and his father, who ironically also lost his wife, my husband's mother, before her death as well.

With love,
Lea

From: Veronice Satoor
Sent: Monday, July 21, 2003 9:12 AM
To: Jane Bay
Subject: Re: Prayers for my daughter Namgyal

Jane,

I am very sorry to hear this news. I know how much she meant to you. You will always have a huge space missing. I too lost someone extremely close to me last year. I cry every day thinking of him. I don't know when it will get better. Everyone tells me it will just take time, and I suppose that is true. Find time for yourself. Feel good when you can.

You are a very special lady and I'm sorry this had to happen.

My love and sympathy to you,
Veronice.

From: Lucille Martin
Sent: Monday, July 21, 2003 9:15 AM
To: Jane Bay
Subject: Re: Prayers for my daughter Namgyal

Dear Jane,

I am so sorry, Jane. I cry with you. I lost my daughter five years ago, June 16, and it doesn't get any easier. I loved the song and it fit my Sue, too. I do not understand why this happens—on the threshold of their lives. I am so sorry. Your grief is my grief.

With love and deepest sympathy,
Lucille

From: Margi English
Sent: Monday, July 21, 2003 9:16 AM
To: Jane Bay
Subject: Re: Prayers for my daughter Namgyal

Oh Jane,

How very, very sad and unfair. I can only imagine your despair. What a shock! My heart is with you. But, I am worried about you. Take some time off work. I would be glad to sit with you or tend to any details for you, just so you can take the time to yourself.

Much love,
Margi

From: Sushma Patel Bould
Sent: Monday, July 21, 2003 9:17 AM
To: Jane Bay
Subject: Re: Prayers for my daughter Namgyal

Dearest Jane,

We just received the devastating news from Sarita and Tommy. Please forgive the coarse medium of e-mail, and please do not feel you have to respond. On behalf of our family, we each extend our deepest, most sincere and heartfelt empathy to you Jane, and to Namgyal's family.

The depth and gravity of your sudden and heartbreaking loss weighs like a boulder of granite in our hearts. Please know that we are here to comfort you in your grief, and offer our unconditional spiritual support in any way that you need during this difficult time and on the journey ahead. Reading your memoirs, hearing your stories, and anticipating the joy of the future have enabled us to see what a ray of sunshine your daughter will always be in your heart. Jane, our arms and love are all around you.

With love, respect, and sincerely heartfelt regret. Our prayers are with you and your family.

Sushma and Fred
and the Patel family

From: Cathy Nilsen
Sent: Monday, July 21, 2003 9:21 AM
To: Jane Bay
Subject: Re: Prayers for my daughter Namgyal

My Dearest Jane,

I write to you with teary eyes. Why, why, why keeps pounding in my head. Yet I take strength in the words of your e-mail. Namgyal's life was enriched tenfold with your love and support. This blessing is a gift for you as well as Namgyal.

Jane my thoughts, prayers, and love are with you and Namgyal. You must let me know if there is anything I can do for you. I will call you later in the week as I am sure you will need time to yourself to begin the healing.

Love and Prayers,
Cathy

From: Nancy Harris
Sent: Monday, July 21, 2003 9:45 AM
To: Jane Bay
Cc: Anne Merrifield
Subject: Re: Prayers for my daughter Namgyal

Dear Jane:

Have just opened this email, immediately called and left a message at your home, and then just spoke to your colleague Anne. I am ccing this to her so that she might include me in any arrangements.

Words cannot express adequately any consolation for the sorrow and grief you must feel. This is unbelievable news. An unbelievable tragedy.

Anne has reassured me that you have had wonderful support over the weekend, and that the appropriate prayers and ceremonies are underway. There is some deep solace in the Tibetan culture concerning death and bereavement, and I am grateful that this is surrounding you now.

With all my love,
Nancy

From: Joanne Shenandoah
Sent: Monday, July 21, 2003 9:50 AM
To: Jane Bay
Subject: Re: Prayers for my daughter Namgyal

My Dearest Jane,

I am sooooo sorry to hear of your loss. The world is such a strange place. Just this weekend a good friend of ours passed on who was just recently married (two weeks ago.) So sad. They were just in the Adirondack Mountains with us camping.

I know you were so looking forward to her visit. In the Iroquois way, we believe that we can talk to our loved ones in our dreams and that her spirit will be around you for ten days.

I am enclosing an article that my husband wrote about passing into the spirit world. The song, "Feather from Heaven" on *Eagle Cries* was written to lift the grief from the loss of a loved one.

You are in my thoughts and prayers, Jane.

With love and hugs,
Jo

Feather from Heaven
Written by Joanne Shenandoah

When the dusk of death has settled on your shoulders
and life has no meaning at all.

I will be there to wipe away your tears
with the soft skin of the deer.

When the dust of death has settled in your ears,
and you can hear nothing at all.

I will be there to brush away the pain,
with the softest feather from heaven.

When the dust of death has settled in your voice
and you can say nothing at all.

I will be there with water pure and clean to wash
away the silence within.

I will be there to wipe away your tears.
I will be there to brush away your fear
and wash away the silence within.

I will be there to wipe away your tears.
I will be there to brush away your fear
and wash away the silence within.

From: Kelly Morris
Sent: Monday, July 21, 2003 10:03 AM
To: Jane Bay
Subject: Re: Prayers for my daughter Namgyal

My dearest Aunt Jane,

I can't tell you how broken my heart is for you. I am terribly sorry to
hear of this.

My thoughts and prayers are with you. If I had any money I would fly
out to be with you a bit. I would love just to give you a hug and hold you.

Isaiah 41:13
For I am the LORD your GOD, who holds your right hand,
Who says to you, do not fear, I will help you.

God bless you!

********************HUGS*****************
I love you!
Kelly

From: Chin Rodger
Sent: Monday, July 21, 2003 10:32 AM
To: Jane Bay
Subject: Re: Prayers for my daughter Namgyal

Dearest, Dearest Jane,

My deepest, deepest, heartfelt condolences for your great great loss. I am so sorry to hear of this. It fills me with such sadness, I can't help but weep this morning reading your mail.

My daughter, Georgia, who is seven came in and hugged me and asked why I was sad. I told her, and this is what she said, " Mommy, tell your friend, just like Kim, she just left her body and she is now a ball of love in your friend's heart" and then she added, "If she wants, your friend can share me with you." It makes me cry even more. This came from Georgia and with all my heart, sometime along the way, if you ever wish to take her up on it, it will be my great joy to share her with you. She brings joy and peace to all in her presence.

Jane, I send you and Namgyal's brothers all my blessings and my prayers. I will go to our temple in Santa Monica tonight and burn a prayer stick for you, Namgyal and Namgyal's family. I know you have many great friends with you right now to be with you. However, I am sending a big big hug with this.

May grace and blessings be with you. I am thinking of you.

With much love,
Chin

From: David Riordan
Sent: Monday, July 21, 2003 11:30 AM
To: Jane Bay
Subject: Re: Prayers for my daughter Namgyal

Jane: I am so sorry this has happened. My prayers are with you and Namgyal.

It seems to be a week of unexpected tragedies. I learned on Friday that a good friend of mine, Lynn Weaver, was one of the dead in that senseless rundown in the Santa Monica farmers market. The shock wave hit me over the weekend. There is no explanation when these tragedies take place. We, the living, are left to grieve and pray for their safe journey to the other side. If there is anything I can do, if you need a hug, anything, let me know.

I love you,
David

From: Lisa Cooke
Sent: Monday, July 21, 2003 11:42 AM
To: Jane Bay
Subject: Re: Prayers for my daughter Namgyal

Dearest Jane,

What can I say? My heart is filled with such sadness for the loss of your beautiful daughter. I don't have the words to express to you the profound sorrow I feel. I am so honored to have shared in her life, through you, and your touching photos of her and her family. I never met Namgyal, but I felt close to her as I experienced her through your love.

I know how heavy your heart must be with grief. Life is such a mystery, and death makes us bow in reverence to the preciousness of living. The depth of one's grief is always measured by the depth of one's love, so I understand how intensely you must be grieving. You will always be Namgyal's mother and she was blessed to have you in her life.

Time does help heal our most profound wounds. And when the wound heals, what will remain is the love you shared with Namgyal. That is forever.

You are in our thoughts and prayers, as are Namgyal and her family.

Please, dearest friend, if there is anything we can do. A walk by the beach, help with a memorial, a hug, a good cry together. . . . . please let us know.

All our love,
Lisa and Jon

From: Paula Boam
Sent: Monday, July 21, 2003 5:03 PM
To: Jane Bay
Subject: Re: Prayers for my daughter Namgyal

My dearest Juanita,

My tears are many. You and I have been through this before. I remember talking with your dear, funny and sweet mother. She was and is a wonderful soul. I think about her and pray for her and ask that she will keep a glint in her eye, for all of us left behind. I was so lucky that I got to know her before she passed away.

Then we had to watch Jeffrey die. I think we all did it with grace and love. I will never, ever, forget the good times and all the love you showered on us. I love you Jane Bay. I will do anything for you, you just have to call.

But, having said all that... I never dreamed we would be facing the death of one of our children. This passing of Namgyal is almost too much to take. So many dreams and hopes. So very much left, you and all of your friends wanted to give her. My heart feels like a bag of sand, so heavy and so helpless. But Namgyal did pass and I believe to a better place. I miss her, though I never touched her or held her. But I wanted to...

I love you, over the moon,
Paulita

From: Carolyn Rangel
Sent: Monday, July 21, 2003 6:12 PM
To: Jane Bay
Subject: Re: Prayers for my daughter Namgyal

Dear Jane,

From one mother to another—family to family, I grieve with you and
your family.

I hope you find this prayer comforting.

With love,
Carolyn

Native American
Unknown Author

Don't stand by my grave and weep,
for I am not there,
I do not sleep.
I am a thousand winds that blow,
I am the diamond's glint on snow
I am the sunlight on ripened grain
I am the gentle autumn's rain
In the soft hush of the morning light
I am the swift bird in flight
Don't stand by my grave and cry,
I am not there,
I did not die.

David and I were married for almost seven years. Shortly after my fortieth birthday, I became pregnant for the first time in my life, only to suffer a miscarriage at ten weeks. The loss of the baby I had longed for sent me into a deep depression. It manifested in my comforting myself with food which resulted in a tremendous weight gain over the next couple of years. Our marriage began to fall apart, and we divorced not long after.

When David showed up at my front door the Monday after Namgyal died with a Native American flute and a Lakota medicine bag in hand, it had been ages since I'd last seen him.

"I can't talk about it, I haven't slept in three days, and I was just going to try to take a nap, but you can come in and sit with me in the bedroom." He said, "I understand," and there was no need for further conversation.

When I told Kitty about what happened that afternoon, she said she thought that in some way, because David and I had conceived a child together, he felt a fatherly connection with Namgyal, too. When I thought about it, I realized that Namgyal had been born the year following my miscarriage. Maybe it had been her consciousness that entered my womb for that brief moment in time.

From: Fu Ching
Sent: Monday, July 21, 2003 7:58 PM
To: Jane Bay
Subject: Re: Prayers for my daughter Namgyal

My dear Jane,

I...I am really so surprised about the bad and saddest news.

First of all, personally, I am so sorry and very sad to hear the news.

And, dear Jane, you should take care, do not be too sad. Yeah, she gone too fast and so this is her Karma. And, let's all pray for her, hope her soul will fly to the sky soon, where she still can feel the warm love. And, also, we still pray for the family, her brothers and wish the Buddha can bless them, bless the saddest family.

And, I also pray for you—my dear friend: Jane Bay. I pray for you, who did and doing lots of things for Namgyal with warm heart. I pray for you, hope the Buddha can bless you. And, I will go to the Manjushri Temple to do the prayer for you soon. Hope this can help you.

Just now, I called to Ms. Yu Jun to tell her the bad news (she is so suprised and said sorry to you) and the appointment canceled.

I called to Mr. Wangdu to cancel the ticket booking. I called Airline Company to cancel the international ticket booking; there will be some charge for that.

I will arrange the refund and mail the paper work back to you.

Yours,
Fu Ching
Kham Trek Adventure Club
Chengdu, China

P.S. Dear Jane, please do not be too sad. TAKE CARE!!!

Dearest Jane,

I cried the minute I saw your message and never stopped today. Every time I think of you and your great loss my eyes fill up with tears and I can't talk. What must you be going through? If there is *anyone* on this earth who I WOULDN'T want to die now, it's this young sweet dear daughter of yours who had so much ahead of her! So much life thanks to you and your love.

I guess I really don't have that positive "meant to be" type of spirituality and understanding deep in my soul during times of tragedy—it's right there when everything is FINE. I *want* to believe that "it's meant to be" but I just can't feel it. 22 years old! NO WAY was it "her time." I *want* to believe it, I really do… "Her time" was to come and have fun with you and to see your beautiful home(s) and meet all of us at work and see what the United States is like. Is that selfish and shortsighted? Maybe she will come back to us soon in another body? Is that what you believe? (I just got chills down my arms when I wrote that which is strange.) I'm so full of grief and sadness, not full of wonderful spiritual soothing thoughts that I can tell you all about…

I did say prayers for both of you (thanking God for your lives, for finding each other, and for caring so much about each other), but mostly I'm just so unspeakably sad right now, Jane. I never KNEW her, just knew the joy that she brought to you, and knew the beautiful plans of love and sharing you had for her.

You have so many people who love and care about you Jane—you are SURROUNDED by our positive love and thoughts towards you.

All my love,
T.

From: Jane Bay
Sent: Monday, July 21, 2003 10:30 PM
To: Tina Mills
Subject: Re: Horrible…

Dearest Tina,

All these feelings you've expressed are exactly the ones that went through me the moment I realized she was gone.

I'll send you a poem Sarita wrote and brought over to the house on Saturday morning that I think will resonate with you. It's called "Your Daughter."

Thank you dear Tina, for sharing your grief with me.

I love you,
Jane

From: Tina Mills
Sent: Tuesday, July 22, 2003 10:00 AM
To: Jane Bay
Subject: Lovely poem

I LOVE the poem that Sarita sent! Just *what* I was lacking… I guess it's just perfect to cry because frankly it HELPS. I had another cry this morning! I think it shows my love for YOU because I haven't cried so much in YEARS. Matt thought my dad had died...

I heard you might be in tomorrow. Don't push it, but it might make you feel OK to be working—whatever feels OK. You can even come and go home again right away if it upsets you. If you want a partner for lunch tomorrow—I'd love to. If you want your privacy (LEAVE ME ALONE) I understand that too.

Dearly love you.
T.

From: Jane Bay
Sent: Tuesday, July 22, 2003 11:00 AM
To: Tina Mills
Subject: Re: Lovely poem

Tina,

This morning, Arjia Rinpoche, the Abbott of Kumbum Monastery in Tibet who defected about six years ago, now living in Mill Valley, came over to perform special prayers for Namgyal. It was such a blessing, and I realized that every day for the first week of Namgyal's death, I need to do some specific Buddhist practices for her, and myself.

I'm not going back to work until next week, but I want to stay close to you in this way. Your love is a great comfort to me now.

Love you,
Jane

By the time I learned that Namgyal had died, she had been dead for over twenty-four hours. Her family in Tibet had already begun the forty-nine day practice of reading *The Tibetan Book of the Dead* to her.

In the Introduction to his book, *The Tibetan Book of the Dead for Reading Aloud*, Jean-Claude van Itallie states:

> The Tibetan Book of the Dead *is a manual traditionally read aloud to the dying and the dead by a spiritual teacher or a friend. It is a teaching expressed through the spoken word.*
>
> *One of the earliest teachers to bring Buddhism to Tibet, Padmasambhava, popularly called Precious Guru (Guru Rinpoche), is said to have composed* The Tibetan Book of the Dead *around the eighth century A.D. It was rediscovered in Tibet...around six hundred years ago and is part of the everyday culture of Tibetan Buddhism.*
>
> The Tibetan Book of the Dead *contains practical*

navigational instructions of urgent use on the journey that starts with dying and continues in the days following death. A guide-book to the "in-between place," it instructs how to avoid the suffering caused by the confusion of constantly discursive thoughts.

The Tibetan Book of the Dead *is also for the living, a meditation manual on how to pay attention despite the distractions of our daily worlds...*

In The Tibetan Book of the Dead, *the traveler-after-death starts "at the top" with an experience of the clear white light of universal mind. This light, most visible at the moment of death, is our best opportunity. If we recognize it as our own fully-awakened nature, we may merge with it. If not, however, the five peaceful manifestations of universal energy each appear in turn. (Presumably these energies appear differently to each person.) Pay attention, says* The Tibetan Book of the Dead: *These peaceful energies are you too. But if we don't recognize these as emanations of our own mind, then the five Universal energies will appear again, this time in angry form.*

If, despite warnings from the Book, *we are blinded by fear, and do not recognize the angry energies as emanations of our own mind, we descend further yet. We attempt to return to our former body. We want our possessions back. The voice of a friend reading aloud the* Book *reminds us that we can't return to the past, we must be fearless, we must take this opportunity not to be reborn into a world of tears.*

But if we allow ourselves to be pushed even further downward by demons, by old habits of thinking, then we must seek refuge in a womb. "Don't grab just any womb" says the Book. *The* Book *gives the dead one instructions on how to consciously choose an auspicious place of rebirth.*

The Tibetan Book of the Dead *reminds us, in living as in dying, to stay alert, to be fearless and undistracted...reminding us that we are ourselves manifestations of universal energy.*

I, too, would read aloud to my beloved daughter from this ancient book of wisdom during her forty-nine day transition through the Bardo.

From: Glynda Rich
Sent: Tuesday July 22, 2003 11:08 AM
To: Jane Bay
Subject: Re: Prayers for my daughter Namgyal

My Dearest Jane,

My heart cries for you and your lovely daughter. What a terrible shock. I wish I could be with you and just hold you in my arms. Please know I am thinking of you and holding you in my heart.

I don't know all that happened. Our cell phone doesn't always give us the messages as they come in, however, I know Jim has been calling. I tried to call but missed him.

Take care of yourself and know that Roger and I love you.

With great sympathy,
Glynda

My first cousin, Glynda Hatcher Rich, was named after my daddy, Glenn Stead Morris, her mother's youngest brother. Daddy was adored by Grandmother Morris and his sisters who spoiled him rotten, his being the baby in the family.

When Kitty, Jim and I took our road trip to trace our family history, we met up with Glynda and her husband, Retired Rear Admiral Roger Rich, in Swainsboro, Georgia where they happened to be staying at the time in their traveling mobile home.

Glynda took us over to Wrightsville to the house she lived in as a child, and where I spent several months following my mother's "nervous breakdown." Mother suffered from post-partum depression shortly after Jim was born, and my father's shameless philandering drove her to the nut house. The pain had been too much to bear and one day she had a psychotic break. She woke up in a mental institution where she was confined for six weeks, and given electric shock treatments which were standard procedure in the 1940s to treat psychiatric disorders. Mother was amazingly resilient, however, and years later said she thought it had been the best thing for her because it blotted out the pain.

Daddy packed Jim and me off to Georgia to be cared for by his older sisters, Aunt Dhalia and Glynda's mother, Aunt Agnes. I was only four years old at the time, but I have very vivid memories of Glynda. She was like a big sister and became my protector, but I carried the fear of losing my mind like my mother did throughout adulthood, until I began to look at life from a Buddhist perspective.

From: Jane Bay
Sent: Tuesday, July 22, 2003 12:45 PM
To: Sarita Patel
Subject: Your poem

Dear Sarita,

I hope you don't mind my sharing your poem. It's so hard to comfort others right now, and you have given me this beautiful gem which is like a shining crystal of light cutting through the dark sorrow we're all feeling. I read your poem to Dickey and her friends and several other people, and in the reading, it comforts me again and again.

I've set up a shrine for Namgyal on an oval-shaped, flat wicker tray sprinkled with pink and red rose petals from my garden on which I placed a 3 x 5 framed photo of her taken at the park behind the Potala Palace in Lhasa. I draped a pendant necklace that Namgyal had given me of Garuda (the Hindu god/bird deity with the head and wings of an eagle, thought to be the destroyer of obstacles), over the frame. I added a two-inch white marble statue of Buddha that I'd gotten in India; a Chocolate Rasberry Caramel Silk Truffle candy wrapped in pink paper and tied with gold ribbon, a small Tibetan butter candle lamp I got in Lhasa, and a brass heart-shaped paperweight with an angel and flowers made of copper and silver on top that Deborah gave me last Christmas. I placed your poem, standing upright, against the frame of the photo of my precious daughter.

The shrine is on the foyer table welcoming friends when they come to call, and in my view every time I walk by.

Thank you, dear friend.
I love you so very much,
Jane

From: Lynn Nicholas
Sent: Tuesday, July 22, 2003 1:00 PM
To: Jane Bay
Subject: Re: Prayers for my daughter Namgyal

It is unbelievable to hear such news, Jane.

Let her go, her Karma will bring her where she belongs and you know this is important for you to let her go and wish her a successful journey for forty-nine days from this life. It's very hard to accept the death of such a young woman with a future, but this is her future.

I feel sad for you and I know the best we can do for her and you is to breathe her freedom to a better place. The teachings in which she was brought up into and her rebirths are her journey to being the Bodhisattva Buddha she deserves to become. Our prayers and acceptance of this journey are especially important for these forty-nine days.

I imagine you have been blessed by helping her in this lifetime. I am glad I had the opportunity to meet her as a young girl when we were in Dharamsala together. I will always remember that day.

With much love and compassion,
Lynn

From: Sarita Patel
Sent: Tuesday, July 22, 2003 7:31 PM
To: Jane Bay
Subject: Re: Your poem

Oh Jane,

I love you so much. I know how much your heart is hurting. I am always here with you—in good times and bad. It makes me feel grounded to know I have helped you in this way with mere words.

Love you so,
Sarita

From: Laurie Bauman
Sent: Tuesday, July 22, 2003 7:52 PM
To: Jane Bay
Subject: Re: Prayers for my daughter Namgyal

Dear Jane,

There are no words that can express both the shock and the sadness I felt when I heard the news of Namgyal. To be so young and filled with such promise then snatched away is an unspeakable tragedy. No, I don't think its Karma, either. I think life sometimes delivers those unexplainable whammies to remind us just how unpredictable and precious it is.

I remember back twelve years ago just before we moved up to the Northwest. Women friends on opposite coasts died young and suddenly, ironically one from a brain aneurysm, one from a heart attack, both of them in their early to mid-thirties, each with two small children. The shock that attacked was both fierce and numbing and for me it took a year to feel like the ground wouldn't swallow up my loved ones in the blink of an eye.

It grieves me so much that the relationship you forged with Namgyal has no more forward momentum, but I know that the joy you derived from creating and sustaining such a bond is as precious as breath itself. Love is bigger than life, continues after life, and takes on a place of its own.

My love and thoughts are with you.

Love,
Laurie

From: Wangdu
Sent: Tuesday, July 22, 2003 9:14 PM
To: Jane Bay
Subject: Re: Prayers for my daughter Namgyal

Dear Jane,

This morning my first call was from Fu Ching and he told me this saddest news. (Sorry I was unable to check my email, since out of Lhasa—to Terdrom Hot Spring and back to Lhasa late Monday evening). This evening I went to Jokhang with butter lamp and prayer money that is the only thing I can do for Namgyal Youdon.

Jane please take care of yourself, as you said it is her Karma. You did so much for her and at last have to accept such sad fact. Being a friend thanks for all you have done for her—at least you give her a feeling of being a child with hope and bright future, especially came to Lhasa to celebrate Losar with her and discuss her future plan. She is lucky to be your daughter.

Once again PLEASE TAKE CARE OF YOURSELF and let me know anything need to do in Tibet on behalf of you.

Yours,
Wangdu

From: Melene Smith
Sent: Tuesday, July 22, 2003 9:48 PM
To: Jane Bay
Subject: Re: Prayers for my daughter Namgyal

Dear Jane,

I am so shocked and saddened to hear about Namgyal's death. My heart breaks for you Jane for I have felt the depth of your love for Namgyal and your hopes for her future. I wish I could give you a hug, but know you and Namgyal are in my thoughts and prayers.

Love,
Melene

From: Anne Millikin
Sent: Tuesday, July 22, 2003 11:27 PM
To: Jane Bay
Subject: Sympathy

Thinking of you...

Dear heart, yes, thank you for letting me know that Sunday was her sky burial. I wish we could have been there in person. Was it at Drigung Monastery? When I was saying my prayers for her yesterday as well as sending love to you, it felt so strongly that she was being released. What a blessed burial way they are still able to honor, thank goodness.

I cannot imagine the loss and heartache you must be experiencing, but if I can help you in any way, or if you just wish to talk, please call on me.

My love,
Anne

I didn't leave the house for five days, and then only to go to the grocery store. On the way home, driving west on Sir Francis Drake Boulevard, the setting sun was directly in front of me, blinding my sight. I couldn't continue driving and turned right at the next street that happened to go up to the top of Red Hill where my veterinarian's office was located. I pulled into the driveway, facing the car toward the setting sun, and parked. The sky was a blazing streak of red and orange.

Sunset is my favorite time of day. Something about the sun slipping below the horizon is calming. Even though my thoughts were preoccupied with Namgyal, my body was warm and more at ease than it had been since I learned of her death.

I noticed an animal walking across the street, directly in front of the car, heading toward the trees up the hill. It was a fox. It paused momentarily, looking straight at me, and in that moment of eye contact, I felt Namgyal's presence.

From: Anne Merrifield
Sent: Wednesday, July 23, 2003 9:00 AM
To: Jane Bay
Subject: Checking in

Dearest Jane,

You have been in my prayers all week, so that you have strength to cope with the loss of Namgyal. My prayers also go to her spirit for a peaceful transition. I fed the hummingbirds this afternoon and added a prayer, then watched them soar upward toward the sky.

Here is the information I found on the Internet about the fox:

Foxes are seen as totems throughout the world: the Chinese believe they can take human form, in Egypt the fox brought favor from the gods, there was a fox god in Peru. Foxes help the dead get to the next life in Persia. Cherokees, Hopi and other American Indian tribes believe in its healing power, the Apache credited the fox with giving man fire.

Since the fox lives "between times"—on the edge of land, visible at dusk and dawn, they can guide the way to the faerie realms.

Take care of yourself and come back when you are ready.

Love,
Anne

From: Jane Bay
Sent: Wednesday, July 23, 2003 9:30 AM
To: Anne Merrifield
Subject: Re: Checking In

Dearest Anne,

Thank you for the beautiful note, and the information on the fox. I'm sure it was a sign...

I've decided not to return to the office until Monday, July 28, but will check my email daily. If you would like to come over sometime before Monday, I would welcome a visit maybe over the weekend?

I'm having a very difficult time talking to people about it, telling them the details or talking about my feelings. It's so hard for me to comfort others right now, so I'm avoiding the telephone. It's much less difficult to communicate by email (bet you never thought you'd hear me say that). I am talking to Dickey everyday, and Tenzin Tsering as well.

Thanks for taking care of everything at the office.

Love,
Jane

The Peace of Wild Things
Poem written by Wendell Berry

When despair for the world grows in me
and I wake in the night at the least sound
in fear of what my life and my children's lives may be,
I go and lie down where the wood drake
rests in his beauty on the water, and the great heron feeds.
I come into the peace of wild things
who do not tax their lives with forethought of grief.
I come into the presence of still water.
And I feel above me the day-blind stars
waiting with their light. For a time
I rest in the grace of the world, and am free.

From: Tina Mills
Sent: Wednesday, July 23, 2003 9:42 AM
To: Jane Bay
Subject: Namgyal's Spirit

Dearest Jane!

I'm so glad to hear you are spending your time this week in such a beautiful and positive way! You truly continue to be the loving mom and person that Namgyal fell in love with. I told my mom what happened today (through MORE tears) and she started crying too! It's sad to say, that people die every day, and they are dearly missed by their loved ones, but the circumstances of her death and your anticipation for her arrival make this a real tragedy...

I hope you are feeling a bit better and stronger every day. I'm so glad you are surrounded by beautiful spiritual people who can help you and that you are opening your heart up to their blessings. You are a VERY special person, Jane, and deserve endless love and attention and devotion now.

Thinking of you every second of the day,

T.

From: Kelly Morris
Sent: Wednesday, July 23, 2003 10:00 AM
To: Jane Bay
Subject: Rhododendron Seeds

Dear Jane,

I wanted to send you something you could grow in your garden to remember Namgyal. Something native and typical to the Tibet that is so dear to your heart. It was going to be a surprise but the gentleman who will be sending the seeds can actually get them from any part of Tibet... so I wanted to ask you what part of Tibet did Namgyal come from or is there an area that is very dear to you that you would like? He sent me a list of the areas of Tibet that he has seeds from. He also said that they should grow very well in your area. Looking at the list below from my friend, John, is there an area closer to your heart that you would like your flower seeds to come from?

Love,
Kelly

> If you know the location in Tibet we can possibly match the rhodie collection site to the location your aunt's daughter came from or perhaps close by. Below is a listing of the collection sites:
>
> Locations:
> *L 1 Basum Tso, site 2-01, N30o00'17.3", E93°55'32.9", 3468m
> *L2 Doshong La, site 13-01, N29°29'30.7", E94°55'43.8", 3690m
> Doshong La, site 13-02, N29°29'15.9", E94°56'50.8", 4233m
> *L3 Sirchem La, site 4-02, N29°33'45.4", E94°34'20.7", 3839m
> *L4 Tra La, summit, site 10-05, N29°44'43.5", E94°45'57.4", 4008m
> *L5 Rong Chu, site 9-04, N30o00'32.3", E94°57'27.8", 2268m
> *L6 Sirchem La, site 5-01, N29°37'01.9", E94°37'26.8", 4270m

*L7 Lang to Zetang, site 16-01, N29°01'46.4", E92°21 '57.5", 4548m
*L8 Tangme to Lunang, site 9-01, N30o01'22.5", E95°00'24.8", 2029m
*L9 Tra La near Lunang, site 10-02, N29°44'56.4", E94°45'08.6", 3404m
*L 10 Sirchem La, site 5-03, N29°57'14.4", E94°49'34.4", 2531m
*L 11 Tra La, near summit, site 10-04, N29°44'27.4", E94°45'34.8", 3722m
*L 12 Tra La, site 10-03, N29°44'56.8", E94°45'16.6", 3533m
*L 13 Beijing, site 18-01
*L 14 Bomi to Tangme, site 8-02, N30o03'23.8", E95°12'44.9", 2375m
*L 15 Sirchem La, site 5-02, N29°51 '00.7", E94°45'53.9", 2980m
*L 16 Lhasa to Basum Tso, site 1-05, N29°42'33.7", E92°11'56.6", 4200m
*L 17 Tangme to Lunangs, site 9-01, N30o01'22.5", E95°00'24.8", 2029m
*L 18 East of Bomi, site 7-01, N29°50'47.3", E96°05'52.4", 3208m
*L 19 Sirchem La, site 4-03, N29°33'58.4", E94°32'51.8", 3406m

---

From: Jane Bay
Sent: Wednesday, July 23, 2003 11:45 AM
To: Kelly Morris
Subject: Re: Rhododendron Seeds

My darling Kelly, this is such a sweet and beautiful gesture. The area that Namgyal is from is #16 Lhasa to Basum Tso. It would be truly wonderful to have seeds from that location.

Rhodies are one of the few flowers that thrive in the harsh high altitude of Tibet, and I will plant these seeds with the thought of new life for Namgyal.

Any word on whether you can come to Santa Fe for Christmas? I talked to your dad yesterday, and he is going to try to get some time off work. It would be great to be with the Morris family during the holiday season this year.

All my love,
Jane

From:	Jon Berg
Sent:	Wednesday, July 23, 2003 12:34 PM
To:	Jane Bay
Subject:	Re: Prayers for my daughter Namgyal

Dear Jane,

I have found it extremely difficult to put into words my sorrow for your profound loss. I hold you, the memory, through you, of Namgyal and her family in my heart and in my prayers. If there is anything that I can do, please, only ask.

I join with all who love you and Namgyal in hopes that you pass safely through this most painful of experiences. Be kind and gentle with yourself, as Namgyal would have wished.

In Peace and Love,
Jon

From:	Jo Donaldson
Sent:	Wednesday, July 23, 2003 5:19 PM
To:	Jane Bay
Subject:	Re: Prayers for my daughter Namgyal

Dear Jane,

I'm so sorry to hear about Namgyal. I know you must be devastated.

I hope you will be able to take off from work so you can adjust to your loss and grieve properly. If you need anything, please let me know.

xxoo
Jo

CHAPTER THREE

Grief

Give sorrow words. The grief that does not speak
whispers to the overwrought heart, and bids it to break.
—William Shakespeare—Macbeth

From: Jane Bay
Sent: Wednesday, July 23, 2003 4:39 PM
To: Dear Friends
Subject: Grief

Dear Friends,

Thank you for your emails, cards, flowers, and phone calls. I've been
having a difficult time talking with people on the telephone, or face-to-
face, about Namgyal's death so I hope you will bear with me as I use
this way (via email) to share my feelings with you.

On the seventh day of Namgyal's passing, I went down to Oyster
Point Marina to rescue live fish from being killed. I released the fish
into the open water of the Bay to help guide and comfort Namgyal on
her journey through the Bardo (in Buddhism, the stages between
death and rebirth are known as the Bardo). Then I said goodbye to
her and threw flower blossoms on the water that floated out to sea. I
will be doing special prayers for her every seven days throughout the
forty-ninth day, which will be on Wednesday, September 3.

I am beginning to regain my balance, somewhat, from the terrible
shock of her death, but there are so many emotions lurking around

that I know will continue to surface during the ebb and flow of this wave of grief that is washing over me.

My grief is as great as my love for Namgyal. Yet, there are other feelings beginning to arise, and when I can "calm my mind" a little, which is not often, I begin to open up to other emotions. What I have vowed NOT to do is stifle my feelings. I no longer fear the pain will be too great to bear. I know it will not kill me or drive me mad. I can stand in the pain and not run from it. I owe it to Namgyal and myself to be authentic, to be totally present with my feelings, whatever they are. My meditation teacher, Yvonne Rand, has taught me that even pain has the mark of impermanence... and everything changes. She also said the Chinese character for "change" translates as "dangerous opportunity." It's almost impossible to imagine what opportunities can come out of this magnitude of grief.

I want to share with you a poem Sarita Patel wrote for me the morning after I learned of Namgyal's death when I thought I was inconsolable. I've reread it a million times since, and it is helping to relieve some of the terrible grief I'm experiencing from losing her. I hope it will comfort you as well.

Your Daughter
Poem written by Sarita Patel

She was meant to be noticed by you.
She was meant to change you forever.

She had a purpose where time
was not relevant –
But where meaning and beauty
meant everything.

This angel, your daughter,
felt the meaning of life in ways
many cannot even begin to imagine –
And her journey included you.

Your journey continues
with the greatest gift
of having been chosen to know her.

Cry, grieve, celebrate —
Be grateful for her life.

I am, and send you oceans of love,
Jane

From: Betty Nelson
Sent: Wednesday, July 23, 2003 7:50 PM
To: Jane Bay
Subject: Re: Grief

Dear Jane,

I appreciate your willingness to connect with your friends in this way—
email. You've been very much on my mind. I continue to hold you and
Namgyal in my thoughts and prayers.

With warm regards,
Betty

From: Jane Bay
Sent: Wednesday, July 23, 2003 9:27 PM
To: Joanne Shenandoah
Subject: Feather from Heaven

Dearest Jo,

Thank you so much for your email. Music is for me the food of love,
the great healing balm, the connection to the Divine. I have your
Eagle Cries and *Peace & Power* CDs and listening to "Feather
from Heaven" is such a comfort to me at this devastating time.

And thank you for sending Doug's beautifully written article "Passing into the Spirit World." I was very interested to find many similarities between Iroquois and Tibetan Buddhist cosmology. I pray Namgyal has peacefully entered the spirit world.

I'll be in Santa Fe from August 9 to 24 and hope to see you before I leave. Please call me when you get in.

With love and gratitude,
Jane

Passing into the Spirit World
Written by Doug George-Kanentiio

The death of a family member or someone we truly care about is the most tragic of human experiences, yet the ancient teachings of the Iroquois give the bereaved assurances spiritual consciousness does not end with the demise of the body.

As Iroquois we are taught our souls are not of this earth but originated in another dimension to which we return when our time on this land is completed.

It is said the movement into physical death takes the soul into warm, living light where we are met by our spiritual guardians and taken along a journey into the sky. We are told this "walk along the stars" follows the path of the Milky Way galaxy.

As the last breath is expelled from the dying the soul rises above the body where it experiences a sense of peace. The soul is aware of the circumstances of death but the initial feelings of trepidation are replaced with a profound sense of release.

Nothing in nature truly ends; the cessation of life in one organism means sustenance for another and the subsequent transformation into something else. The Iroquois believe we as humans have been given this form of life so we may become sensual beings, to learn what it is like to understand birth, struggle, love, death and renewal.

Iroquois who have had near death experiences recall it as a form of knowing. They tell of rising to an all encompassing light, towards a place without pain where they are greeted by beloved relatives and friends. It is from this place the soul is guided towards a celestial home.

In Iroquois cosmology there is no "heaven" or "hell", nor is there a singular, all powerful supreme being waiting to exercise divine wrath against those who have violated sectarian law.

There are two forces we acknowledge as "creators:" one with the power to bring beauty and goodness to the earth, and the other, a lifetaker and carrier of evil. In Iroquois society the challenge was to achieve goodness by living in a condition of material simplicity while performing acts of kindness.

The resulting peace is called the "good mind" which, when achieved, makes the transition to the spirit world a simple one.

Those who violate the good Creator's instruction by committing acts of evil will suffer by having their souls confined between the spiritual and physical worlds; they are prevented by their own deeds from returning to the Creator but at the same time are helpless witnesses to the living. It is said there is no greater agony.

By no means did the Iroquois look forward to dying because they believed life was a great gift to be cherished in all of its infinite forms. In addition, traditional Iroquois are taught all people had important obligations to the living which cannot be casually discarded.

In traditional families there is a ten day mourning period which begins when the loved one passes on. If the person who has died is of the wolf clan then the bear and turtle families will take care of the funeral arrangements from the preparing of the body to the exhuming of the grave.

Services are usually held in the communal longhouse with each person sitting according to their respective clan. A speaker, perhaps a chief or faith keeper, is selected to deliver the words of condolence to the relatives of the deceased.

These words were carefully chosen many generations ago and are meant to relieve sorrow by assuring the mourners their loved one is beyond suffering and in a place where they are being embraced by their ancestors.

All are encouraged to dwell in peace in knowing that when their life's journey is complete there will be a "welcome" for them in the spirit world.

From: Lynda Beth Unkeless
Sent: Wednesday, July 23, 2003 10:32 PM
To: Jane Bay
Subject: Re: Grief

Dear Jane,

There is so much emotion that is arising in me that I would also like to share, but like you, it is just so difficult to talk about much of it at all, so I find myself rendered speechless and ripped open at the heart by her death, and the profound loss and grief it engenders in my heart, yours and all the people who love you.

I spent a lot of time today trying to quietly meditate and reflect on her death, and her life, and our communication yesterday, and feeling toward you and wanting so much in some wider and deeper way to soften your grief. It is so painful to feel all the feelings and not just the ones that I want to feel, I am discovering.

I thank you for sending your beautiful email this afternoon, and I am continuing to think and pray for you and your daughter's passage now.

I have also created a memorial space for her on my altar in my bedroom.

With all my love, and deepest affection,
Lynda Beth

From: Roger Christian
Sent: Wednesday, July 23, 2003 11:15 PM
To: Jane Bay
Subject: Re: Grief

My beautiful Jane, I was ill after reading your email and could not reply.

My heart goes out to you. I have never shared with you my experience but I lost an angel, a soul mate who was sent to me, and who I lost when she saved another woman's life and sacrificed her own. My week in hospital in Mexico with her on life support never coming to, with nasty Catholic nuns was hell in itself.

I went to the depths of darkness, but was blessed with a healer who has basically guided my spiritual path for years. She took me in hand and helped me stand in the pain and not run from it.

What was very important was that she took me to a spirit guide to help me, and it was my friend Toni. It took me a year of intense work. I was able to have the time sent by the grace of spirit to go three times a week, four hours a day. After nine months I reached the place of silence.

I reached the place where I realized she had given me a gift. Love. She had in fact released all in me and this is truly the realization of non-attachment. You know instinctively what to do. Jack Kornfield and Krishnamurti wrote the words that helped me the most.

Love and loneliness deal so well with the pain of this. It is the worst. I am sure like me there are moments that you do not want to go on, and you want to join her, but you need to be here for her. You must shine for her, for she is now in your heart forever, and you will find you have two times the love you share. You were a guide to her, to give her love and support and that is the only gift there truly is.

Destinies are so strange but we are all guided to where we need to be. Toni's mother thanked me on the day after we cremated her. She thanked me for giving her daughter true love before she went, and she told me that her daughter was an angel and could only love a mirror of herself. It was of great comfort to me, and I tell you the same words, for that is why Namgyal found you and you found her. She has resolved her Karma in this world and with your help she is able to fulfill her true destiny spirit. She is with you always. When you meditate into the silence to let her enter your heart, she will.

This is Tagore's poem I placed in Toni's coffin, just two years ago. It's for you, as you will understand these words now for your beautiful angel of a daughter....

My heart beats in waves
on the shore of the world
and writes its name in tears
with these words,
"I love you"

I love you and bless you,
Roger

From: Jane Bay
Sent: Thursday, July 24, 2003 11:09 AM
To: Sarita Patel
Subject: Email from Namgyal's elder brother

Sarita,

I want to share with you an email I received this morning from Namgyal's brother who is studying at Tibetan Medical College in Dharamsala.

Dear Jane-la,

I can understand and feel your feelings at this very moment and I hope the grief that enslaved you would vanish soon. Namgyal's soul would be happy to see you with no grief and she would rest in peace.

Since you have great love and care for your daughter Namgyal Youdon, I am certain that this Karma will bring Namgyal to you as your daughter again someday and feel your motherhood with her gentle hands and bright smile.

We brothers always consider you as our beloved mom. We and our prayers are always there for you. I and on behalf of my brother Tenzin Tsering would like to thank you for raising the memorial fund. Your love and sympathy for us will be remembered and cherished forever and ever.

Today I asked for a leave from the college and went for offering butter lamps and prayers for my beloved younger sister Namgyal Youdon and you at various monasteries in Dharamsala. I believe our sincere prayers will bring everlasting happiness for all.

Please take very good care of your health.

With love and regards, yours' lovingly,
Tsetan Khensur

I love you, Sarita.
Jane

From: Sarita Patel
Sent: Thursday, July 24, 2003 11:30 AM
To: Jane Bay
Subject: Re: Email from Namgyal's elder brother

Oh my god—this is the most incredible letter I have ever read.

Do you know how many people have changed because of the relationship you had with Namgyal? Do you know how many hands are touching when they may never have touched before?

Do you see souls awakening after your souls united in their own journey? How can you ever not feel like you had the chance to be a mother when you have always been one and will continue to be one to these boys—these boys who were also left behind. I am just sobbing with feelings for you now.

I love you so,
Sarita

From: Sue Branch
Sent: Thursday, July 24, 2003 11:45 AM
To: Jane Bay
Subject: Re: Grief

My darling Jane, here is something I love. I don't know who wrote it, but I know you will love it, too.

> "I am standing upon the seashore. A ship at my side spreads her white sails to the morning breeze and starts for the blue ocean.
>
> She is an object of beauty and strength, and I stand and watch her until at length she is only a speck of white cloud just where the sea and sky meet and mingle with each other. Then someone at my side exclaims, 'There, she's gone.'
>
> Gone where? Gone from my sight, that is all. She is just as

large in hull and mast and spar as she was when she left my side, and just as able to bear her load of living freight to the place of her destination. Her diminished size is in me, not in her.

And just at the moment when someone at my side says, 'She's gone,' there are other eyes watching for her coming and other voices ready to take up the glad shout, 'There, she comes!'"

All my love,
Sue

From: Goldie Hawn
Sent: Thursday, July 24, 2003 12:00 PM
To: Jane Bay
Subject: Re: Grief

Dear Jane,

I too am going to do a puja for her passing through the Bardo with ease. I am grieving for you my love and from the bottom of my heart I send you love...so much that it will soften your heart and clear the path for peace and gratitude to take the place of tears. Death is always difficult. You will see her again in so many ways. All the beauty of the earth will remind you of her deep and evolved soul. We serve each other in so many many ways. For this we share gratitude.

I love you xx
Goldie

From: Chin Rodger
Sent: Thursday, July 24, 2003 12:02 PM
To: Jane Bay
Subject: 7 week long prayers and offerings for the departed

Again, my prayers and blessings to you at this moment in time.

It is very honorable of you to honor and follow Namgyal's tradition/culture by making offerings for her onward journey. The Tibetan rituals must be similar to the Buddhist upbringing I had in Malaysia. My Grandma's passing when I was ten years old, still remains alive in me.

I remember my family making daily offerings of delicious food and delicacies with prayers and joss-stick/incense for seven days, then every week for the next six weeks and we wore black till the forty-ninth day. I remember them as joyous times somehow—I remember not being sad with all these continuous remembrances and "celebrations." For us, besides the offerings and also of releasing a live caged bird into freedom, we had a puja set up—a space with a photo of Grandma with candles, incense and special stuff of hers.

This has brought back enormous memories of those special days of remembering my Grandma who meant so much to me. If it is okay with you, I wish to offer daily prayers by lighting incense for Namgyal and invoke the presence of all the Siddhas and saints to guide her onward on her journey, following the tradition daily until the seventh day and weekly until the seventh week.

Jane, my love and blessings,
Chin

From: Shana Chrystie
Sent: Friday, July 25, 2003 1:15 PM
To: Jane Bay
Subject: Quick note…

Dear Jane,

Just a note to let you know I'm thinking of you. If you want any company or to go to a movie or something this weekend, I'm around. And if you don't, that is fine too. Do what you need to do to take care of yourself during this time—that is the most important thing and I support you in that.

I'm glad to hear your willingness to be open to all the feelings that may arise. It takes courage. One of the things that Stephen said to me last year in the midst of all my pain was "... Just keep softening into deeper layers, allowing more. That's what will heal you." My experience continues to be that this is really true.

Hope that your release of the fish was meaningful yesterday—such an interesting symbolic thing to do.

Love,
Shana

From: Dennis Leonard
Sent: Saturday, July 26, 2003 10:56 AM
To: Jane Bay
Subject: Grief

I do think and continue to pray for you and Namgyal....

My feeling is that she is so ok! Her incarnation was supercharged, you were such a catalyst in her life, she came to know someone from far away, and felt so much love, so much wonderful love from you. Tears fall as I write this, I feel she is very ok. I pray for you to find understanding and comfort...She was done here...And we all still have work to do before we move on....

With Much Love and Prayers,
Dennis

P.S. I'm going back on the road with Mickey and the Grateful Dead folks. Should you ever want to talk, call on my cell.

From: Jane Bay
Sent: Saturday, July 26, 2003 3:28 PM
To: Dennis Leonard
Subject: Re: Grief

My darling Dennis,

You are right, she was done here, and day by day I understand that more. Thank you for your continued prayers. Namgyal's forty-ninth day is September 3.

Would you please tell Mickey about Namgyal's passing. He was such a big part of my awakening into Tibetan Buddhism, and I realized when you said you were going out on the road with him that I don't have his email address so I doubt he has heard about her death.

I keep reading the poem that my friend Sarita Patel wrote and would like for you to share it with Mickey, too.

Vaya con Dios, my darling.

I love you,
Jane

From: Dennis Leonard
Sent: Saturday, July 26, 2003 6:34 PM
To: Jane Bay
Subject: Re: Grief

Jane,

I was wondering if Mickey knew. I will share with him and ask that during drums one night, he dedicate some of his wonderful cosmic energy to her soul's travel.

I have been spending quite a bit of time with Billy Kreutzman, the other drummer in the band. Billy recently found great peace and understanding thru the Sufi way. We share prayers just about every time we spend time together at shows. I will pray with him as well.

I know *you* will be all right, and whatever the lesson, *you* will learn it, and be stronger as a result.

We suffer, we grow. Now my heart is glad for the growing soul of

Namgyal, (I felt a benevolent force when I wrote that!) she is a great one! My heart also aches for you, I cry a bit for you, and everyone else who loses a loved one.

Love,
Dennis

From: Fu Ching
Sent: Sunday, July 27, 2003 6:28 PM
To: Jane Bay
Subject: Re: Pray Namgyal and Jane

Hello, dear Jane

How are you now? First of all, I wish you are OK.

I went to Manjushri Monastery, and I did pray for Namgyal in the monastery one hall by one hall, and also I did pray for you. I stayed there the whole morning time. We arrived there the very early morning time, and that time it was very quiet, so I can speak more to Buddha. And, wish Jane can have a nice life!

Any requests, please feel free to let me know. I will try my utmost!

All the Best!

Yours,
Fu Ching

From: Jane Bay
Sent: Sunday, July 27, 2003 8:10 PM
To: Fu Ching
Subject: Re: Pray Namgyal and Jane

My dear friend, Fu Ching,

Thank you so much for your prayers for Namgyal and me at the Manjushri Monastery. Next time I am in Chengdu, will you please take me there?

On Thursday, Namgyal's seventh day since her passing, I released some fish into the San Francisco Bay and threw flower blossoms on the water that floated out to sea. I said goodbye to her and prayed for her safe and peaceful journey through the Bardo. I am feeling more peaceful every day and will continue my morning and evening prayers for her through the forty-ninth day.

And, I will dedicate my meditation practice to her for an entire year from the day of her death. In my prayers to the Buddha, I have found great relief from the terrible suffering I am experiencing, and am very thankful for this. My sadness is lifting, and I am more able to remember the wonderful time I spent with her in Tibet. In fifteen days, we became closer than many mothers and daughters are ever able to achieve, and she will always live in my heart.

I had dinner with Shana Chrystie/GeoEx last night, and told her I want to return to Tibet for Sakadawa at Mt. Kailash next year, on June 3, and want to spend time with Namgyal's family in Lhasa. So, I will arrange my schedule to come to Chengdu on my way to Tibet sometime in late May 2004.

Do you want to hold the remainder of the money from Namgyal's ticket for my expenses next year, or would you prefer to send me a refund after you have deducted your expenses and the ticket cancellation fee? Please let me know what would be best.

Thank you again, Fu Ching, for all your help and support.

With great appreciation, yours fondly,
Jane

From: Fu Ching
Sent: Sunday, July 27, 2003 9:17 PM
To: Jane Bay
Subject: Re: Pray Namgyal and Jane

Hello dear Jane,

It is so great to see that you are better and better, and I am sure that Namgyal she can feel you love and your prayer can help her to Bardo peacefully. And, for me I will go to Manjushri Monastery again, to do pray for Namgyal and you again, hope this can help you. Or I will drive out to a small town where there is a small monastery that has relationship with Gelukpa, and inside a statue of Tsongkhapa. This monastery is very holy.

It is great for you to go to Kailash during Sakadawa. So that we can meet again in Chengdu and we can go to Manjushri Temple again.

For the money, which way is better for you? Let me keep the money or wire transfer to you? If you want me to wire transfer the money, please let me know your bank account or credit card number?

Would you please let me know your address, so that I can mail the paperwork to you. Any questions, please let me know.

Buddha bless you!

Yours,
Fu Ching

From: Dennis Leonard
Sent: Monday, July 28, 2003 10:46 PM
To: Jane Bay
Subject: Re: Grief

Dear Jane,

I'm in Florida now. We start our tour here. I told Mickey the sad news, and he was quite shaken. He just could not believe it... My reaction as well when first I got your mail. I'm sure he will be in touch...

We will be doing a show in Mountain View on September the 19th, (no, I'm not out till then, back in two weeks, then just four days the 18th-21st of Sept.) I would be glad to host you there. The Dead have always been an uplifting force and it might be a good distraction for you. Please feel no obligation, it's just a small something I can offer. I cry again, so I guess you can cry that much less.

I Love You so much my sister, please be well...

Forever Your Friend,
Dennis

From: Jane Bay
Sent: Monday, July 28, 2003 11:16 PM
To: Dennis Leonard
Subject: Re: Grief

My dear brother,

You won't believe this, but I have NEVER been to a Grateful Dead concert. This seems like the appropriate time....

I love you, Dennis,
Jane

P.S. I received two dozen red and pink roses from Mickey.

CHAPTER FOUR

Live Today Today

From: Jane Bay
Sent: Wednesday, July 30, 2003 3:53 PM
To: Dear Friends
Subject: Live Today Today

Dear Friends,

Yesterday, July 29, was the day Namgyal was supposed to arrive in San Francisco for her two week summer vacation from Tibetan Medical College, and it was an especially sad day for me.

But today is another day, and I want to share with you a letter I received from Anna Hamilton Phelan, the woman who is interested in writing a screenplay of *Precious Jewels*, that was handwritten on July 22, 2003 with ink pen on crisp ecru-colored monogrammed stationery.

> Dear Jane,
>
> It's unimaginable. Absolutely unimaginable. And you must be utterly heartbroken. I'm in L.A. and went to St. Monica's to light a candle for her this morning. It was dark and cool in the church, peaceful. And I began thinking about something I had read recently in one of the books you lent me...about impermanence. The Dalai Lama was quoting an earlier incarnation who said, 'Young people who seem strong and healthy, but who die young, are masters who teach us about impermanence.' This is difficult for my western mind to hold, yet I know it's true.

I didn't know your daughter, Namgyal, and was so looking forward to meeting her just for the pleasure of it but also for the more mercenary reason... to study her with the intent of creating/writing a character that captured her true essence. But somehow I do know that she would want you to be at peace with her leaving...which had nothing to do with you or even with her physical self:

Her soul had its own schedule.
While she checked the clock,
talked on the phone, prepared
for her day, made her plans
for the future,
her soul consulted its
inner ledger, asking:
'Have I done what I came to do?'
'Have I touched who I needed to touch?'

While the cat licked his back,
while the water boiled, while
she decided what she would
wear that day
her soul tallied each victory
with its pain and joy and asked:
'Have I made my mark?'
'Have I set things right?'

While the car engine sputtered,
And the tea steeped
her soul — full of longing —
stood in the doorway, and asked —
'Can they live without me?'
On Friday she answered: 'Yes.'

I told my dear friend, Carol Burnett about you and Namgyal and about Namgyal's death and Carol (who lost her daughter Carrie to lung cancer six months ago) sent this thought to you through me: Be gentle and kind to yourself over these next weeks. Nurture Namgyal who now <u>lives</u> in you. And sooner than you think you will find yourself laughing about something silly and you will know you are on the mend.

With warmest affection,
Anna

It's funny, my second ex-husband used to say talking to my family was like being on *The Carol Burnett Show*...

My heart will mend, I know, slowly but surely.

Love to you all,
Jane

From: Margi English
Sent: Wednesday, July 30, 2003 4:10 PM
To: Jane Bay
Subject: Re: Anna's letter

How completely lovely. I look forward to that day when you can laugh again "about something silly." Until then cherish yourself.

Much, much love,
Margi

From: Noah Skinner
Sent: Wednesday, July 30, 2003 5:15 PM
To: Jane Bay
Subject: Hello

Dear Jane,

It was really good to see you Monday and give you a hug. Please know that I'm here for you if you need anything. I will be off duty for a few days but you can always contact me through fire safety or on my cell phone anytime for anything.

I have been praying for Namgyal while she goes on her journey through the Bardo. His Holiness will be in the Bay Area two days after her forty-ninth day and I thought this might be the perfect way to start Namgyal on her new journey.

The attached is an article my father sent about the Dalai Lama teachings that I thought you might be interested in reading. It also has a picture of the Kalachakra mandala that my dad helped build with Arjia Rinpoche.

> This existence of ours is as transient as autumn clouds. To watch the birth and death of beings is like looking at the movements of a dance. A lifetime is a flash of lightning in the sky, rushing by like a torrent down a steep mountain.
> —Buddha (c.563-c.483 B.C.)

Take care,
Noah

From: Mark Lefever
Sent: Wednesday, July 30, 2003 5:36 PM
To: Jane Bay
Subject: Re: Live today today...

Dear Jane,

I'm not one to share my heart so openly, but you have done so with the passing of Namgyal, so I wanted to respond from mine.

With each of your letters my heart has been touched even more than your last letter. Every thought of Namgyal brings me closer to the loss of my oldest brother John who left us at a young age thirty-six. Like Namgyal, he left before we were ready to say goodbye and without any warning. I have now learned to cope with his departure, but in the back of my mind, I will always await his return. No one has ever shed so much laughter, love and joy on so many as he did. As with Namgyal, he was a

155

chosen one for which we will never understand why. I some times awaken to the thought that maybe I'm just stuck in some extended dream, and when I am awake, my brother will be there for me. But the reality is my brother now lives through me and my family, as Namygal will live on through you. Look at how many people she never met, but whose lives will have changed forever through your love and messages.

Warmest thoughts and lots of prayers,
Mark

As I heard the stories of loss that my friends have suffered, I thought of the Buddhist parable about the mustard seed that Dr. Howard C. Cutler recounts in his book *The Art of Happiness*:

> In the time of the Buddha, a woman named Kisagotami suffered the death of her only child. Unable to accept it, she ran from person to person, seeking a medicine to restore her child to life. The Buddha was said to have such a medicine.
>
> Kisagotami went to the Buddha, paid homage, and asked, "Can you make a medicine that will restore my child?"
>
> "I know of such a medicine," the Buddha replied. "But in order to make it, I must have certain ingredients."
>
> Relieved, the woman asked, "What ingredients do you require?"
>
> Bring me a handful of mustard seed," said the Buddha.
>
> The woman promised to procure it for him, but as she was leaving, he added,
>
> "I require the mustard seed be taken from a household where no child, spouse, parent, or servant has died."
>
> The woman agreed and began going from house to house in search of the mustard seed. At each

house the people agreed to give her the seed, but when she asked them if anyone had died in that household, she could find no home where death had not visited—in one house a daughter, in another a servant, in others a husband or parent had died. Kisagotami was not able to find a home free from the suffering of death. Seeing she was not alone in her grief, the mother let go of her child's lifeless body and returned to the Buddha, who said with great compassion, "You thought that you alone had lost a son; the law of death is that among all living creatures there is no permanence."

Kisagotami's search taught her that no one lives free from suffering and loss. She hadn't been singled out for this terrible misfortune. This insight didn't eliminate the inevitable suffering that comes from loss, but it did reduce the suffering that came from struggling against this sad fact of life.

From: Tenzin Tsering
Sent: Wednesday, July 30, 2003 6:50 PM
To: Jane Bay
Cc: Tsetan Khensur

Dear Mom and bro,

Today is day for the second week of Namgyal's death. All the aunties's and others are going to different monastery for the butter lamp pouring. Myself and Lhakyi will be going to Jokhang this evening to change the butter lamp near the Shakyamuni. Leave the butter lamp for whole tonight. Usually it always change the butter lamp every after an hour due to others need to change the butter lamp too. We still believe she is alive and it feels to us like a dream and not a real situation. But it is a real happened.

Mom you too take care. We all miss you a lot and hope to see you soon.

Yours' lovingly,
Tenzin

From: Jane Bay
Sent: Wednesday, July 30, 2003 7:09 PM
To: Tenzin Tsering
Cc: Tsetan Khensur

Dearest Tenzin,

It seems like a dream to me, too, a nightmare actually, but every day
I am more calm and accepting this sad situation. I will be doing special
prayers for Namgyal tomorrow (Thursday, July 31) U.S. time around
2:30 PM here at Skywalker Ranch where I work.

My friends are getting fish for me to release in Lake Ewok, a small
freshwater lake here in the high valley where my office is located. It's
very beautiful and peaceful, and the fish will have a long and happy
life in this lake and will help guide Namgyal on her journey through the
Bardo.

Please give my love to all your aunties and uncles, and their children
Tsedon, Kaltsun, Tsepal and Tsechoe, and much love to you, Lhakyi, and
my beautiful granddaughter Tenzin Monkyi. I miss you all so very much.

With love from your mom,
Jane

From: Robyn Brentano
Sent: Wednesday, July 30, 2003 8:41 PM
To: Jane Bay
Subject: Re: Prayers for my Tibetan daughter Namgyal

Dear Jane,

Please know that I have been holding you and Namgyal in my heart since I received your sad news, and will continue to send you healing energy/prayers as the days carry you forward. I can't begin to imagine how you must be feeling but I am sure you are drawing strength from the profound love you have for her and the unique karmic connection between you.

Thank you so much for sharing this very special event in your life with me. When you first told me about Namgyal and your book, I didn't realize that you had met at TCV and then she returned to Lhasa, so now I understand the import of the title of your book. The children of Tibet are indeed precious jewels. It pains me to know how at risk they are, especially in Tibet, where they have so little opportunity to fulfill their potential. I am sending a donation in memory of Namgyal to TCV and will continue to remember her and you in my prayers.

With warmest regards,
Robyn

From: Lynne Hale (JAK Productions – Sydney)
Sent: Thursday, July 31, 2003 2:51 AM
To: Jane Bay
Subject: Re: Live today today...

Jane,

This is one of the most beautiful messages I've ever read. So wise. All of your friends are learning life lessons through your experience. Thank you for sharing with all of us. I hate being so far away when you are going through such a difficult time but I'm comforted by the fact that you have so many amazing friends to take care of you. If you don't mind, I'd like to forward your letter to Jeanne. I think it would help her with Travis' death.

I'm going to keep your letter forever. It contains wisdom that will help me throughout life. I miss you, Jane, and wish more than anything that I could give you a huge hug.

Lots of love,
Lynne

From: Stephen Simmons
Sent: Thursday, July 31, 2003 7:47 AM
To: Jane Bay
Subject: Re: Live today today...

Dear Jane,
It is so hard to express, especially through e-mail, my thoughts for this loss. Having two children myself strikes an even closer chord to my home. My thoughts are with you. God Bless.

What a wonderul prose your friend inked. Take care Jane and obviously if there is anything... please do not hesitate.

Stephen

From: Jane Bay
Sent: Thursday, July 31, 2003 8:30 AM
To: George Lucas (JAK Productions – Sydney)
Subject: Bereavement Leave

Dear George,

Thank you for phoning last week when you heard about Namgyal's death. I'm sorry I missed your call. I had turned the phone off because it's so difficult to talk about it, but I check the messages every day.

I'm back at work this week, and most of the day passes smoothly, but it's harder than I thought. People are naturally concerned, and sometimes talking about Namgyal dying brings up all the pain of losing her. I need a little more time.

The company gives us five days for bereavement leave which I took last week. I checked with the HR department, and they suggested I take some of my sick days since I'm still behind on vacation from my trip to Tibet in March. We accumulate ten sick days per year, and I currently have twenty days in my sick leave account. I've used only one sick day this year.

I'd like to take ten days of sick leave to extend my bereavement leave, so please sign the Absence Report that I faxed over to the production office.

Thank you, George.
With love,
Jane

P.S. Hope all is going well on the movie.

From: Jane Bay
Sent: Thursday, July 31, 2003 9:00 AM
To: Lynne Hale (JAK Productions – Sydney)
Subject: Re: Live today today…

My dearest sweet friend, I don't know why, but I just broke down again when I read your message. It is harder than I thought to be back at work, so I'm going to Santa Fe for an extended bereavement leave on August 9 - 24.

Today is Namgyal's second seventh day since her passing, and an important milestone during the forty-nine day transition, so I'm doing another fish rescue and release for her, this time at Lake Ewok here at the Ranch. Mike Thomas and Tom Forster have arranged to get the appropriate fish, and a few of my friends from Ranch Ops/Fire Safety will be helping me.

I don't know if I told you, but last Thursday at Oyster Point Marina on the boat ramp just after I had finished my prayers for Namgyal, I stepped closer to the water's edge and slipped and fell on some green slime, landing on my tailbone on the concrete ramp. I had the bucket of fish in my hand and when I fell, some of the fish jumped out of the

161

bucket onto my lap where I was sitting waist deep in the water.

Karen, Dickey's assistant who was helping me, was so upset that I had fallen. She wanted to help me get up, but I said, "No, I'm just going to sit here in the water with the fish, and finish my offering," and that's exactly what I did, throwing the flower blossoms onto the water's surface, and watching them float out to sea.

I thought better of going to the Oyster Point Inn for lunch since I was soaking wet from waist to toe, slime squishing out of my tennis shoes as I walked back to the car. It was quite a funny sight. I'm black and blue all over, and I'm going to see the doctor tomorrow because my tailbone is still very sore, and I want to make sure there isn't a hairline fracture or something nasty wrong with my back.

Jeanne was on the blind recipient list for Anna's letter, and she came over yesterday afternoon with the most beautiful card and message, and a small wooden statue of a "grieving Yogi" that I can give my grief to who will help carry some of this burden for me. It was so touching...

Keep me in your prayers these coming days. I need them more than ever....

I love you so much, Lynne.
Jane

From: Paula LeDuc
Sent: Thursday, July 31, 2003 12:06 PM
To: Jane Bay
Subject: I love you Jane

Oh my dear Jane,

Ashley forwarded your messages about your daughter Namgyal's sorrowful passing. I am so taken with grief for you and her family. I send love with heartfelt deep sadness, Jane, as I know this must be an unbearable and difficult time. My heart is broken for you.

God has His way of working, ways which are not clear at the time or ever, nonetheless, what we must trust as the way it must be. You gave her so much and she to you. Savor the moments and the gifts you shared. I know you do. She carries all the treasures you bestowed upon her as she passes into her next life and you will carry for your lifetime all those she bestowed upon you. Carry those Jane, as the proud mother you were to her. She is so much richer having had you in her life. What blessings you were to one another.

Life's twists and turns can be so sudden, making understanding it impossible. Just know that God loves you both. I am so sorry Jane and love you so much. If I can help in any way please let me know.

I am requesting prayers for you and Namgyal at St. Vincent de Paul. I volunteer in the free dining room every Monday with the Sisters and Brothers of St. Vincent de Paul and we start the day with Mass. You and Namgyal will have special intention prayers on Monday and for the entire week.

Thank you for sharing the beautiful poem and message from Anna. How beautiful the sentiments.

My spiritual guide, Robert Skillman, and I will say a special prayer for both of you in our session on Tuesday evening. Prayers of peace and comfort.

My love and affection,
Paula

From: Jane Bay
Sent: Thursday, July 31, 2003 12:38 PM
To: Paula LeDuc
Subject: Re: I love you Jane

Thank you so much, dearest Paula. It means a lot to me that you are doing prayers for us, and they will be of great benefit to Namgyal on her journey.

I love you,
Jane

From: Tom Hunter
Sent: Thursday, July 31, 2003 2:16 PM
To: Jane Bay
Subject: Namgyal

Dear Jane,

I am stunned and deeply saddened to learn that Namgyal, whom you loved so purely and unselfishly, has passed from this physical realm. I take comfort in this, however: I know how deeply and profoundly your time spent with her changed you as a person, and fertilized a spiritual growth in you that is not capable of description.

I know this even though we spent too little time together for me to have perceived these changes with my worldly senses; I know this because you wore the immense and indescribable joy and happiness of your love for Namgyal like a beautiful garment.

It became you and you it. It will never leave you, even though your daughter has commenced this next journey so much sooner than you would have wished, and even though you are grieving from the loss of her presence in your physical life. Her journey, and yours, will be greater, more fulfilling and more meaningful for the time you shared together and for the beautiful relationship that miraculously resulted.

Jane, you are such a wonderful soul, and because of that, all of your friends share the pain of your loss and want to comfort you. I am honored to count myself among them. But comfort is difficult to find in the face of such profound loss. Keep the wonder of your Precious Jewel at the forefront of your consciousness and do not try to push the feelings you are having to a less accessible place, for the sadness that may accompany thoughts of Namgyal by its nature co-exists with the feelings of great joy, gratitude and pleasure that your relationship has brought.

Sooner than you can imagine, your thoughts will come to focus on the positive, and the pain you are feeling will begin to recede, like the tide.

Please know that my thoughts and my prayers are with you.

With much love and affection,
Tom

From: Jane Bay
Sent: Thursday, July 31, 2003 2:23 PM
To: Tom Hunter
Subject: Namgyal

Dear Tom,

I've been wallowing in grief and self-pity, but you have so poetically described another perspective on this horrible tragedy that is so much more hopeful and helpful.

I've put a copy of your email in my filofax to have close at hand as an antidote to grief when the blue meanies creep back into my consciousness again.

Thank you for your beautiful message. Your thoughts and prayers mean so much to me.

All my love,
Jane

From: Gretchen Elbert Brice
Sent: Thursday, July 31, 2003 2:33 PM
To: Jane Bay
Subject: 2:30 At The Beach

I'm unable to leave the office at this moment to join you all at the beach, but I'm taking a silent moment here to join your hearts and spirits in prayer.

God bless you and Namgyal and everyone whose life she touched.
Gretchen

From: Margi English
Sent: Thursday, July 31, 2003 2:39 PM
To: Jane Bay
Subject: Fish release ceremony

My prayers are with you both right now.
Margi

From: Jane Bay
Sent: Thursday, July 31, 2003 3:48 PM
To: Margi English
Subject: Re: Fish release ceremony

It was a lovely, sweet ceremony. Several of my dear friends from
Ranch Ops came, and I was especially happy to see some of the
Skywalker Firefighters, Stan Lopes, Frank Wells, Jeanne Capozzi and
Noah Skinner, whose father helped Arjia Rinpoche construct a three-
dimensional model of the Kalachakra Mandala Palace that was
recently exhibited at the Smithsonian. Noah gave me a khata, a white
blessing scarf, and a string of Tibetan prayer flags. I'll tell you about
the ceremony when you come up.

Please continue to pray for us, Margi. It will be a tremendous benefit
to Namgyal, and a great comfort to me.

Much love,
Jane

There was more to tell about the fish release ceremony.
Mike Thomas, who works in the Landscape Department at
Skywalker Ranch, had gotten two fish from a bait shop in
Bodega Bay, and he brought them to Lake Ewok in a five-

gallon plastic bucket half filled with water.

Before we began the ceremony, I explained a few details about the purpose of releasing fish for someone who has recently passed (to rescue the fish from certain death so they can help guide the person who has died on their journey) and said that I was going to recite the Tibetan mantra of compassion, Om Mani Padme Hum, seven times before releasing the fish. Everyone was invited to say it aloud with me, or silently offer a prayer on their own.

I stepped to the water's edge, and after finishing the mantra recitation, poured the bucket of water containing the fish into the lake. All of a sudden, the little fish jumped out of the water and scurried across the surface to a cluster of reeds on the side of the beach.

In hot pursuit was a big trout looking for its dinner. I couldn't believe it. Here I was, trying to rescue the little fish from a fate of being used as bait, and their certain demise, and I'd put them in harm's way of being eaten by a bigger fish.

My dear friend, Tom Forster, who is the Ranch Manager at Skywalker, said, "Jane, don't worry if they were eaten, it's all part of the natural cycle of life." I knew Tom was right, but I wanted to believe that the little fish had reached the safety of the reeds.

From: Jane Wyeth
Sent: Thursday, July 31, 2003 3:54 PM
To: Jane Bay
Subject: Re: Live today today…

Oh Janie,

Thank you so much for sharing Anna's beautiful poem. When I read the last line (On Friday, she answered, "Yes."), my eyes welled with tears.

I immediately thought of my daddy, whose birthday was two days ago, when he would have been ninety-three. He died eleven years ago. I celebrated his birthday by going to the Bronx Zoo with my dearest friend (whom I met at Sotheby's in 1973, only a few months after I'd started working there). When I was a child growing up in Providence, my father frequently used to take us kids to one of the two great zoos in Rhode Island. So I celebrated his birthday by being taken by my closest friend to a place my daddy would have absolutely loved.

I also, right after that, thought immediately—and spontaneously—of my mom, who died two years ago July 24th. She was eighty-seven and had been diagnosed three weeks earlier with very terminal brain cancer after being in excellent health until that fateful day. I was blessed enough to be visiting her anyway (for the Fourth of July week) when she had a tiny seizure right in front of me, and I then, of course, stayed with her around the clock for the three subsequent weeks it took before she succumbed.

None of us five kids wanted to be the one to tell my mom the diagnosis, or the prognosis, so we asked her doctor, whom she adored, to tell her himself, the morning after she'd been admitted to the emergency room. Right after the doctor told Mummy, in answer to her "How much life (she didn't say "time") do I have left?", and he answered, "A few weeks to a few months," she smiled gently, looked at him (with my baby sister and me right there, 'cause the three other kids hadn't arrived yet), and said, "It's OK; I'm eighty-seven, I'm ready." ('Course, then she laughed and said, "But I'll be damned if I'm going to take my vitamins any more!") Anyway, sweet Janie, my point is that on that Friday, Namgyal was obviously ready, although no one else in THIS world knew it.

So, be at peace, knowing that your daughter is watching over you now and forever. More important, know that Namgyal is loving you from afar.

And by the way, as I wrote you previously, do NOT expect to "find yourself laughing about something silly sooner than you think." My own experience was that the grieving process for my mom took almost an entire year. I KNOW that I didn't have one good time that whole period. But then, one of my very closest friends died in an accident eleven months later, and then someone else who was very, very special to me for many, many years, too, died in another accident only three months after THAT.

I found that I could not think happy thoughts at all while I was STILL grieving so much and hurting so much on the inside. Maybe you'll be lucky and heal sooner. If you do NOT, however, don't chastise yourself. Everybody's different in terms of how much she loves and how much she then hurts when the loved one is no longer here.

Much, much love, to my dear, dear Janie.
Janie W

From: Jane Bay
Sent: Thursday, July 31, 2003 5:11 PM
To: Jane Wyeth
Subject: Re: Live today today...

Oh, Janie, your stories are so inspiring. Thank YOU for sharing them with me. And, I'm from the South, and we don't do anything with alacrity down there... in my own sweet time...

Much love to you, dear friend.
Jane

From: Jane Bay
Sent: Thursday, July 31, 2003 5:52 PM
To: Shana Chrystie
Subject: It's so hard

Shana,

It has been much harder than I thought to return to work, and Tuesday I tortured myself with thoughts every hour starting at 12:15 PM when Namgyal was supposed to arrive at SFO until midnight when I finally collapsed in bed. I plunged deep into the almost exquisite agony of grief. But it was exhausting, unsatisfying, and difficult to escape from. I'm trying to focus on the joy of knowing Namgyal, but it so hard.

Love you,
Jane

From: Sylvia Boorstein
Sent: Thursday, July 31, 2003 7:54 PM
To: Jane Bay
Subject: Re: Live today today...

Dear Jane,

I am so very, very sorry.

I've lit a candle for Namgyal, a long burning one in a glass, and I'll keep her in my prayers. There really is nothing to say to someone whose heart has been broken, other than I hold you in my prayers as well.

Every blessing of consolation,
Sylvia

From: Lynne Hale
Sent: Friday, August 1, 2003 3:19 AM
To: Jane Bay
Subject: Re: Live today today...

Dear Jane,

I'm so glad that you are going to Santa Fe—you need to get to a beautiful place to heal. It's too difficult to try to concentrate on work when your heart and mind are with Namgyal. I couldn't believe your story about Oyster Point—I love that you just sat in the water and finished your offering! I hope that tailbone of yours is feeling better.

It's been a long week here. I have lots of stories to tell, but it needs to be a phone conversation. I may come in tomorrow morning just to use the phone. If so, I'll give you a call.

Try to continue to do things that comfort you. I'm glad that you shared the letter with Jeanne and that she responded with such a beautiful gift. You two now share a powerful bond.

Lots and lots of love coming to you from Australia.

Lynne

From: Shana Chrystie
Sent: Friday, August 1, 2003 10:24 AM
To: Jane Bay
Subject: Re: It's so hard

Dear Jane,

Sorry not to answer yesterday. I left early to do a session with Stephen.

Thanks for sharing Tom Hunter's email with me. It is beautifully written. Good to keep these things that support you during the rough times. Keep on softening into what comes — just as you are.

I know I've sent this poem of Stephen's to you before, but thought it might be appropriate again.

Be
Poem written by Stephen Dinan

Be the ache of love,
The sweet forgetting of oneness
The delicious hunger for what already Is.

Be the honey of loss,
The death of cool emptiness
Into the searing heat of Form.

Be it all:
The drunken kiss, the pained pulse
The stolen caress, the shared giggle
The betrayed pang, the flowing wound.

Love excludes nothing from Her tender Arms.

Sending you much love,
Shana

From: Tom Pollock
Sent: Saturday, August 2, 2003 2:16 PM
To: Jane Bay
Subject: Re: Prayers for my daughter Namgyal

Jane,

Peggy and I were shocked and depressed to hear the news about the death of your daughter. What universe could have taken such a person so young? I know you speak of Karma, but where is the solace in that?

Our hearts are with you at this terrible time,
Tommy

From: Gordon Radley
Sent: Sunday, August 3, 2003 12:43 PM
To: Jane Bay
Subject: Re: Prayers for my daughter Namgyal

Jane,

I am astounded and devastated for you. I can only imagine what it must be like for you. My prayers and deepest sympathies go out to you and are in my heart. (I just returned from Africa to read your e-mail.)

As I have learned from my African friends as they go through their devastating losses, there is a reason for such early and inexplicable losses and it is known to God even if it is so difficult for us to comprehend and accept. I am so, so sorry. I know that her life and memory will live on inside you like a jewel that is unseeable to others but a source of love, beauty and nourishment to you.

All of my love...
Gordon

From: Joanna Lovetti
Sent: Sunday, August 3, 2003 5:28 PM
To: Jane Bay
Subject: Thank you

Jane,

Thank you for sharing with us what is helping you. Anna Hamilton Phelan's letter about impermanence and the poem from your other friend that you sent a week ago — beautiful and helpful to us all who feel so helpless at a time like this — when someone you love is in so much pain. I heard a deep piercing and plaintive wail when you first sent the news. We are all so connected, for the sorrow and the joy of it all.

Adam has a close friend who is dying and he was over at her place mucking out the horse stalls because she can no longer do it. Her name is Peg. She believes she acquired this illness to teach her compassion for others, because she had little of it before.

Adam was saying how each of us must do our individual work as part of the greater lesson. We took the time to ask each other what we thought our individual work might be. He thinks mine is to learn about humor.

We were brought together to help each other with these things. I don't know what yours is, Jane, maybe that's private, but knowing you is a gift. Thank you.

Sending light and...

Love,
Joanna

From: Jane Wyeth
Sent: Sunday, August 3, 2003 5:50 AM
To: Jane Bay
Subject: Re: Live today today...

You're a SOUTHERN girl????? My goodness, Scarlett, I had no idea.... Please remember now to take care of YOU, sweet Janie, — and not everyone else, for a change, OK???

Much love,
Janie

From: Will Channing
Sent: Tuesday, August 5, 2003 8:27 AM
To: Jane Bay
Subject: Re: Live today today...

Jane,

I'm here in Connecticut with my eighty-eight-year-old aunt and my eighty-year-old mother. It isn't easy yet I still think of your robbery and place things in perspective. I remind you of the beautiful words of one of my favorite authors, Rabindranath Tagore, "Faith is the bird who feels the light and sings while the dawn is still dark." I am with you in prayer and spirit.

Deepest love,
Will

From: Jane Bay
Sent: Tuesday, August 5, 2003 12:22 PM
To: Will Channing
Subject: Re: Live today today...

Dearest Will,

Tagore is one of my favorite authors, too, and I'm glad you reminded me of this beautiful thought. It, and your love, is a comfort to me now, and always.

Love,
Jane

From: Louise Riley
Sent: Wednesday, August 6, 2003 6:08 AM
To: Jane Bay
Subject: Re: Thank you

Dear, dear Jane:

I've been away for three weeks (traveling around Scotland and England, visiting with Eamon's family) and have just returned home, only to read your e-mails regarding the recent loss in your life. As I read each word, I can feel some of the pain you've experienced the past several weeks. Namgyal brought you joy and now sorrow. Isn't that what love is — joy, sorrow, and all those wonderful emotions that we experience when we love someone.

Knowing you, I'm sure you will go through this ultimately knowing what you gave to each other, something most people won't experience in their lifetime. Continue your journey with all the zest and passion you have, knowing you made a difference in people's lives.

Love,
Louise

From: Ruth de Sosa
Sent: Wednesday, August 6, 2003 2:52 PM
To: Jane Bay
Subject: Your beautiful precious daughter

Dear, dear Jane!

I am still in shock and deep sadness over the news of your very special daughter Namgyal. I am beyond sorry for the grief I know you carry that is deeper than words can ever do justice to.

All I know is: Love crosses all time, all space and all eternity. Your love for her, and her love for you, even though she is no longer physically with us, is and always will be a strong and guiding light of purpose for you forever.

I know nothing can replace her EVER, but I get the strongest intuitive "hit" that your little granddaughter really needs you. And all the lessons you are learning and the wisdom of your experience that you so willingly share with us, bless us all, and will continue to do so. Thank you for forwarding those amazing emails.

I do not know why life has to carry such deep and painful lessons... but your story and her story is far from over. What incredible Karma the two of you share. I continue to say special prayers for her.

My own tears mixed with yours. Bless you, Jane. I am truly so sorry...again, beyond words.

Sincerely,
Ruth

From: Roger Christian
Sent: Thursday, August 7, 2003 11:23 PM
To: Jane Bay
Subject: Re: Prayers for my daughter Namgyal

Dearest Jane,

Just to let you know that you are in my prayers. Now is the darkest moment and she will be trying to come to you to enter your heart forever. One day her gift to you will blossom in your heart as all the pain and sorrow turn back to the love it came from. You have the blessing of being evolved in spiritual truth. This will guide you through.

Much love to you,
Roger

From: Lisa Cooke
Sent: Friday, August 8, 2003 12:28 PM
To: Jane Bay
Subject: Hi, my friend…

Dear Jane,

What a wonderful place to heal! (New Mexico). My thoughts will be with you.

I lost someone very dear, unexpectedly, two years ago. It is a wondrous process to experience the excruciating grief gradually transform into a profound thankfulness for having had the chance to feel such deep love for the one that was lost. Not everyone gets to feel that exquisite texture in their lifetime.

Enjoy the quiet beauty of the desert. I hope to see you when you get back.

Much love.
Lisa

From: Glynda Rich
Sent: Tuesday, August 19, 2003 4:41 PM
To: Jane Bay
Subject: Thinking of you

Jane,

Roger and I are deep in the Amish country of Ohio. We left home Aug. 8th and will return around the 30th of September. Retirement is wonderful! I wish you were here for it is a peaceful place. Everyone seems to move slower and thus does life. The rolling hills are full of the most beautiful corn we have ever seen and it is good too!! There is a lot to be said for living a simpler life.

I pray you are doing better. Grief takes so much from a person. Please give yourself time to heal and treat yourself with a great deal of kindness. Whatever brings you joy, regardless of how small, is what you need now. Eat well, be with dear, understanding friends, go to special places that are peaceful and healing, write in your journal, spend time in nature. Simply, be good to yourself.

I love you, Jane. Please stay in touch.
Glynda

From: China Galland
Sent: Sunday, August 24, 2003 8:29 PM
To: Jane Bay
Subject: Re: Prayers for my daughter Namgyal

Dear, dear, Jane,

I am SO sorry to only now be responding to this terrible, sad news. My heart goes out to you and to Namgyal's family. I know how much you loved her and how eager you were to have her here. May her spirit be free to inspire us all now!

Blessings, prayers and condolences,
China

From: Katie Lucas (JAK Productions – Sydney)
Sent: Sunday, August 26, 2003 10:55 AM
To: Jane Bay
Subject: Sorry

Dear Jane,

I was sad to hear about your daughter. I'm sorry it took so long for me to email you, but I didn't know what to say. I am so sorry — she was such a lively and vibrant spirit, and I was looking forward to getting to know her better.

I love you so much and I miss you.
Katie

From: Jane Bay
Sent: Tuesday, August 26, 2003 4:39 PM
To: Katie Lucas (JAK Productions – Sydney)
Subject:

Dearest Katie,

Thank you so much for your sweet note, and don't worry about not knowing what to say. Your thoughts about Namgyal are very precious and I will treasure them always.

I love you, Katie, and hold you in a very special place in my heart.
Jane

CHAPTER FIVE

Angels & Incense

From: Jane Bay
Sent: Wednesday, August 27, 2003 5:31 PM
To: Dear Friends
Subject: Angels & Incense

Dear Friends,

I've just returned from a two-week extended bereavement leave in Santa Fe and am feeling stronger every day. But as my cousin recently wrote, "Grief takes so much from a person. Please give yourself time to heal and treat yourself with a great deal of kindness. Whatever brings you joy, regardless of how small, is what you need now. Eat well, be with dear, understanding friends, go to special places that are peaceful and healing, write in your journal, spend time in nature. Simply, be good to yourself," and that's exactly what I'm trying to do.

I have been doing special prayers in the Buddhist tradition for Namgyal every seventh day until her forty-ninth day (the time in which her consciousness goes through the stages of death to reincarnation/rebirth). On the fifth seventh day, I went with my beloved sister, brother-in-law, and Reno Myerson and Cynthia West to a Tibetan Buddhist Stupa (shrine), high up on a mountain overlooking the Santa Fe basin, to offer my special prayers for Namgyal. Out of nowhere, it seemed, a lovely young Asian woman about Namgyal's age appeared wearing jeans, a T-shirt, and hiking shoes, and she sat down next to me on a flagstone bench in front of the shrine. She smiled, but didn't say a word.

My brother-in-law handed her a stick of incense. I leaned toward her and said, "We're going to have a special prayer ceremony for my twenty-two-year-old Tibetan daughter who died recently, and you're welcome to join us." She looked at me with a peaceful expression on her face and said, "Such a young age to die…" That's all she said, but I felt an enormous warmth coming from her that I know was love. The next thing I knew, she was gone…. I think she was an angel, sent by Namgyal to comfort me, and to let me know Namgyal was okay and not to worry about her.

We lit incense, said prayers, and hung Tibetan prayer flags in a nearby juniper tree so that our prayers for Namgyal would be carried on the wind up into the heavens.

As the sun was setting, creating a golden halo around the stupa, I read a Confucian poem recited by Tu Weiming on the *Graceful Passages* CD that I listen to every night at the end of my evening prayers for Namgyal.

> Your vital energy is returning to the Source,
> Like the flowing stream returning to ocean.
>
> Heaven is our Father, Earth is our Mother,
> All people are our brothers and sisters,
> And all things are our companions.
>
> In this gentle, peaceful journey,
> You are forming one body with heaven and earth.
>
> Entrust yourself in the transforming
> and nourishing care of the Cosmos.
>
> Listen to the voice of love in silence.
> You have heard the Way.
> Return home, in peace.

I went back to the shrine, alone, the next week at sunset. Sitting on the flagstone bench, I felt Namgyal's presence very strongly and was filled with gratitude for having known her in this lifetime.

Peace, Love and Light,
Jane

From: Nancy Harris
Sent: Wednesday, August 27, 2003 10:54 PM
To: Jane Bay
Subject: Re: Angels & Incense

Dear Jane:

So good to hear from you, and your words are very healing to me. I will print some of this and take it along with me. Your experience and process is a beautiful way to make sense of the bottomless whorl of grief and loss that affects many of us who deal with unclosed deaths big and small in our professions and path.

Thank you for giving this great advice on how to care for oneself and others in a healthy and self loving way. Your words bring much wisdom and acquiescence in the face of the Mystery, which is often inexplicably painful.

Much much love to you.
Nancy

From: Ruth de Sosa
Sent: Thursday, August 28, 2003 1:28 AM
To: Jane Bay
Subject: Re: Angels & Incense

Dear Jane!

You write SO beautifully...it is as if I am there with you. What an amazing journey you are on...thank you so much for sharing your magical story...I DO believe it was Namgyal coming to you as an angel as well.

I know your grief is something that she didn't want you to have to go through...and I know she is comforting you and is re-affirming your mutual love for each other.

Again, the photos you sent were so JOYFUL, just like the two of you belonged together always. I send you a HUGE HUG and lots and lots of love! I am ever, ever so sorry you have to go through this, and yet, it is all so incredible how it is unfolding...your trip to Santa Fe sounds like the perfect place to pray and meditate and be in nature. I can see the prayer flags in the wind in my mind's eye...

Your continued truthfulness in following life's path - no matter how rocky or difficult - gives one courage to live each day as best one can.

Thank you for that. I, too, through your words, can feel Namgyal floating on the breezes and playing...her Spirit fully free!

Love,
Ruth

From: Lynda Beth Unkeless
Sent: Saturday, August 30, 2003 5:08 AM
To: Jane Bay
Subject: Re: Angels & Incense

Dear Jane,

Reading your email gives me faith that the healing and grieving process you are undergoing now is a graceful passage of hope and love.

All my love to you,
Lynda Beth

From: Tenzin Bob Thurman
Sent: Thursday, August 28, 2003 11:24 AM
To: Jane Bay
Subject: Re: Angels & Incense

Dear Jane,

All our love goes with you and Namgyal. I hope you have been reading for her the prayers and passages from the *Book of the Dead* for the various days. I have done so several times.

Lots of love,
Bob & Nena

From: Frank Wells
Sent: Tuesday, September 2, 2003 12:49 PM
To: Jane Bay
Subject: Re: Angels & Incense

Dear Jane,

I just wanted to express to you how much I admire the grace with which you are walking this difficult path. This sacred journey is a deeply personal one, and I thank you for sharing your experiences with me. And though my heart mourns for your loss, following your growth continues to lift me up and comfort me.

You are in my thoughts and prayers.

Love,
Frank

From: Chin Rodger
Sent: Tuesday, September 2, 2003 11:10 PM
To: Jane Bay
Subject: 49th day

Jane,

Tomorrow, the forty-ninth day of Namgyal's passing, my prayers and blessings are with you and will be offered in love to Namgyal — may she continue to be in the bliss that is already hers and may that bliss flow forth to you, dear Jane.

Tomorrow, as each of us gather wherever we are, to pray and invoke blessings for Namgyal, know that it is an auspicious time, collectively our prayers do reach Namgyal and everyone involved "when a group gathers to recite prayers, there descends upon them the divine presence, mercy covers them, angels spread their wings over them, and God mentions them to those close to Him."

Thank you, too, for sharing this difficult time. I tried to bring forth words to comfort you, but Jane — it is you who is comforting me. Although, I miss Kim so very much, I know too that she is o.k. and that she is so in bliss.

Your sharing, so selflessly, has been very helpful. We are also very fortunate to have a spiritual path to support us so that we may have a greater understanding, and also the great Shakti-energy and Grace in our lives.

Much love and blessings,
Chin

From: Jane Bay
Sent: Wednesday, September 03, 2003 1:38 PM
To: Tenzin Tsering
Subject: Namgyal's 49th day

Dearest Tenzin-la,

As Namgyal's forty-ninth day arrives, I want you to know that I will be doing special activities for her. This weekend I will be going to a public talk with HH on Friday night that is being sponsored by The American Himalayan Foundation. I'll spend a day in silent meditation at my house on Saturday, then on Sunday my teacher, Yvonne Rand, will be holding a Buddhist ceremony for children who have died. I will be attending that for Namgyal as well.

Know that you and your family are in my daily prayers for your good health and prosperity.

With much love from your mom,
Jane

From: Richard Nelson
Sent: Monday, September 08, 2003 12:20 PM
To: Jane Bay
Subject: I Love You

Dear Jane,

I have been thinking about you and want to express my profound sadness for your loss. As I am sure you know, no matter what we think and know, grief will have its way with us in its own place and time.

When it comes all we can do is let it have its way. It's healing. Let it flow. Judy is doing so well and I am so proud of her. She has such courage and strength. I pass on this picture of her to bring you joy.

I love you,
OXOXOX Richard

From: Joanne Shenandoah
Sent: Tuesday, September 09, 2003 7:44 PM
To: Jane Bay
Subject: Re: Angels & Incense

Jane Bay,

You are an angel. I wish you could have come to the Symphony – as we tributed a song "Feather in the Wind" to all those who have passed on. It is a natural progression, one which I am beginning to believe balances the joy of the incoming of Life.

I was delighted to see you in Santa Fe, if just for a short while. Here's hoping our next meeting will include more music and time to share the joining of spirits.

With love,
Jo

From: Vanessa Whitford
Sent: Tuesday, September 09, 2003 11:13 PM
To: Jane Bay
Subject: Hello, Jane Bay :)

I know it is late and you are probably not awake at all, but I thought I would write to you nonetheless.

When my Mom told me the news of the recent tragic events that have happened in your life, although I of course wanted to console and lend myself to you in any way I could, somehow I had hesitations. I felt immediate pain for you. After mulling over the events in my mind for a while, I tried to think of what I could say to you, what I could give you, that would be something besides the the same meaningless comments that people who don't really know me often say to me when I am sad, and I realized that I had nothing to say.

Even though I have thoughts in my head and feelings in my heart, they are inexpressible in writing, or spoken words, or gestures, at least by me. I have never experienced the type of loss that you are experiencing, so I don't want to say meaningless chatter like, "I know how you feel," and "I'm sorry," because I'm not. To me that makes no sense. I have done you no wrong, so why would I be sorry in consequence? (I hope you know that was in no way intended to offend you).

So, I decided to wait until something happened, (although I did not know what it would be at that time), that would inspire words that I felt could be of any consolation to you. Therefore, here they are:

Jane Bay, I can only offer you the deepest empathy in my heart and an ear that will listen wholeheartedly whenever you ask.

I love you, and I hope this letter reaches you in good spirits,
Vanessa

From: Jane Bay
Sent: Tuesday, September 12, 2003 12:43 PM
To: Vanessa Whitford
Subject: Re: Hello, Jane Bay :)

Dearest Vanessa,

Your email touched my heart and filled it with love. I could wish for nothing more from you because love is the great healing balm.

Thank you, precious jewel, for your great heart of compassion.

With oceans of love to you,
Jane

From: Jane Bay
Sent: Thursday, September 16, 2003 4:11 PM
To: Richard Nelson
Subject: Re: I Love You

Dearest Richard,

Forgive me for not responding sooner to your loving email last week. It was my first week back at work full-time since Namgyal's death, and it's been hard to get into the rhythm of the Ranch again. But I loved your message, and you're right on about grief having its way with us in its own place and time.

And thank you for sending that beautiful photo of Judy. I love her smile, and when she shines her light on me, I don't have a care in the world.

I love you, dear friend.
Jane

CHAPTER SIX

Love & Loss

From: Jane Bay
Sent: Wednesday, September 17, 2003 2:09 AM
To: Dear Friends
Subject: Love & Loss

Dear Friends,

The heavens rumbled with thunder the morning of Namgyal's forty-ninth day. No rain, just thunder and lightning due to unusual atmospheric conditions. I liked it, all that energy whirling around in the cosmos.

The day before, however, had been an emotionally critical day. Spontaneous outbursts of tears, anxiety about letting her go, the sadness of saying goodbye, the end of this time of prayers and mourning during her transition through the Bardo. But I woke up refreshed on September 3, with the full day ahead to make my prayers and offerings for her, and time to consider the consequences of Namgyal's life and death on my life, and the rest of my life without her.

I'd like to share with you an excerpt from a letter I received from Tom Hunter. It read in part,

> I know how deeply and profoundly your time spent with Namgyal changed you as a person, and fertilized a spiritual growth in you that is not capable of description. I know this even though we spent too little time together for me to have perceived these changes with my worldly senses. I know this

because you wore the immense and indescribable joy and happiness of your love for Namgyal like a beautiful garment. It became you and you it. It will never leave you, even though your daughter has commenced this next journey so much sooner than you would have wished, and even though you are grieving from the loss of her presence in your physical life. Her journey, and yours, will be greater, more fulfilling and more meaningful for the time you shared together and for the beautiful relationship that miraculously resulted.

That night, Namgyal's cousin, Dr. Dickey, and her friend, Mary Ann Wong, came over for a fire puja (ritual) in the garden outside my bedroom where Namgyal's altar was set up. I had ordered a fire pit from the Smith & Hawken catalogue, (a large copper bowl that rests on a wrought iron stand about eight inches off the ground) that I placed on the gravel patio. We made a fire of juniper, kindling, and the powdered incense Dickey brought back from her recent trip to Lhasa to see her and Namgyal's family. Dickey spoke the prayers in Tibetan, and then the three of us recited Om Mani Padme Hum (the mantra of Compassion) together seven times.

Shortly after Namgyal died, David Riordan had come over with his flute and Lakota medicine bag, and he offered songs and prayers in the garden for her, for me, and for all creatures and sentient beings on the earth. He made 49 Prayer Ties (small bundles of tobacco wrapped in red and white cloth that were strung together on a long cord) that I placed on the burning embers in the center of the fire pit during the puja. As the smoke from the Prayer Ties curled and drifted upward toward the waxing moon, Dickey, Mary Ann and I joined hands in a circle around the fire, and in the silence, I heard the voice of love.

Two days later, I went to Davies Symphony Hall in San Francisco to hear the Dalai Lama give a talk about "A Human Approach to World Peace." Being in the presence of the Dalai Lama is always inspiring, and I was fortunate to have the opportunity to shake His hand which was a great blessing. The essence of His talk, it seemed to me, was about dialogue, discussion, talking, communicating more from the heart, from the heart of compassion, and less from the mind.

Serendipitously, Yvonne Rand was performing a "Ceremony for Children Who Have Died" the Sunday after Namgyal's forty-ninth day at Goat-In-The-Road, the center in Muir Beach where she is Resident Teacher. The ceremony, in the Zen Buddhist tradition, involves the Bodhisattva of the Earth Womb, Jizo, who is depicted as a Buddhist monk and is worshipped as the protector of women, children, and travelers.

That afternoon there were people from many different faiths and spiritual traditions participating in the ceremony which was performed in silence except for Yvonne's instruction and guidance, and the occasional sound of soft, muffled cries and tears from some of the men and women. We were invited to make an offering to place on an altar with statues of Jizo, as well as statues of Mary and the Baby Jesus; Quan Yin, the Goddess of Compassion and Divine Mother aspect of Buddhism; and Avalokiteshvara, the Bodhisattva of Compassion. (The Dalai Lama is the reincarnation of Avalokiteshvara).

Yvonne supplied red cloth (in Japan the color red is associated with a true heart), needle and thread, scissors, paper and pencils, and red string, blessed by the Dalai Lama specifically for this ceremony, as well as a rubber stamp of Jizo, and a red ink pad. She also cut sprigs of rosemary, the herb of remembrance, from her garden.

Not knowing how to even sew on a button, I made a paper wind chime, stamped with the image of Jizo, and added a small talisman made of the red string tied at the bottom. I cut a heart-shaped piece of red satin cloth, wrapped two small sprigs of rosemary in it, making a little ruffled bundle to attach at the top of the paper with more red string so it could be hung outside or placed over a statue. On my paper wind chime I wrote in pencil so it would last longer, "In Remembrance of Namgyal Youdon — Beloved Daughter of Jane Bay."

At the end of the ceremony, one by one, we placed our offering on a statue on the altar, mine going on Avalokiteshvara. We were encouraged to release our child into the arms of compassion, and with Yvonne, we recited aloud, seven times, the Heart Sutra:

Gate Gate Paragate Parasamgate Bodhi! Svaha!

Gone, Gone, Gone Beyond, Gone Utterly Beyond!

What Freedom!

Driving home, I felt an enormous relief, a lightness of being, and an awareness that the veil of grief that had enveloped me for the past forty-nine days was lifting.

There's one more story I want to share with you before I close. Recently I received an email from a former colleague I have rarely seen since she left Lucasfilm several years ago. Here's what she wrote:

From: Cheryl Forberg
Sent: Saturday, August 23, 2003 10:13 AM
To: Jane Bay
Subject: hello

Hi Jane,

I hope this note finds you well and happy!

Jane, next week it will be eight years (!!!) since I lost my dear friend Michael. Since that time, I have written way too many sympathy notes to friends who have lost a loved one. In each note, I close with the wonderful words you shared with me when I lost Michael. "May the love of family and friends bring you comfort. May time bring you peace." Those words never lose their warmth and depth.

Thanks so much for sharing them then. They still mean a lot to me.

All best to you,
Cheryl xo

From: Jane Bay
Sent: Wednesday, August 27, 2003 12:54 PM
To: Cheryl Forberg
Subject: Re: hello

Dear Cheryl,

It's so amazing that you should send this message. My Tibetan daughter died on July 18 and I have been heartbroken and grief stricken ever since. These words are exactly what have sustained me, too, and I know in time I will find peace.

Thank you for giving this back to me just at the moment I needed it most.

With love,
Jane

And so, my dear friends and family, thank you for your love, for it has given me strength and courage to face the loss of my precious jewel, Namgyal. My grief is diminishing every day, and my gratitude for her being in my life increases with every breath I take. My love for Namgyal is eternal.

Life goes on, one day at a time, one moment at a time. I'm looking forward to returning to Tibet again next year to see Tenzin Tsering and Namgyal's family in Lhasa, and on to Mount Kailash for Sakadawa, the annual celebration of the Buddha's birth and enlightenment. Then to India to meet Namgyal's other brother, Tsetan Khensur, who is studying at the Tibetan Medical College in Dharamsala. I'm their mother, too.

I love you all,
Jane

From: Margi English
Sent: Wednesday, September 17, 2003 6:07 AM
To: Jane Bay
Subject: Re: Love & Loss

Dearest Jane,

I have been gone in Italy for the last two weeks and feel at a loss for not being part of your forty-nine days.

But, what struck me as I read this last e-mail of yours, was not just your beautiful, expressive writing style, although that has obviously deepened and developed during this process, but the amount of love and community that you have in your life.

Seeing it from the distance, I am so touched. There are so many, many people who love you and this is obviously a direct result of your love and compassion. What a painful way to have to experience the circle of love that you have created, but you should be so proud of the lives that YOU have touched.

We all knew Namgyal because of the way you gave her to us so freely in the passion that you expressed in your words, both written and spoken. Thank you, Jane for letting me into your life. You are such a brave and generous soul.

Much, much love,
Margi

From: Sylvia Boorstein
Sent: Wednesday, September 17, 2003 6:27 AM
To: Jane Bay
Subject: Blessings to you

Dear Jane,

Blessings on your journey, and on Namgyal's, as well. And thank you so very much for including me in the circle of friends who share your experience. My own losses sit easier, and my own understanding deepens, as I read your personal process.

I thought, as I read, "I wish I could read this description of the Jizo ceremony to my class." I know about it, of course, and what happens there, but a personal account is always so much more moving. And the rituals of the fire ceremony, as I read them, were evocative for me of the religious ceremonies I know that honor passings, and it is confirming to know, this is what human beings do. They say "good-bye" in ways that sanctify a relationship and its ending.

And, I thought as I read your sentence about the lightness of being, at the end, that it is so important to notice that moment of relief, and tell other people about it. I won't, of course, say anything of what you've written unless you tell me it would be all right. And, telling would be extra. You have been healing to me already.

Blessings,
Sylvia

From: Jane Bay
Sent: Wednesday, September 17, 2003 6:45 AM
To: Sylvia Boorstein
Subject: Re: Blessings to you

Dear Sylvia,

Your message touches me deeply. Of course, you may share my letter with your class. Writing is part of my healing process, and if it can be of any benefit to others, I will be glad.

Thank you so much for your kindness.

Love,
Jane

From: Sylvia Boorstein
Sent: Wednesday, September 17, 2003 7:32 AM
To: Jane Bay
Subject: Re: Blessings to you

Thank you so much, Jane, and may your healing continue and may my telling of your experience, when it is right to do it, be of benefit to all beings.

Sylvia

From: Jane Wyeth
Sent: Wednesday, September 17, 2003 7:56 AM
To: Jane Bay
Subject: Re: Love & Loss

Oh Janie,

I've been thinking of you so often in the last few weeks, knowing that Namgyal's forty-ninth day was approaching. I didn't want to call or e-mail you until AFTER that day, as I wanted to respect your need for solitude during those forty-nine days. And then, in this morning's e-mail, I found your beautiful note.

Janie, I'm so happy (wrong word, but you know what I mean) that your grief is, actually, diminishing day by day. Cheryl's recent words to you, quoting yours to her after her terrible loss eight years ago, made even more tears fall down my face. (My tears began with the first sentence of today's e-mail.)

I particularly loved your description of the ceremony that Yvonne performed — and your version of sewing the red cloth filled with sprigs of rosemary, for remembrance. What a wonderful idea.

If it's not inappropriate, do you think it would be OK for me to make something similar to yours (heart-shaped, of course, too) and containing a sprig or two of rosemary to hang somewhere special in my home

— for my own Mummy, whom I miss so very, very much (even two and a half years after she died), I still talk out loud to her every morning in the shower.

I can't remember if I wrote you that a few days before she died and I was with her all day long for the four weeks before she died — I asked Mummy, as I was holding her hand as she lay in bed dying,

"Mummy, what am I going to do after you're gone? I won't be able to talk to you anymore."

Her response was, "Yes, you will."

And then she gave me a HUGE smile and added, "You just won't be able to hear my answer."

I realized just the other day, however, that even though I can't hear my mom's side of our conversation, I actually CAN hear it, because I know pretty much exactly what she would have said to everything I tell her or ask her. I hope that you continue talking to Namgyal, because she will hear you.

And OF COURSE you're the mother of Tenzin and Tsetan, too. I knew that when you first wrote of Namgyal's brother. So even though Namgyal was your "official" daughter, her brothers are obviously your children, too. So you are blessed again, as you still have two sons.

Ever since Victoria (now twenty-four) was born, I would tell her, "I love you up to the sky and down again." I love you, too, dear Janie.

xxx Janie W

From: Ree Whitford
Sent: Wednesday, September 17, 2003 8:43 AM
To: Jane Bay
Subject: Re: Love & Loss

Dearest Jane,

I'm grateful that you have included me in your circle of friends that have received the letters about your journey through grief. Thank you. What you have shared inspires and comforts me. Your love is beautiful.

I know very little of the spirituality that you experience, but I do know that it is a powerful and positive force. I have nothing to offer but my love and sympathy as another mother and your friend.

With love, Ree

P.S. By the way, Jane, I have a guesthouse here in Studio City. Should you ever need to be in L.A. and want to avoid the hotel scene, we would be delighted to have you stay with us. I think you might enjoy my garden — as I have enjoyed yours.

From: Tina Mills
Sent: Wednesday, September 17, 2003 10:27 AM
To: Jane Bay
Subject: Re: Love & Loss

You are such a beautiful writer Jane!! But without these true feelings deep in your heart you wouldn't be able to write so movingly... I love hearing about the amazing "coincidences" (not) surrounding you and Namgyal and all the people around you who love you so much! Your travels are certainly not over (spiritual or physical)!

Thank you so much for sharing your life and love and loss with us. I *love* it when you laugh, but I am honored to be a part of your suffering as well...

T.

From: Mark Parnes
Sent: Wednesday, September 17, 2003 10:51 AM
To: Jane Bay
Subject: Re: Love & Loss

Jane,

Thank you so much for sharing this email with me. My thoughts and love are with you and Namgyal. Please know that, even though we do not get together that often, I am grateful for your friendship and for the time we have spent together, particularly in Tibet. You have touched many lives in wonderful ways and I am proud of you for facing the loss and pain but remembering the love. Be well my friend.

Love,
Mark

From: Jane Bay
Sent: Wednesday, September 17, 2003 12:25 PM
To: Jane Wyeth
Subject: Re: Love & Loss

Dearest Janie,

Please, by all means, make an offering for your mother, and have your own ceremony of remembrance for her. I'm so happy that you resonated with this experience and can bring it into your own life. I got goosebumps when I read your mom's reply, and I know that Namgyal will always hear me, too, and that I will know her reply as well.

Thank you, dear Janie, your love and friendship mean so much to me.

Love you,
Jane

From: Jane Bay
Sent: Wednesday, September 17, 2003 1:21 PM
To: Margi English
Subject: Re: Love & Loss

Dearest Margi,

You have been on my mind so often, and I had planned to call you last Sunday, but was having chest pains and was somewhat disoriented in the sweltering heat (109 degrees in the shade in San Anselmo last weekend). I went to the doctor on Monday, and it seems I have a condition called Costochondritis which is an inflammation of the cartilage between the ribs and the breastbone. I'm taking anti-inflammatory drugs to fix it, but my doctor is sending me in tomorrow for a heart scan just to be absolutely sure that's the cause of the pain.

The pain in my heart actually started two weeks before Namgyal died. I had a premonition that I was going to die and set up an appointment with my local attorney to make a will, naming Namgyal as the primary beneficiary. The appointment was scheduled for the Friday after she passed away, which was canceled, of course, but I assumed the pain had been some sympathetic intuitive response to her dying and that it was her heart that failed, not mine.

It wasn't until after Namgyal's forty-ninth day that I realized the pain was still there, and had worsened. I had been so preoccupied with my prayers and practices for her that I hadn't really noticed it. I've heard there is a medical condition that occurs from a broken heart.

I wondered if you wanted to come up during the Mill Valley Film Festival October 2-12? I don't know what tickets I'm getting yet, but I'll try to get something on Saturday, Oct. 4 and Saturday, Oct. 11.

Hoping to see you soon and thank you, Margi, for your thoughtful message. I am truly blessed by the friendships in my life.

Love,
Jane

From: Jane Wyeth
Sent: Wednesday, September 17, 2003 5:10 PM
To: Jane Bay
Subject: Re: Love & Loss

Thanks for your so very prompt reply. I look forward to searching for the red cloth out of which I will cut a heart. Not so sure how easy it'll be this time of year to find fresh rosemary, but if necessary, I can always buy the yucky "fresh" packaged kind at the local supermarket. I'll just have to leave a section of the edge of the heart open, so I can replace the rosemary with good sprigs next summer. Or isn't that appropriate? Should I just leave the original sprigs inside or replace them when the aroma dissipates, like an old sachet?

By the way, my daddy's daddy was a tailor, so my father is the one in our family who sewed all the buttons. My mom probably knew how, but she pretended that she didn't have a clue. I, on the other hand, inherited my mom's inability to sew a botton on straight. However, as you and I both know, in this case, it's very much the thought that counts.

All my love,
Janie

From: Jane Bay
Sent: Wednesday, September 17, 2003 5:20 PM
To: Jane Wyeth
Subject: Re: Love & Loss

Any type of rosemary is just fine, and if you have to go with store bought, you could certainly replace it any time in the future. The important thing is that you make this "your" offering, something that you're comfortable with. That's what's important. I used satin fabric because I like the feel of it, but any red fabric, cotton/wood, etc., that you like will do.

Love you,
Jane

Dear Jane,

We all love you, too. Thank you for once again sharing such compassion and insight with me. I do pass your emails on to my family.

I want you to know what a profound effect you are having on Lexsea. I thank you for this — being a sixteen-year-old with only these few years of living experience it has been very moving and enriching to see her becoming more enlightened by your letters and I feel this is making her a more compassionate human being. We have your photo from the *Precious Jewels of Tibet* standing on a white ledge in the studio alongside the photo you so kindly gave to me of Namgyal and yourself at the same exact spot with arms stretched wide...

Loss is strong, but Love is so much stronger. A day does not go by that I do not think of my beloved brothers, Stephen and Andy, who have died during the last ten years. So even though time goes by, I do not forget them. I truly enjoy all the memories I have. Your daughter was so beautiful in spirit and body —what a treasure.

We are happy to hear you are returning next year to visit Namgyal's family in Tibet. You are blessed with so many loving friends and family.

All my love,
Lis

From: Ruth de Sosa
Sent: Wednesday, September 17, 2003 9:01 PM
To: Jane Bay
Subject: Re: Love & Loss

Dear Jane, Beloved Mother of Namgyal!

Again, what a beautiful letter. Thank you for sharing the continuing journey of your loss, your renewal, and the realization that you are still a mother with a rather large family who need you and love you here on this physical plane.

I am so glad you saw the Dalai Lama. What blessings surround you.

Much love,
Ruth

From: China Galland
Sent: Thursday, September 18, 2003 11:20 AM
To: Jane Bay
Subject: Re: Love & Loss

Dear Jane,

Thank you for including me on your list to receive this beautiful letter. I have tears in my eyes as I write back.

Bless you for opening up your heart to us all, and letting me in on Namgyal's journey with you. Both your names are on my altar.

I was also so happy to hear about Yvonne Rand and to know that she's your teacher. She's done marvelous work and has been so deeply kind to me on many, many occassions. I have great respect for Yvonne and have had the benefit of her wise counsel over the years at critical moments. Can you please send me an e-mail address or some way of getting notices for Goat in the Road events? It's been entirely too long since I've paid my respects to Yvonne.

Love and blessings,
China

From: Jane Bay
Sent: Thursday, September 18, 2003 1:46 PM
To: Lis Blackwell
Subject: Re: Love & Loss

Dearest Lis,

Please tell Lexsea how much I appreciated her beautiful handmade card and message. And I'm so touched that you have shared my emails with her.

With love and gratitude,
Jane

From: Jane Bay
Sent: Thursday, September 18, 2003 3:31 PM
To: China Galland
Subject: Re: Love & Loss

Dear China,

I am grateful that I had the opportunity to take your writing workshop several years ago. What I've come to realize is that writing is part of my healing process, and I am compelled to share it with others because I cannot do this alone. The exchange of feelings/emotions between me and you (circle of friends), is what cultivates the ground for me to "experience" this most difficult and challenging experience. It puts things in perspective in a way that I could never have realized without your being part of it. If it can be of help to others, I am glad. So, truly, thank you for being in the circle.

Yvonne has a wonderful website: www.goatintheroad.com where you'll find the calendar of events, contact numbers, etc. I am so fortunate to have been studying with her since 1991 and she has helped me enormously with the loss of Namgyal. I know she would be pleased to hear from you.

With love and gratitude,
Jane

From: Susan Branch
Sent: Tuesday, September 23, 2003 5:39 AM
To: Jane Bay
Subject: Love & Loss

Hi Sweetheart,

Oh yes, I have been getting your emails, and printing them and giving them to Joe, and we have been touched by your journey and cry when we read about it.

What happened to you has never happened to me, I haven't lost a family member or anyone close to me, only my Grandma, and it is easier to live with when the person is ninety-two. I guess I am so programmed to "help" that I feel completely at a loss in profound heartbreak, except to say I am here and I love you and I do think about you every day. I have been wanting to call you again and hear your voice.

I am ambivalent about death you know, I don't know what to think, I basically think it is part of life, and then I try not to think about it anymore. I pretty much have planned to cross that bridge when I come to it, and then I hope I can do it just like you. Every spiritual, nature embracing move you made was beautiful to me.

All is well here. I am still face down in the creation of the Autumn cookbook. I've been here (San Luis Obispo) since last March, and very much resemble "the blob." I am two-thirds done. Joe left for France yesterday — he is doing the same sailboat race he did last year, and in two weeks he flies to Chicago to meet my train and ride the rest of the way east with me to the Vineyard where we will have an eight-day visit to see the house, friends, and to take Fall pictures for the book.

OK honey, talk about a blabbermouth! Sorry, hope every day gets better for you. I am sure there is a hole in your life where Namgyal is supposed to be right now, planning Christmas without her. :-(I am so sorry dearest Jane.

I love you very much, your friend for life,
Sue

From: Jane Bay
Sent: Thursday, September 25, 2003 3:07 PM
To: Dennis Leonard
Subject: The Dead Concert

My dearest Dennis,

Thank you so much for the wonderful experience I had last Friday night. I'm sorry I didn't see you at the concert, but I was obsessed with getting a hot dog during the intermission (my friend nearly choked on hers) and I thought I'd see you at the end of the evening. Then, it went so late that I worried about being too tired to drive back to Marin and left just at the end of the encore. We came backstage and saw Howard Cohen. I hope he told you I was there.

You won't believe this, but it was one of the most wonderful concerts I've ever attended. I really loved the music, the energy, the good vibes and contact highs. I especially loved Mickey's song "Plead My Case to the Court of Paradise" (I think that was the name of it). And, when he started playing those huge round drums at the back of the stage, I felt every vibration in my body, and all the grief and sorrow I have been holding since Namgyal died just melted away.

My friend, Karen Mullarkey, who was the photo editor at *Rolling Stone* magazine in the seventies/early eighties, was in hog heaven. She's a Dead Head from way back. We had so much fun, laughing and reminiscing about the good old days. Karen and I've been friends for thirty-three years. I met her in L.A. one afternoon, stoned on acid, sitting with my boyfriend at the time on the front lawn of her apartment that was across the street from mine on Beachwood Drive, just below the Hollywood sign. I have no idea why we were sitting on her lawn instead of mine, but she invited us up to her apartment. We were really hungry, just coming down from our trip, and Karen fed us the most delicious herbed chicken from a recipe she had gotten from Joan Didion. We've been friends ever since. So it was like going back in time to be at a rock concert together again, and it was a blast.

My only regret is not seeing you. I'm so sorry I had to leave before giving you a big hug. Hope to do that soon. Just let me know when you'll be back at the Ranch, and I'll come to you...

I love you, dear friend.
Jane

From: Tenzin Tsering
Sent: Thursday, September 25, 2003 8:29 PM
To: Jane Bay
Subject: Bank Account

Dear Mom,

I received 1500 usd on 25 Sept 2003 from Bank of China Lhasa branch. Also sending message for your friends.

Yours' child,
Tenzin

From: Jane Bay
Sent: Friday, September 26, 2003 10:44 PM
To: Tenzin Tsering
Subject: Re: Bank Account

Dear Tenzin,

I'm happy to know the money arrived at the Bank of China in your account number. I set up a repeating wire transfer system on that account and would prefer to use it, so I don't have to fill out new forms when I send you money again in the future. I hope this is acceptable to you.

I'll print your thank you note and send it to the people who contributed to the fund in memory of Namgyal. My friend, Benina Gould, is going to Dharmasala in October and will give Tsetan Khensur his money from the fund. I'm also sending him photographs that I took in Lhasa of you, Tenzin Monkyi, Namgyal and your father, and some of Namgyal and me.

Tenzin Monkyi is probably growing up very quickly. Please send me recent photos of her and your family from time to time.

Much love from your mom,
Jane

From: Jane Bay
Sent: Friday, September 26, 2003 1:14 PM
To: Dear Friends
Subject: Thank you note
Importance: High

I'm enclosing a thank you note from Namgyal's eldest brother, Tenzin Tsering, the father of my beautiful twenty-one month old granddaughter who I'm going back to Tibet to visit next year. Tenzin and his brother, Tsetan Khensur, are grateful for your generosity in contributing to the memorial fund in honor of their beloved sister, Namgyal Youdon.

Dear Mom,

This is message to all the people who kindly made contribution to us:

Thank you very much for your kindness even though we live far from each other and culture is totally different. Even though we are strangers to each other your concern is worth much more than someone in the Tibetan culture.

Your kindness that I never forget forever and I always pray for you all wishing you a great prosperous life and enjoyable forever. I will pray to the God to bring you to me. I definitely not waste this amount and use this on the study that my job is here sustainable for all.

Any effort I can make from Tibet that you all want I will definitely send to you all for instance Tibet souvenir stuff. I don't know how to express my feeling in the very best way, but anyway thank you very thousand much to all.

We will be a same family link forever. When you have the time to visit Tibet I will invite you all to my home with my daughter and wife and whole family. Hope to see you and return your gratefulness.

Sincerely yours, Tenzin

With love and gratitude from me, too.
Jane

From: Tenzin Tsering
Sent: Monday, September 29, 2003 12:41 AM
To: Jane Bay
Subject: Photos

I think you will get recent photos of us that taken by your friend Melene Smith. No problem for account it is fine. We recently sent a small gift to you as well. We gave a small statue of Avalokiteshvara to Melene and video about Tibet as gift to her. Right now I think she will be on way to Everest and hope we will see her after a week. We miss you a lot.

Yours' child,
Tenzin

From: Jane Bay
Sent: Monday, September 29, 2003 8:46 AM
To: Tenzin Tsering
Subject: Re: Photos

Dear Tenzin,

That's wonderful news. I can hardly wait to see the photos, and thank you for the gift. I look forward to receiving it when Melene returns to the States.

I really appreciate your kindness to my friend. I miss you and your family, too. I will be very happy to see you again next year. I'll email my schedule to you soon.

Much love from your mom,
Jane

From: Tenzin Tsering
Sent: Monday, September 29, 2003 9:07 PM
To: Jane Bay
Subject: Namgyal's astrological chart

Dear Mom,

I forgot to give Melene the astrological chart. I am sending it now.

Namgyal's astrological chart's meaning:

• When she was died her mind was attracted to eldest brother, that may be when she was fall she may thought if eldest brother is near her then eldest brother will help her to lift her up.

• Some women were not allowed to look her dead body. It will harm her to Bardo to the sky burial.

• During the last year September her soul was already collected from a cave up in one of monastery.

• She will be reborn in the very rich family in western culture.

• Her death deity is Vajrapani.

This is the main meaning of the astrological chart and I am very sorry not to give you a detail as AC chart need to burn with the sky burial.

Yours' child,
Tenzin

From: Jane Bay
Sent: Tuesday, September 30, 2003 9:00 AM
To: Tenzin Tsering
Subject: Re: Namgyal's astrological chart

Dear Tenzin,

Thank you for sending the astrological chart. I'm sorry to say I don't really understand it. Could you explain the comment about her soul was already collected in a cave up to the monasteries? Also, who were the women that couldn't look at her body? Was Auntie Drakpa one of them? It's very interesting. Hope to hear more about it.

With love from your mom,
Jane

From: Aleja
Sent: Wednesday, October 01, 2003 10:55 AM
To: Jane Bay
Subject: Your daughter

Jane,

Sept. 28, I climbed this mountain in honor of your daughter. 14,000+

feet. It is just above Telluride. I thought of you with your beautiful smile and warm heart. Prayers also recited for my mother, my brother and your daughter. It was such a glorious day.

Love to you,
A.

Aleja—Telluride mountains, Colorado Photographer: Aleja

From: Jane Bay
Sent: Wednesday, October 01, 2003 11:22 AM
To: Aleja
Subject: Thank you

Wow, Aleja. You are awesome!!!!! Thank you so much for this sacred offering you made in memory of Namgyal. It looks like a very challenging mountain to climb, and I am grateful for your efforts on my daughter's behalf, and your prayers for me.

I had an emotional breakdown over the weekend, and your prayers were probably what helped me through it. I know the pain of losing her will surface again and again, but it was so unexpected because I had gone on a half-day meditation retreat on Saturday. Just couldn't get past the grief until Sunday night with the help of my massage therapist, Lynda Beth Unkeless. Woke up refreshed on Monday morning.

Thank you, dear friend.

With love and gratitude,
Jane

From: Benina Gould
Sent: Wednesday, October 01, 2003 11:33 PM
To: Jane Bay
Subject: Your emails

Dear Jane,

Thank you for sharing the emails you wrote. They gave me strength to imagine if I could endure the worst. I feel your love and courage throughout everything. I hold you and Namgyal in my prayers. I am happy that we are all together for each other.

Love,
Benina

From: Tenzin Tsering
Sent: Thursday, October 02, 2003 3:27 AM
To: Jane Bay
Subject: Re: Namgyal's astrological chart

Dear Mom,

It did not say any particular women. I will write a Tibetan version here and you can ask someone in States know about that:

mo rang ki laa gonpa shik kyidraphung tro nay kyel

Otherwise it is very difficult for me to explain for you. I hope you understand it

Yours' child,
Tenzin

Unfortunately, I was never able to find the meaning of this statement. Dickey couldn't translate it either without seeing it in the original Tibetan language and that document was burned at Namgyal's sky burial. It remains a mystery.

From: Louise Riley
Sent: Thursday, October 02, 2003 12:49 PM
To: Jane Bay
Subject: Re: Love & Loss

Dear Jane:

I feel blessed that you continue to share your family and friends what you have, and are still going through. I read your letters over and over again and through your words of wisdom and love, I find myself going down a road that I have not yet traveled.

Love,
Louise

From: Thupten Donyo
Sent: Tuesday, October 07, 2003 12:21 AM
To: Jane Bay
Subject: Gyuto Monks

Dear Jane,

Thanks for the note and I'm so sorry for my late reply. As you know we have moved to a new location but still in the San Jose area. The following address is our new contact information.

I'm so sorry to hear about your daughter Namgyal's lost. It was very sad to hear about your lost. Last month our friend Howard Cohen told me about this news and right away we the monks did prayers and lit 108 candles for her. I also mentioned to our teacher who is 78 years old reincarnated Lama and requested him to do prayers for her as well. We all hope and pray that she take good rebirth.

I thank you so much for helping Namgyal. I'm sure she must have had a very good time during her study in Lhasa because she had a second good mother in America. You gave her very good opportunity to study in a medical field but it was unfortunate that she could not live long.

I know how you feel about your lost but what can we do. I used to sponsor a monk who was in his late forties, and he was always sick. Since 1990 I promised to send him some money to buy medicine for him and I also had a great deal of hope that he'll recover from his illness. However, after four years of medical treatment, he could not survive and I was so upset that I could not keep him alive. But what can I do. I did my best to keep alive but no success. Because of that sometimes I still get upset. So I understand how you feel now. We will continue to pray for her time to time to have a good rebirth.

Take care and Tashi Delek.

.

Thupten Donyo
Gyuto Vajrayana Center

From: Jane Bay
Sent: Tuesday, October 07, 2003 4:32 PM
To: Thupten Donyo
Subject: Love & Loss

Dear Donyo,

I will send you an email entitled "Love & Loss" that I sent to friends shortly after Namgyal's forty-ninth day. Thank you so much for your prayers for her. The 100th day will be Friday, October 24.

Hope to see you soon.
Warmest regards,
Jane

From: Thupten Donyo
Sent: Tuesday, October 07, 2003 5:04 PM
To: Jane Bay
Subject: Re: Love & Loss

Dear Jane,

We will have a prayer service for Namgyal on October 24th, at 10 AM – 11 AM. I know it is a long way for you to come for the prayers, but if you would like to come, we can make arrangements for you. If not, then we'll do without your presence.

Thank you,
Thupten Donyo

From: Becky Winding
Sent: Wednesday, October 08, 2003 11:30 PM
To: Jane Bay
Subject: prayers

My dearest Jane:

I am sitting here weeping looking into the eyes of Namgyal. I am shocked and can't begin to comprehend or absorb a fragment of your pain and grief. I can only in this moment comprehend the love of a mother and her daughter and that unto itself is indescribable and overwhelming.

I am so deeply touched by the series of e-mails. You were so right...I cannot yet talk about this to Cami. I need some time to find the words.

I know you will once again work through all of this pouring your heart out on paper to share with all of us who are blessed to be on this earth with you...perhaps through your writing you will find the meaning of such a seemingly unjust and senseless loss.

Namgyal was so blessed to have you as a mother, if only for a short time in this place...

I pray for your peace and I give you my love,
Becky

From: Tsetan Khensur
Sent: Sunday, October 12, 2003 7:54 AM
To: Jane Bay
Subject: thank you!!!!

Dear Mom,

Thank you so much for sending the $1500. gift in memory of Namgyal. I am also very happy to receive your wonderful book (*Precious Jewels of Tibet*), and those photos. It's a great pleasure to see you for the first time. I was so excited to go through some chapters of your wonderful book including your search for Namgyal, and so deep it touched within me by knowing how hard you tried in search of Namgyal, and also your support and sympathy for the people of Tibet.

Please accept my gratitude. I am so grateful to you for sending the $1500 gift and convey my words of thanks to all of your friends. I assure you that I will make the best use of the money and wouldn't waste a single coin on any unnecessary things.

I have sent a card to you in the hand of Mrs. Benina and a photo of mine. Hope you like it.

With oceans of love. Yours' lovingly,
Tsetan

From: Joanna Lovetti
Sent: Tuesday, October 14, 2003 6:36 PM
To: Jane Bay
Subject: hello

Dear Jane,

Just wanted to tell you I was thinking about you. Thanks for sharing the loving messages. I'm so glad that so many people have been there for you in your hour of need. It was moving to hear that David was there.

I have wanted to do something for you, too, but other than pray and love you, I have felt pretty helpless. But I did think of one thing, if you would like. You know I hadn't drawn in over twenty years, and I picked up a pencil again last year. It was wonderful. It's startling how little time I have spent at something I enjoy so much, and it occurred to me that I could do a drawing of you and Namygal, if you would like. If this appeals to you, let me know. You'd have to give me pictures, but I thought you might like it.

Have been buried in the editing room on this series. I haven't been in a very good mood. Adam and I had such momentum on our film co., and unfortunately everything is on hold with it til this job is over. I'm lucky to have it, so I shouldn't complain, but...

Adam sends his love from New Mexico. I have asked for some time off to go see my mother in Florida in a couple of weeks. She had a mild stroke this summer, and she's never met Adam, so we're going there the end of this month. This editing job may go until the end of the year, but I do plan to be in New Mexico at Christmas, so I'll see you then.

Take care, Jane. Love always,
Joanna

From: Jane Bay
Sent: Wednesday, October 15, 2003 10:01 AM
To: Joanna Lovetti
Subject: Re: hello

Dearest Joanna,

I would be honored for you to do a drawing of Namgyal and me. Maybe you could select the pictures you want to use sometime in Santa Fe. I'll be in Santa Fe for a week at Thanksgiving, and two weeks for Christmas and New Year's. Of course, I'll have my annual holiday party, but it will be smaller this year, just my closest friends like you and Adam. I don't think I'm ready for a crowd of people yet.

Sorry to hear about your mother's stroke. My mother had a stroke, too, several months before she passed away. I had been told by mother's doctor that she could live another ten years, but when I went to see her, I took that opportunity to tell her how much I loved her, that she had been the best mother, and I didn't discuss any old baggage or disappointments. She died a week after I left Florida, and I was so glad I had that connection with her. I've always wanted the last words I say to someone to be positive because you never know if it will be the last words they ever hear from you (The old adage, don't go to sleep angry.). So, those are my thoughts about your visit to your mother, for what it's worth.

Much love to you, Joanna.
Jane

From: Jon Berg
Sent: Saturday, October 11, 2003 11:01 AM
To: Jane Bay
Subject: Thinking of you

Dear Jane,

I just wanted to let you know I'm thinking about you. I greatly appreciate you sharing so many of the wonderful and beautifully expressed thoughts that so many others have had. I lack their eloquence, but there hasn't been a day when you and Namgyal haven't been in my thoughts. I hope you're doing well.

Love from us both,
Jon and Lisa

From: Jane Bay
Sent: Wednesday, October 15, 2003 10:15 AM
To: Jon Berg
Subject: Re: Thinking of you

Dear Jon,

Thank you for your thoughts and love, it means so much to me. Namgyal's 100th day is next week, Friday, October 24

I saw a program on PBS last night, "The Wisdom of Dreams" about Carl Jung, and was thinking this morning about the meaning of family and community. I realized that, through the Internet, I have been connected with my "family" all over the world during these months of mourning for Namgyal. I feel very close to you and Lisa, and your emails have been the link that connects us to the web of life.

Much love to you, dear friend.
Jane

CHAPTER SEVEN

---

100 Day

From: Jane Bay
Send: Wednesday, October 22, 2003 12:11 PM
To: Dear Friends
Subject: 100 Days

Dear Friends,

During the first forty-nine days after Namgyal died, I was totally focused on prayers for her and had the time to be present with the shock of it all. Since returning to work full-time, it feels good to turn my attention to the tasks at hand. Life is settling into a comfortable and familiar routine, engaging with colleagues and friends. So, it was a surprise how spontaneously I could have a meltdown.

Marshall Turner, one of the board members of the George Lucas Educational Foundation, arrived for the board's quarterly meeting a few weeks ago, and he stopped by my office before the meeting began. "I'd love to see the photos from your trip to Tibet to see your daughter, if you still have them here at the office," he said with great enthusiasm. It took my breath away, but of course he had no way of knowing what had happened, and he was stunned by the news of Namgyal's death.

What followed was a slow, quiet sinking, deep down into the familiar grief pit, and by the following morning, which was Saturday, I was wallowing in despair. I had been cheated, robbed of my most precious jewel. It was a cruel karmic twist of fate. What life lesson could I possibly learn from losing her?

By nightfall, I tried to distract myself with television, and while surfing the channels, came upon a musical program celebrating World Children's Day on a local PBS station. But it was more torture, all those children singing along with superstars like Celine Dion and Josh Groban, and when they sang a duet of "The Prayer," the song written by Carole Bayer Sager and David Foster, I completely broke down.

The next thing I knew, an announcer was telling me to get up and go to the telephone and make a pledge to the station. In an almost Pavlovian stupor, I followed his instructions. Through my sniffling tears, I made a pledge of $100 and charged it on a credit card. When the going gets tough, the tough go shopping. I felt better immediately, but didn't even know which station it was until the invoice arrived in the mail a week later.

What's hard is seeing people who don't know. I can't pretend it didn't happen, can't say I'm fine when someone I haven't seen for a long time asks the question, "How are you?" Telling the story inevitably brings up the sadness again, and sometimes I feel like it's just too much to bear. Then, in my head, I hear the exhortation of a Japanese Zen Master, "No matter how hard or heart-rending it is to live, do not wear a tearful face. Let's keep walking steadily and live out our lives."

Every year around the first of October, I look forward to the Mill Valley Film Festival. I hadn't been to the movies since Namgyal died, and as I circled the films in the program I wanted to see, a theme began to become apparent. They were all films about love and loss. Films from Iran, Denmark, France, Canada, UK/Luxembourg, China and the USA. I saw at least one film a day, frequently two, during the ten days of the festival. The director of the festival, Mark Fishkin, had kindly given me a "Fast Pass" that provided easy access in and out of the screenings.

Early on, I ran into Robert and Terese Payne, who asked "The Question." I've known them for many years through my association with Mount Tamalpais School. Terese had given my book, *Precious Jewels of Tibet*, to their daughter, Samantha, when she went off to college back east a few years ago. I showed them several pictures I carry around in my purse that were taken of Namgyal during my trip to Tibet in March. I couldn't hold back the tears, nor could Terese. We sat together at the screening that night, and several other nights, and being in their company made me feel protected in a way, and that it was safe to go out into the world again.

On another night, sitting on the aisle at the Sequoia Theatre, I saw Gordon Radley as he entered the theatre, and I called out for him to take the empty seat next to mine. Gordon knew about Namgyal, but it was the first time I'd seen him since he left Lucasfilm about eight months ago.

Gordon talked about the poignancy of her death. He said the timing and circumstances were both inexplicable and yet somehow purposeful, fulfilling a destiny that is unknowable, but integral to some greater meaning and purpose. He told me about the recent death of his African goddaughter, a thirty-two-year-old woman he had named when she was born while he was in the Peace Corps in Africa. He had recently returned to her village and was concerned about her health. She died subsequently, possibly from AIDS-related complications, but she had written a letter to Gordon that didn't arrive in the U.S. until after he had learned of her death. He said it was like receiving a message from the grave. She was telling him not to worry about her.

Gordon had sponsored an Iranian film, *Paradise is Somewhere Else*. It was one of the films on my list. The night of the screening, I noticed a tall, lithe woman in flowing robes who had a bald head, walking toward Gordon in the theatre lobby. I thought, "Another Marin County woman going through chemo." But, it was Susan O'Connell, a former Bay Area film producer who several years ago had taken vows as a Buddhist priest at Green Gulch Zen Center in Muir Beach. It had been ages since we last saw each other.

When she asked "The Question," I told her the story of losing Namgyal. As we talked, I had the sensation of everything else around us falling away, and saw only her face. Looking into her eyes felt like being connected straight through the heart, and in that moment, a soothing calm came over me.

The next day, I received the following email:

Dear Jane:

I thought the reason I was going to the festival on Tuesday night was to spend some time with Gordon and see some new films. Now I see it was to connect with you, and hear your heartbreaking story.

I will do a memorial service for your daughter. Would it be all right if we do the ceremony on Wednesday afternoon, Oct. 22? (The next observance for Namgyal is Friday, October 24, the 100th day since her passing). And, if it is ok with you, I would like to read the poem that you sent with the first email, telling your friends of her death.

After reading the love soaked letters you sent, I feel that your "motherness" which was evoked by the commitment you made to your daughter, and developed and sustained by the depth of your wish for her happiness, is something that is vital and alive in you – and is a radiating gift to the world.

Thank you for sharing your journey with me. I am comforted in knowing that such a great pain can be sustained and lived through. I will pass along your story as an example of skillful action to anyone I meet who has suffered loss, which means basically everyone.

Love,
Susan

It doesn't feel skillful. It's a constant struggle to keep my balance, and it's exhausting. This is hard work. Yet, I am beginning to have a taste of relief that I think comes only when I look straight into the face of suffering and realize that the wound will heal, even though a scar will always remain.

In every single film I saw at the Mill Valley Film Festival, I felt a symbiosis with the characters as they struggled to overcome the terrific suffering in their lives. Their suffering was no different than mine, and through the medium of film, I felt connected to the human condition of all beings. It didn't matter that these were movies; the stories were very much alive. Art imitating life or life imitating art, it doesn't really matter.

Being a single woman, with no other children, and living alone, I have been afraid of isolation. It is what compels me to write these emails, just as I was compelled to write *Precious Jewels of Tibet* as a way to cope with losing Namgyal the first time. When we were reunited in 1998, shortly after *Precious Jewels* was published, I told her we would never be separated again in this lifetime. It never occurred to me that her lifetime would be so short, but I can honestly say I feel we made the most of the time we had together, and about that, I have no regrets. If there is one thing I've learned from this excruciating experience, it is the realization that I am NOT alone, and there exists a deep sense of interconnectedness with each of you, and all sentient beings on earth.

In closing, I want to share a beautiful poem sent to me by a friend.

Full Succulence
Poem written by Stephen Dinan

In the swirl of forgettable days
There emerges a knowing:
We are not here to taste
A life drained of beauty
But to savor the full
Succulence of the Divine life.

There is a catch, however,
For the Divine does not
Flow through light alone:
Suffering, fear, and dread
Are part of the
Full Godly meal.
Some spices singe
While others soothe.

To savor the full succulence
Means to expand the Heart beyond
Its safe compass, to let it be bowed
And broken, delighted and dazzled,
Humbled and honored until there is
No experience from which we
Shrink.

Thank you for letting me share this journey with you. It is an integral part of the healing process.

With love and gratitude,
Jane

From: Cathy Nilsen
Sent: Wednesday, October 22, 2003 2:06 PM
To: Jane Bay
Subject: Re: 100 Days

My dear Jane,

You are a gift in my life and so many others. I continue to learn and feel so many of life's emotions from your emails. It is difficult to accept that we are here to experience all that life has to offer not just the joys. Knowing this I still wish that I in someway could ease your pain. You must however know that your life has brought joy and knowledge to so many of us and Namgyal has touched us through you.

Lots of love,
Cathy

From: Lisa Cooke
Sent: Wednesday, October 22, 2003 12:24 PM
To: Jane Bay
Subject: Re: 100 Days

Dearest Jane,

It was with the greatest honor I read your email and shared your grief for Namgyal. I only knew her through your love, but feel a deeply intimate connection to her, because her brief life shed sacred light on the potential for love in all of us.

May the tears I shed reading your words become part of the healing balm that will eventually close the wound in your heart. We are all one. We are all love.

You are a dear friend and I thank you for sharing your incredible journey with me. Love to you and Namgyal. You are forever mother and child, one and the same.

Namaste,
Lisa

From: Lis Blackwell
Sent: Wednesday, October 22, 2003 12:41 PM
To: Jane Bay
Subject: Re: 100 Days

Dear Jane:

You sign your beautiful painful letter, "With love and gratitude"… It is gratitude and love I feel towards you and deep honor that you call me friend.

You are never alone — I pray daily that your pain lessens.

All my love,
Lis

From: Lynda Beth Unkeless
Sent: Wednesday, October 22, 2003 5:07 PM
To: Jane Bay
Subject: Re: 100 Days

Dear Jane,

"Delighted" and "dazzled," "honored" and "humbled" — those 4 words contained in the poem you sent so aptly describe how I feel that the journey of my life somehow...miraculously! intersected with the journey of yours.

Thank you very much for your amazing and beautifully written email this afternoon.

All my love,
Lynda Beth

From: Ree Whitford
Sent: Wednesday, October 22, 2003 6:30 PM
To: Jane Bay
Subject: Re: 100 Days

Jane,

You are an inspiration. By that I mean I feel enlarged and enriched by hearing of your journey. You are certainly not alone. There is no need for your giving spirit to be isolated. We all share reality and the only thing that interferes with real understanding and community is our own desire to bury reality. Acceptance defeats barriers.

I'm just going to mention again your standing invitation to the Pool House, so that you won't forget, if you seek sanctuary in L.A.

With love,
Ree

From: Gloria Borders
Sent: Thursday, October 23, 2003 6:59 PM
To: Jane Bay
Subject: Re: 100 Days

Dear Jane,

Once again your e-mail has moved me to tears, but I do think it's a good thing. Thank you so very, very much for including me on your journey. Karen and I are traveling to Santa Fe today for a couple of days of relaxation since work has been so hard lately.

I find the trip so much more meaningful now that I know about Friday being the 100th day. We will have a special moment of prayer for you and Namgyal. I will be back to the Ranch on November 4th to finish *Peter Pan* and am still looking forward to the hug I promised.

Love,
Gloria

From: Ruth de Sosa
Sent: Friday, October 24, 2003 3:07 AM
To: Jane Bay
Subject: Re: 100 Days

Dear dear Jane,

Thank you as always for your wonderful e-mails that so honestly express the journey you are going through no matter how painful... I moved, as I told you, and your beautiful card and the pictures of you with Namgyal are here with me...and I am so amazed at how ALIKE the two of you look...truly like mother and daughter...and how you found each other, lost each other, found each other and lost each other again...and yet, ultimately she always lives inside of you and inside of all of us, too.

Grief is the most unusual taskmaster...especially now when it is all so new and different...you are back at work and back in your life and yet you are forever altered, deeply changed, not knowing how loss will find you in any given moment. My heart so goes out to yours.

And you are right, grief and loss have touched all of us in so many large and small ways over the years...and what always floors me is when it hits me, so many days, months and even years later...it can surprise me by the depth of its freshness all over again... sometimes a dull ache, sometimes deeply buried so I am barely aware of it, other times tears and slashing pain...all triggered by something as simple as the smell of a certain flower, the color of something out of the corner of my eye...a phrase of music on the radio...or just thoughts late at night when I can't sleep...yes, LOSS...definitely part of the human condition. It seems never ending sometimes.

And yet, I am so happy that you were and are a mother still! Such a gift! Both of you a blessing, one to the other.

I am glad that so many wise and caring and loving individuals are all around you. Yes, the hardest is when you have to tell people who don't know yet and it is all still so new and immediate...100 days...it is hard to believe.

Love,
Ruth

From: Sylvia Boorstein
Sent: Friday, October 24, 2003 6:08 AM
To: Jane Bay
Subject: Re: 100 Days

Dear Jane,

As always, I am tremendously touched by the depth of your grief and your willingness to share it. Your insights into moments of hope sustain me in the griefs that I am holding.

Blessings to you and to the spirit of Namgyal,
Sylvia

From: Roger Christian
Sent: Tuesday, October 28, 2003 5:54 AM
To: Jane Bay
Subject: Sorrow

Dearest Jane,

I understand your sorrow. We think we are stoic and practice nonattachment as we understand it and feel the joys of release for our dearest loved ones, but suddenly from nowhere the pain hits, and it is a pain that no human beings should have to endure. It contains sorrow and sadness, anger and confusion and loss and a feeling of being so alone.

Pain is the worst feeling of helpless and inconsolable grief. You may want to die, too, but you have to stay and use the gift she had given you. You have to let go of everything. Namgyal's love will be with you. She will live in your heart forever, you will have double the love to give that you already had.

All I can tell you is it is normal, and as Krishnamurti and Jack Kornfield say you have to stand in it, stand in the pain until it transcends back to the love it came from, and that is guaranteed it will.

The suffering though can be unbearable at moments but you have to go through it to transcend it. It's all okay. I wonder at the world we are in. We are not karmic recipients as that suggests punishment and that does not fit the true essence of spirit. However, we have been chosen by angels to be there when they transcend. You are strong enough to do this, though it may not seem so some days.

I can only send you love, Jane, and remember that there is a gift somewhere in this of gold. Love is all there is. You have been privileged to love. Most people never find this in their lifetime.

I will send you strength and love. Be blessed and cry until you can't any more. You won't believe how much water can come from a human being.

Love,
Roger

From: Jane Bay
Sent: Tuesday, October 28, 2003 9:44 AM
To: Roger Christian
Subject: Re: Sorrow

Thank you dearest Roger, from the bottom of my heart for your wonderful words of wisdom. Your words are like the sound of a bell of clarity ringing in my head. I'm especially grateful for the reminder, "We are not karmic recipients as that suggests punishment and that does not fit the true essence of spirit. However, we have been chosen by angels to be there when they transcend." Yes, I know in my heart this is true. It's just in the meltdown that I lost sight of the true nature of reality.

All my love to you, dear friend,
Jane

From: Jane Bay
Sent: Tuesday, October 28, 2003 11:25 PM
To: Dear Friends
Subject: Pilgrimage to Mount Kailash and Dharamsala

It has become very clear recently that I want to return to Tibet again, to physically be with Namgyal's eldest brother (father of my grand-daughter) and his family sometime during this year of mourning. I've decided to go on May 18, 2004, for my sixty-third birthday, and will spend almost a week in Lhasa visiting Namgyal's relatives who so graciously welcomed me into their hearts and homes at Losar in March of this year.

It will probably be my last trip to Tibet, so I am planning to fulfill my long standing dream of going to Mount Kailash, Tibet's most sacred mountain, to celebrate Sakadawa, the festival that commemorates Buddha's birth and enlightenment. Then after spending time at the sacred Lake Manasarovar, south of Mount Kailash, I'll drive down to the Nepal border and on to Kathmandu. With a few days' rest in Kathmandu, visiting Bodhnath, the largest Tibetan Buddhist stupa in Nepal, I'll fly to Delhi. Then by train, I'll go to Dharamsala, the home of the Dalai Lama and the Tibetan government in exile. Namgyal's elder brother is studying at Mentseekhang (the Tibetan Medical College) in Dharamsala. I'm eagerly looking forward to meeting him in person for the first time.

Geographic Expeditions has organized an itinerary that we're calling *A Pilgrimage to Mount Kailash and Dharamsala*, and I would like to invite you to join me on this journey. It would be a great pleasure to intro-duce you to my Tibetan family, and the Tibet I love and know so well.

Enclosed is a detailed itinerary, and a schedule titled *Tibet '04*. If you are interested in going on the trip, or any part of it, say just the Lhasa/Mount Kailash/Kathmandu leg, that could be worked out with GeoEx, too.

I'll need to confirm the number of friends on the trip by January 1, 2004, so let me know as soon as possible if you're interested, and I'll ask someone from GeoEx to contact you directly.

With love,
Jane

From: Jane Bay
Sent: Wednesday, October 29, 2003 1:03 PM
To: Arthur Holcombe
Subject: Greetings

Dear Arthur,

Thanks for your note acknowledging my contribution to TPAF (Tibet Poverty Alleviation Fund). It's still very painful and difficult to accept Namgyal's death, but I am getting stronger as time goes by. I so appreciated hearing your impressions of Namgyal when we met you at the Kyichu Hotel in Lhasa during the New Year's celebrations.

By the way, I shared your letter and the brochure with George Lucas, explaining that Namgyal's brother worked with TPAF, and Lucasfilm will also make a contribution in Namgyal's memory. It's comforting to know these gifts may possibly be of some benefit to young Tibetan women of Namgyal's age.

I've decided to return to Tibet next year in May. I'll be in Lhasa for a week visiting Tenzin Tsering and his family. Then, I'm heading out to Mount Kailash for Sakadawa. Sorry I'll probably miss you.

With all good wishes,
Jane

From: Arthur Holcombe
Sent: Wednesday, October 29, 2003 5:21 PM
To: Jane Bay
Subject: Re: Greetings

Dear Jane,

In many respects we are a program for young women — loans,

skills training, improved reproductive health services and sex education. We may miss you in Lhasa this time, but my daughter lives in S.F. and I will try to contact you the next time I'm in California.

Glad to hear that you are working through the loss.

Thanks for thinking of TPAF.

Best wishes,
Arthur

From: Jane Bay
Sent: Thursday, October 30, 2003 8:00 AM
To: Tenzin Tsering
Subject: Greetings

Dear Tenzin,

Thank you so much for the lovely gifts you sent with Melene. I especially like the mala with the wood beads, jade swastika, and gold threads. I wear it as a necklace. Thanks for the video and *Treasure of Tibet* book, too. Melene printed several photos that she took of you, Lhakyi, Tenzin Monkyi, Uncle Losoel and your mother-in-law. The photos are wonderful, and it makes me so happy to see the baby growing up. I can hardly wait to see you all again.

I have a lot of news to tell you. I got a letter from Arthur Holcombe in September that included a brochure about TPAF, and I was happy to see your picture in the Lhasa group. I decided to make a $500 contribution to TPAF in Namgyal's memory, and received another letter from Arthur thanking me for it. He said he was terribly sorry to hear about Namgyal — she was a lovely, bright and dynamic young woman who had so many prospects for the future. Lucasfilm is going to make a contribution to TPAF in Namgyal's memory as well.

I have finalized the itinerary for my trip to Tibet next year. There is a possibility that several of my friends in the U.S. will be coming with me. It's very important to see you and your family again during this first year since Namgyal's death. I think it will help me let go of my attachment to her. It's still very painful to think about her being gone. Arthur's comments were so true.

Another friend of mine, Benina Gould, recently went to India and saw Tsetan Khensur. She took the $1,500 contribution for him, and he sent an email saying that he had received it. I'm looking forward to seeing Benina this weekend to hear all about her visit with him.

Much love from your mom,
Jane

From: Tenzin Tsering
Sent: Tuesday, November 4, 2003 10:17 AM
To: Jane Bay
Subject: Re: Greetings

Dear Mom,

Sorry for the delay reply as internet in Lhasa is not working very well. Anyway it was very great news and I am very happy to hear that. I am so lucky to hear about George Lucas and his kind concern for Tibet Poverty Alleviation Fund. I saw him in the television interviewing for the *Star War* movie. I am so proud that I can hear some Tibetan dialect in the *Star War* movie. Thank you for Mr George Lucas and thank you mom for such a great concern for us and for people of Tibet.

I am so happy to hear all the great news and especially you met Melene for our wishes. We are so eager to meet you as soon as possible and we are always prayer for our late Namgyal her great next life will be most prosperous. We really miss her a lot.

Yours' child,
Tenzin Tsering

From: Jane Bay
Sent: Thursday, November 06, 2003 12:31 PM
To: Dear Friends
Subject: My Tibetan Family

Dear Friends,

Melene Smith recently returned from Tibet where she met Namgyal's family, including my granddaughter, Tenzin Monkyi, who will be two years old on December 25, Christmas Day 2003.

Included in the enclosed photographs are Namgyal's brother, Tenzin Tsering, his wife Lhaki with a monk at the Johkang Temple in Lhasa, Lhaki's mother with Tenzin Monkyi and her cousin, and Namgyal's Uncle Losoel (gray-haired gentleman) on her mother's side of the family. Uncle Losoel has become the head of the family since Namgyal's father died on June 9 of this year, six weeks before her death.

Aren't they beautiful...

Love to all,
Jane

Tenzin Tsering and family in Lhasa
Photographer: Melene Smith

Uncle Losoel, Tenzin Tsering and Tenzin Monkyi

Lhakyi's mother, Tenzin Monkyi and cousin Tenzin Saldon

Lhakyi and monk at Johkang Temple in Lhasa

From: Jon Berg
Sent: Wednesday, November 26, 2003 10:10 AM
To: Jane Bay
Subject: Giving Thanks

Dear Jane,

Thinking of you and giving thanks for you being in our lives.

Love,
Jon & Lisa

From: Jane Bay
Sent: Tuesday, December 2, 2003 4:44 PM
To: Jon Berg
Subject: Re: Giving Thanks

Dear Jon & Lisa,

Santa Fe was a sanctuary for Thanksgiving, and in spite of everything, I have much to be thankful for, especially the love and friendship we share.

I would love to see you before I go back to New Mexico for the Christmas/New Year holidays. Would you be able to come to the Ranch for lunch? Yesterday, I decorated the Main House Christmas tree, and the house is filled with warmth and good cheer. Please come...

Love,
Jane

From: Lisa Cooke
Sent: Tuesday, December 02, 2003 8:36 PM
To: Jane Bay
Subject: Re: Giving Thanks

Dearest Jane,

We'd love to see you! I just spoke of you this afternoon to Rose Duignan who is facing some difficult times, and is embracing Buddhism. I told her about your beautiful daughter, Namgyal, and the excruciating grace with which you said goodbye to her, and she was very touched. I drove home thinking about Namgyal and her brief, but beautiful life, and realized that she was the purest embodiment of love, reflected in you.

I came home and looked into the deep forest of my sweet old cat's eyes, and realized the wisest among us often need to live the shortest number of years. Animals teach us that everyday.

I wish I could travel with you to Tibet on your next journey, but my father's health doesn't make for comfortable extended periods of time away from him or my mother.

A big Jane Bay hug would be a wonderful holiday treat. What day works for you?

Love,
Lisa

CHAPTER EIGHT

Celebrations

From: Jane Bay
Sent: Thursday, December 18, 2003 12:50 PM
To: Dear Friends
Subject: Celebrations

Dear Friends,

When I lost Namgyal this past summer, I felt the joy of my life had disappeared forever, and I would never feel like celebrating anything again, but with the changing of the seasons and the coming of the Holy Days, my spirits have lifted.

It's not as difficult to talk about now, and I'd like to share with you an email I received in response to my last missive. Jim is right about the passage of time healing the wound.

> From: Jim Ringseis
> Sent: Wednesday, October 22, 2003 2:44 PM
> To: Jane Bay
> Subject: Re: 100 Days
>
> Dear Jane,
>
> Having just read your letter I was deeply touched. You express your thoughts beautifully.
>
> The best advice I could give you right now is to expect melt-

downs. They will continue to appear at the strangest times. I found that you have to let them in whenever they occur. Your friends who have experienced loss will understand.

After an undetermined amount of time (I'm sure it differs for everyone) you will be able to live through "The Question," and even find that it becomes easier to face these uncomfortable emotions. But until then, you have to cry. You will even find "The Question" comforting at some time in the future, because it will give you the opportunity to remember the good memories of her.

I know this sounds strange, but trust me on this. It has been thirteen years since losing my little brother, but even now on rare occasions someone will ask what Tom is doing. After telling them that Tom is gone, I somehow have warm feelings just being able to speak of him.

You are exactly right when you say that the scar will always be there. But in time even the scar becomes a warm reminder of the beautiful daughter you had the fortune of knowing and loving.

Thank you for your letter,
Jim

I spent the week of Thanksgiving in Santa Fe with friends Cynthia West and her husband, Reno Myerson, whom I've known for over thirty years. I've watched their children grow up and have shared many holidays with their extended families. This year, Reno's daughter, Zia, wanted to prepare the turkey and Thanksgiving meal at the house she is renting next door to Cynthia and Reno's place on Cerro Gordo Road, the Bohemian Embassy, as it's called. Zia's home happens to be where Cynthia lived when she first moved to Santa Fe in the early '70s. It was a little like déjà vu, the gathering of a hippie commune, but all the babies are now adults and they were carrying on the Thanksgiving tradition as the elders sat back and gave thanks for all the blessings of the season.

It was a bittersweet moment. I would have liked for Namgyal to have been there. In fact, we had talked about her being part of my life in Santa Fe when she graduated from Tibetan Medical College. We had planned a future together that was full of promise for both of us. What arose that Thanksgiving night was the realization that I am ready to begin again, to envision a life for myself without Namgyal, but one that carries the joy of knowing and loving her with me every single day for as long as I live.

Recently, I had dinner with Deborah Michie, whose husband of thirty-five years, and my dear friend, Chris, died in March, shortly after I returned from visiting Namgyal in Tibet. I told her about Thanksgiving, and that in reflection, the one thing I don't regret is that I was completely "present" in my relationship with Namgyal since we were reunited five years ago during the summer that *Precious Jewels* was published. Whether by phone, letter, or email, and during the two weeks I spent twenty-four hours a day with her in Lhasa this year, we were totally in that moment for each other.

"So, your relationship with Namgyal was complete."

And so it was…yet, sometimes, it is still so difficult to accept.

Namgyal died five months ago today. Time is passing quickly, and I'm looking forward to my return trip to Tibet this coming year. When I was in Santa Fe for Thanksgiving, I was thinking about being at Mount Kailash on June third for Sakadawa, the celebration of the Buddha's birth and enlightenment, when it occurred to me that Namgyal's forty-ninth day was on September 3 (when she may have entered a womb for her reincarnation), and she might be born nine months later on the very day that Sakadawa occurs on the Tibetan Lunar Calendar in 2004. Now, I look forward to going to Mount Kailash with the intention of celebrating Namgyal's rebirth and the birth/enlightenment of the Buddha on the same day. What an auspicious thought!!!

Today is also Lama Tsong Khapa Day. Tsong Khapa (1357-1419) was the founder of the Gelugpa school of Tibetan Buddhism and Ganden

Monastery. We're having a fire puja for this great Tibetan master, and for my beloved daughter, Namgyal Youdon, tonight at my house in San Anselmo.

Wishing you Good Health, Good Fortune and Happiness in the New Year.

Peace On Earth & Love to All,
Jane

From: Chin Rodger
Sent: Thursday, December 18, 2003 2:33 PM
To: Jane Bay
Subject: Re: Celebrations

Thank you. So right, Jane. Every breath is a new beginning. Namgyal lives in the love you have for her and in the joy and the bliss of being with her in your heart.

Before his mahasamadhi – before he left his body, Buddha said to his beloved disciple, Ananda, "You must know I will never leave you. How can I go anywhere? This body is not me...I live in the dharma I have given you, Ananda, which is closer to you than your own heart, and the dharma will never die..."

Although Namgyal, and I am sure my friend, Kim, have taken birth again or will do so – but the essence of who she is lives in the consciousness of our being...and that is eternal...that is what I am feeling about Kim. Holiday time is tough for Kim's family and me – this last year we were all together – helping them put up their Christmas decorations.

My mom is over for Christmas break, we have not seen her in three years, so we are in bliss – being from Malaysia – she makes the best satay and curries ever...

Enjoy your holidays. I send you great blessings and love for Christmas and for a happy happy New Year.

Much love,
Chin

P.S. Georgia sends you big hugs too.

From: Lynda Beth Unkeless
Sent: Thursday, December 18, 2003 4:01 PM
To: Jane Bay
Subject: Turning the Corner...

Dear Jane,

The past five months have been hell, and despite that fact, you have persevered and you have survived.

However, there comes a time, and that time seems to be approaching faster for you than most people I have witnessed through a grieving process, when you start to THRIVE. You are already thriving and growing far beyond the person you were when your daughter died.

I am happy for you that you are making this transition from surviving to thriving and from merely carrying on to actually thinking about the reinvention of your life.

You are strong, you have all the advantages of the Buddhist traditions and wisdom at your ready disposal, you are practicing your ass off.

ALL GOOD THINGS come to those who practice.

These are my two cents on the matter. I continue to wish you nothing but the best, and your highest good now and in the future....

Lots of Love,
Lynda Beth

P.S. Thanks again for Joan Didion's new book. I did not, however, make her herbed chicken recipe....yet!

From: Goldie Hawn
Sent: Thursday, December 18, 2003 5:52 PM
To: Jane Bay
Subject: Re: Celebrations

Blessings Dear One.

Good you are on the mend! We can't be good for others if our hearts are sad...so time has brought you back to work with spirit on your side. Celebrate Life. It's so precious.

Lovingly,
Goldie

From: Laurent Bouzereau
Sent: Thursday, December 18, 2003 6:13 PM
To: Jane Bay
Subject: Re: Celebrations

Dearest Jane,

Thank you so much for the beautiful letter. In fact, I was just thinking of you last night when I was watching the *Inn of the Sixth Happiness* with Ingrid Bergman – her mission in the film, saving children, completely reminded me of your character. You are ever present in my thoughts and prayers.

Markus and I are here through Christmas, but leave on the 29th for Paris to celebrate New Year's with my family.

We hope to see more of you in the coming year, and send you warm and best wishes.

Love,
Laurent and Markus

From: Jane Bay
Sent: Thursday, December 18, 2003 9:47 PM
To: Laurent Bouzereau
Subject: Re: Celebrations

Dearest Laurent and Markus,

So happy to hear from you dear friends. Thank you for the warm and wonderful wishes, and know that you are always in my heart and prayers.

Love and Light,
Jane

From: Tenzin Bob Thurman
Sent: Sunday, December 21, 2003 12:38 AM
To: Jane Bay
Subject: Re: Celebrations

Dear Jane,

I had just reached Delhi the night of Tsong Khapa's day, and I had a marvelous meditation alone in my hotel, preparing for the conference I inaugurated the next day. I thought of Tsong Khapa's whose body was observed by his disciples to physically return to a child-like form in a swirling of luminous energy during his death process. The next day I received your email.

I am so glad that you are slowly recovering from the sad untimely loss of beloved Namgyal. Jim's advice and experience are awe-inspiring. I will also be there with you at Kailash on Sakadawa most likely as I am leading another trip.

I send you a big warm squeezy hug.

Love,
Bob

From: Sylvia Boorstein
Sent: Sunday, December 21, 2003 6:07 AM
To: Jane Bay
Subject: Re: Celebrations

As always Jane, my soul and my heart are uplifted and inspired by the candor and inclusiveness of your sharing. May your daughter's memory continue to be a blessing to you and to all who knew her through you.

Sylvia

From: Robyn Brentano
Sent: Tuesday, December 23, 2003 12:06 PM
To: Jane Bay
Subject: Re: Celebrations

Dear Jane,

Thank you so much for including me in your emails about Namgyal's passing – not only did you have a deep personal bond, but you were also engaged in her life quest as a Tibetan woman who represented a point of light for the future of Tibet. I am glad that you are beginning to find peace and equanimity with her loss. You are fortunate to have a network of loving and compassionate friends to support you.

Thank you too for inviting me to go along on your trip to Tibet – this is something I've been wanting to do ever since I was there in '87 and now it looks as though I will be going twice this year in connection with Foundation work, in late February or mid-March, and then again in June or July. I'd love to stay in touch with you to see if any synergies develop through either of our trips.

Meanwhile, have a happy holiday season and much peace and inspiration in the coming new year.

Love,
Robyn

From: Fu Ching
Sent: Tuesday, December 23, 2003 7:33 PM
To: Jane Bay
Subject: Merry Xmas

Hello, dear Jane

Warm greetings from China, and wish you will have a happy and relaxed Christmas after the 100 days of your daughter Namgyal. And, the new year is coming, I hope you will have new spirit, just like you say.

And I think that Namgyal she can understand you will have your own life again without her in the future time, but she still can feel that you love her so much.

So, do you have any idea to travel to Tibet again? Hope to see you again, and we can go to the Temple that you had been last time!

Best Regards!

Yours,
Fu Ching

From: Jane Bay
Sent: Monday, January 05, 2004 9:19 AM
To: Tenzin Bob Thurman
Subject: Re: Celebrations

Dear Bob,

It was wonderful to find your email waiting for me after two weeks off for the holidays, which I spent in Santa Fe where I learned for the first time about your trip to Kailash. I immediately called your house in New York to say that I want more than anything to go with you on your trip and to have the opportunity to receive your great teachings.

I'll fill out all the official application forms, etc, right away, but I wanted to mention that I had not planned to do the kora. I discussed this with Shana Chrystie at GeoEx, who assured me it won't be a problem for me to stay at the Guest House while the group makes the trek around the mountain. I hope that's okay with you. I've been suffering from sciatica for the last few years, and I don't want to stress it out because I'm going to India to meet Namygal's elder brother after your group leaves Kathmandu. Just being at the mountain is a huge blessing.

All my love to you and Nena, with great wishes for good health and happiness throughout the New Year.

Jane

From: Tenzin Bob Thurman
Sent: Monday, January 05, 2004 12:30 PM
To: Jane Bay
Subject: HAPPY NEW YEAR

Dear Jane,

It would be wonderful to have you along. Never mind not doing the kora - maybe you can kora around the beautiful lake instead – there is a road nowadays I hear.

Lots and lots of love from us both,
Bob and Nena

From: Francis Ford Coppola
Sent: Monday, January 05, 2004 2:32 PM
To: Jane Bay
Subject: Re: Celebrations

Well Jane, the thing about grief is that it takes time, but you can be sure that with time a healing takes place. The key is to be able to wake up in the morning and not have "that" be the first thing you think of. It took me six years to reach that point, but that was the turning point.

Cheers,
f.

From: Lisa Cooke
Sent: Thursday, February 8, 2004 8:45 AM
To: Jane Bay
Subject: Thinking of you…

Hi Jane,

Just thinking about you. Hope this finds you well and that 2004 is blessing you with many moments of joy and many new adventures.

I sent thoughts of peace to Namygal Monday night when I went to Spirit Rock. I have thought of her often recently. Last week I found a dear friend deceased in her home. She was only fifty years old, and it was a brain aneurysm. It was such a strange feeling to see her Sunday paper on the coffee table, her reading glasses set out, her morning coffee untouched and her music still on. She started her Sunday morning then her soul decided it was time to leave. The coroner said it was a quick, painless way to die.

Her death reinforced the lesson Namgyal taught me as well. Life is very fragile and very resilient all at once. And precious, as are dear friends. Like you. So, I just wanted to say that I think of you often and always with lots of love.

Jon and I are off to L.A. to the premiere of Joe's new movie *Hildago*, a story of great human spirit and love between a man and his horse. I am really looking forward to it.

Take care Jane. Hope to see you soon.

Namaste,
XO Lisa

CHAPTER NINE

Losar

From: Jane Bay
Sent: Wednesday, March 1, 2004 1:14 PM
To: Dear Friends
Subject: Losar – Tibetan New Year

Dear Friends,

Some of you know I'm writing another book. It's something of a sequel to *Precious Jewels of Tibet* in that it begins where *Precious Jewels* ended.

One year ago today, I was in Lhasa celebrating the Tibetan New Year with Namgyal and her family. Following is a chapter from the new book entitled "Losar" about my recent experiences:

Losar, the Tibetan word for New Year, fell this year on Saturday, February 21, based on the Tibetan Lunar Calendar. Last year I had been in Lhasa celebrating Losar with Namgyal and her family. It was the first time I'd seen her in nine years, and the two weeks, twenty-four hours a day we spent together was a deep, intensive retreat in which mother and daughter completely surrendered into the heart of the other. Namgyal was no longer the shy little girl I had met in Dharamsala, but a strong-willed, vibrant twenty-two-year-old young woman with her own opinions about life.

By a serendipitous turn of events, I found myself in Santa Fe on Losar, and I planned to celebrate the New Year with friends and the Tibetan community there. When I woke Saturday morning, a gentle, powdery snow was falling, covering the landscape, similar in so many ways to Tibet, in a sparkling white blanket. It felt like a fresh, new year was blooming.

Namgyal's cousin, Dr. Dickey, had told her friend, Gawa (an older Tibetan man who had been imprisoned in Tibet for many years before escaping to India, then came to the U.S. through the Tibetan Resettlement Project in the early '90s) that I would be in Santa Fe for Losar. Gawa's English is limited, but when I called, he suggested I come to the Tibetan Stupa (temple) early New Year's morning for prayers, then to a celebration at the new Tibetan Community Center in town around one o'clock. And, he invited me to his house for a *chema*, a New Year's offering, afterwards.

I put on my finest velvet and lace, the Mexican serape vest I had worn in Tibet last year, leather gloves and cowgirl boots, a felt hat studded with a silk cactus flower, and headed out to the west side of town to the stupa. When I arrived at nine o'clock sharp, the small stupa was packed with Tibetan men, women, and children dressed in traditional Losar clothing, and a handful of Anglos, sitting cross-legged in tight rows on the hard floor carpeted with Tibetan rugs, facing a Buddha altar decorated with special offerings for the occasion. Several women on the right side of the room motioned for me to take the last remaining seat up against the wall next to two Tibetan gentlemen, one of whom was addressing the assembly. I learned later that he is the President of the Tibetan Community Center, and he, not the lama at the stupa, would lead the morning prayers. A small bowl of barley flour and a bottle of wine were placed on a low dark blue painted wooden table in front of the two men. At various times during the recitation of prayers, one of the men would pour a little wine into a container, and at other times he would sprinkle a pinch of the barley flower over the wine. This was an offering ritual I'd seen many times last year during Losar in Lhasa.

Prayers were recited from Tibetan prayer books, but since I couldn't read the language, I silently recited Om Mani Padme Hum, the mantra of Compassion, counting the repetitions on my amber beaded mala (Tibetan rosary). I was lulled into a soothing trance by the sound of Tibetan voices, and I felt my spirit being transported back to Lhasa, and to Namgyal.

At the conclusion of prayers, the Sangha (Buddhist congregation) was invited to have refreshments in the courtyard outside the stupa. Gawa was one of the people serving bowls of rice with raisins and cups of hot Tibetan butter tea. It was quite cold, and when a chilling wind came up, I decided to leave, but I told Gawa I'd see him later at the Community Center.

My dear friend, Judy Margolis, was at the Community Center when I arrived. Judy, Pat French, Jeff Harbour, and especially Ali MacGraw, had been instrumental in raising money to develop a center for local Tibetans. It had just recently been completed. They invited me to join their group, and I sat in a chair at the side of the main room between Jeff and Judy. There were rugs on the floor in the middle of the room in front of a throne and altar where many of the people who had been at the stupa were sitting. The same man, Guimmey, who officiated at the stupa, welcomed everyone to the center. Khatas, white silk Tibetan blessing scarves, were presented to Judy, Pat, Ali, and Jeff. I was also given a khata, I think because I was sitting with this distinguished group, and we each made a prostration and placed our khata on the altar as the ceremony began.

More prayers followed, but the text had been translated into English which everyone recited after the prayers had been spoken in Tibetan. The final prayer was a Long Life Prayer for the Dalai Lama. Part way through, I felt a wave of sadness from deep inside my being. My throat became constricted, I could barely say the words, and tears swelled in my eyes. Judy reached over and took my hand in hers, and when I looked into her eyes, I knew she knew what was coming up. The great grief of losing Namgyal was arising again.

At the conclusion of the prayers, Guimmey introduced four young Tibetan women, about Namgyal's age, in their traditional Tibetan New Year's dresses, who sang and danced as is customary for the holiday. I wanted to get out of there as fast as I could, but I didn't want to disrupt the happy celebration.

Following the songs and dances, everyone lined up for a special Tibetan New Year's feast. I told Gawa I wasn't feeling well and had to leave. He asked if I could come to his house for a *chema* the next day, but I explained I was going back to California. He insisted we go to his house immediately, and knowing how auspicious it is to receive this invitation, I said okay.

Gawa lives in a modest little apartment a few blocks from the Community Center. The *chema*, an elaborately painted wooden box with two compartments (one containing barley flour, the other barley seeds), was set up in the living room next to an altar. I offered prayers for peace, for good health and happiness for myself, and all beings, during the coming year, and with the middle finger and thumb on my right hand, took a pinch of flour first and flicked it into the air three times. Then, with a pinch of seeds I repeated the same gesture. Gawa instructed me to insert my ring finger into a glass of *Chang* (Tibetan beer), and to flick the liquid into the air three times as well, to complete the *chema*. This is the Losar offering.

It would have been impolite not to eat some of the Losar meal Gawa had prepared: boiled meat, beef jerky, and steamed vegetables. He also made a warm rice pudding on the spot, similar to sizzling rice soup with egg, rice, sugar, and a little Chang. It actually settled my stomach. I was grateful for his hospitality. When the conversation began to lag, I showed Gawa the photographs of Namgyal taken last year at Losar that I carry with me everywhere. He kept saying, "So sorry, so sorry." And so am I...

After taking Gawa back to the Community Center, I drove home and went straight to bed for the rest of the afternoon. It had turned out to be an emotionally critical day. I put Yungchen Lhamo's CD *Coming Home*, a stunning collection of contemporary Tibetan songs of freedom and beauty, on auto-repeat and drifted in and out of a shallow sleep. My thoughts were flooded with memories of the time I spent with my beloved daughter.

Last year, my plane landed in Tibet on New Year's Eve, Saturday, March 1. Namgyal and Auntie Drakpa, Namgyal's mother's younger sister, were waiting outside the Kyichu Hotel when I arrived in Lhasa. We threw our arms around each other in a warm, comfortable embrace as though we had only been separated for a short time. Wangdu, my friend from Wind Horse Travel who had met my flight at

Gongkor Airport, ushered me into the hotel to check in, and accompanied us upstairs to our rooms on the second floor.

Maybe it was the excitement, maybe it was the altitude (12,000 feet), although I had never suffered from altitude sickness on my two previous visits to Tibet, but as we walked up the stairs, I knew I was going to be sick to my stomach. The three of them rushed me into the bathroom where I immediately threw up and pissed all over myself. I was mortified. It didn't faze them a bit. Namgyal and Auntie Drakpa, (who doesn't speak a word of English), helped me wash up, and I joined Wangdu in the sitting room for a cup of Tibetan butter tea.

Namgyal's brother, Tenzin Tsering, arrived shortly thereafter, along with several other relatives on Namgyal's mother's side, and we worked out a schedule to visit each of their families, as well as Wangdu's, for lunch during the coming week which all Tibetans observed as a holiday. Later that evening, Namgyal and I took a bicycle rickshaw to the home of Dr. Tinley (Dickey's mother, Namgyal's father's sister) for Oracle soup, a broth with dumplings, one of which contains a charm to foretell the future for the coming year. Much to my chagrin, I continued to throw up and can't remember what charm Namgyal or I got in our soup. We went back to the hotel and early to bed.

Namgyal had been living primarily with Auntie Drakpa for the last two years since starting Tibetan Medical College located on the other side of town, west of the old city. Auntie Drakpa returned to the Kyichu Hotel early New Year's morning bearing gifts – a thermos of hot, black watery liquid that I was instructed to drink every few hours for the next two days to cure the nausea, and a beautifully brocaded Tibetan satin dress and blouse, complete with traditional striped apron and a hat made of fox fur. All a perfect fit. Auntie Drakpa's tailor had made everything from seeing my photograph (taken at Yamdrok Lake) on the cover of *Precious Jewels of Tibet*. I had sent Namgyal a copy of the photograph when we were reunited shortly after the book was published. She knew about the book, but I couldn't take a copy to Tibet for obvious reasons. Auntie Drakpa helped me dress, and braided my hair with ribbon in the Tibetan style of a married woman (in my case a formerly twice-married woman).

Namgyal had a new dress as well that was more oriental with a Mandarin collar. It was in the style worn in Amdo, a province in Central Tibet and the birthplace of the Dalai Lama. She announced, "Mom, I'm a tomboy. The only time I wear a dress is for Losar." And sure enough, the rest of the time I was there, she wore jeans, a sweater and sneakers. But a very pretty tomboy she was. One morning, I was surprised to see she had on a New York Yankees baseball cap. "Are you a baseball fan?" Laughing, she said, "No, Mom, don't you see, NY is for my name—Namgyal Youdon."

Before we left the hotel, the manager, Lhundup Phuntsok, and his wife invited us to their apartment for tea and a *chema*. We then headed out to Namgyal's father's apartment located next door to the Jokhang Temple. The plaza in front of the Jokhang was swarming with men, women, and children, all dressed up in their Losar clothing, but there was one little boy in a traditional outfit wearing cowboy boots and a cowboy hat. Smoke billowed from the huge incense burners, prayer flags were flying high, and the air was filled with optimism and great expectations for the coming year.

Namgyal's father, Dr. Namgang, had been seriously ill for the last six months, suffering from heart and lung disease. He had recently moved into the apartment building where his brother, Nawang, lived so Nawang could look after him. Dr. Tinley also lived nearby. Uncle Nawang had been a political prisoner for eleven years in Drapchi Prison, the most notorious political prison in Tibet, for publicly celebrating the Dalai Lama's birthday. He had been given an early release from his thirteen year sentence because his health was deteriorating, and the Chinese didn't want him to die in prison, however, he was still under house arrest.

When we arrived at Dr. Namgang's apartment, Dickey's brother, Tsedor, and his wife, Lhakpa, (who I had met briefly New Year's Eve at Dr. Tinley's house), and Tenzin Tsering were already there. It was a poignant moment. I had been fraught with worry that Dr. Namgang might die before I got to Lhasa. It seemed important we meet to have a physical experience of each other. I wanted to assure him I would take care of Namgyal for the rest of my life. Even though he had been on oxygen and couldn't get out of his sickbed, Dr. Namgang embraced me with the warmest and most generous handshake. Then, placing a khata around my neck, he looked me straight in the eyes and smiled.

Since only Namgyal and her brother spoke English, Tenzin Tsering translated a story I wanted to tell Dr. Namgang. When he had become so critically ill the previous year, my friend, Tommy Sullivan (he and his wife Rita were Namgyal's American godparents) had made a 'promisa' for Dr. Namgang one morning at Mass during the Christmas holidays. I said, "So, Tommy, what's a 'promisa?'" He replied, " You make a promise to God that if you give up 'something' for a specific period of time, your request will be granted." "And, what did you promise?" I asked.

Tommy had pledged to give up eating meat for six months as a sacrifice for Dr. Namgang's health improving. "For SIX MONTHS?" I asked. "Oh yeah, once before when I made a 'promisa' for my business to pick up again after 9/11, I gave up meat for a whole year. And my wish was granted."

Tommy's wish was granted in this case, too, as Dr. Namgang's health had improved considerably just before I arrived in Tibet for Losar. Everyone laughed and enjoyed the story. It broke the ice, so to speak, and we spent the rest of the visit in casual conversation as several other relatives came and went. We all had Tibetan butter tea, holiday sweets, and pastries, and we participated in making a *chema* at Dr. Namgang's altar.

Later that afternoon, Namgyal, Tenzin, and I went over to Auntie Drakpa's house for lunch. She had prepared a delicious Losar meal of both Tibetan and Chinese style pork, boiled radishes and carrots, fried yak meat with red peppers, and a green vegetable that looked and tasted like chard, but no one could think of the English word for it. I was happy to be in the house where Namgyal was living so I could visualize where she was when I talked to her on the phone, or when she was at her computer sending an email, or studying, or preparing food. I had been told that Namgyal was an excellent cook.

That night, we had dinner in our room at the Kyichu Hotel. It became a ritual that we continued every evening during my visit. The hotel has an exceptionally good restaurant specializing in Tibetan and Nepalese cuisine. Namgyal especially liked the chicken chow mein, which I enjoyed, too, but I pretty much went through the menu, one night even ordering a very tasty yak burger on a bun with lettuce and tomato, and a side of fries.

We sat at a small round table by the window that overlooked the garden and courtyard at the back of the hotel. After dinner, Namgyal said, "Mom, I have some important things to tell you," and thus began our nightly after dinner conversations in which she told me the story of her life. She talked and cried; I cried and listened.

Namgyal began her story by saying, "I love my father, but I blame him for my mother's death. He was too attached to Tibetan medicine as the only way to treat her. He knew she had headaches and a bad heart, and if he had taken her to a hospital, she could have been saved by Western medicine. Tibetan medicine doesn't work to treat emergency situations."

I let her talk, asking a few questions now and then, but never challenged her assumptions or how she had come to these conclusions. Namgyal was only nine months old when her mother, Dickyi Yangzom, died, and according to Dr. Dickey from whom I'd heard the story of Namgyal's mother's death several years ago, her mother collapsed in the living room of their house during the day, and when Dr. Namgang returned home, her life force was completely gone. There had been no prior warning. Namgyal's mother was only twenty-nine years old when she died, and twenty-two years ago, there would have been no Western medical facilities in Lhasa or procedures that could have prevented a brain aneurysm or a heart attack. In fact, there are none available even today.

Namgyal went on to say this was the reason she hadn't wanted to study Tibetan medicine, but when she learned that doctors in the West were incorporating Tibetan medical techniques in their practices, she thought it would be a good opportunity to get a degree in Tibet, then study Western medicine when she was able to get a visa and work permit in the U.S.

We talked late into the night, and the rest of the story about her father was something like a television soap opera. Apparently, when her mother died, Namgyal and her two brothers were sent to live with relatives. Namgyal and Tsetan Khensur went to Dickey's mother's home, and Tenzin Tsering went to live with Uncle Losoel, Namgyal's mother's half-brother. Dr. Namgang who had become overwhelmed with grief because of the death of his young wife, took to drink with disastrous consequences, and at some time later, he was taken in by a couple who had been their friends before Dickyi Yangzom's death.

Namgyal got up from the table, and sat down on the bed facing me.

"That woman, Pasang, is a witch. She had control over my father and had relations with him. Do you remember that teenage boy who came to my father's apartment this afternoon? He's my father's child! She wanted to get rid of me and my brothers, and she made my father send us to India, and I was only eight years old. I hate her. She tricked my father into giving her my mother's jewels, and her shoes and dresses, and I don't have anything that belonged to my mother," she sobbed.

Abandonment, rejection, betrayal. I sat next to Namgyal on the bed, put my arms around her and held her as we both cried.

"Namgyal, I'm glad you told me these things, and I want you to know that I will always love you, and care for you, but you've got to tell your father how you feel. Ask him to give you a piece of your mother's jewelry. You have a right to ask. And, my darling, your father may not live much longer. For your own peace of mind, you must try to forgive him."

Between tears and gasps for breath, she said, "It's too late, there's nothing he can do to change the situation."

When I was back in the U.S., I heard from Dickey's mother that Namgyal had been very sweet and kind to her father after I left Lhasa, cleaning his apartment, cooking, and taking care of him. However, he died on June 9, and she had never talked to him.

From: Jane Bay
Sent: Monday, March 17, 2003 3:56 PM
To: Namgyal Youdon
Subject: Back in the U.S.

Dearest Namgyal,

Wanted you to know I arrived safely this morning after a very grueling flight. I'm so tired I can hardly keep my eyes open, so this will be a short and sweet message.

Getting to know you was one of the most wonderful experiences of my life. You are a beautiful human being, and I am so thankful that we have been reunited.

Hope school has gotten off to a good start, and that you have reconnected with all your friends. More from me later, I must get some rest now.

All my love, your mom,
Jane

From: Namgyal Youdon
Sent: Tuesday, March 18, 2003 3:58 PM
To: Jane Bay
Subject: so happy!

Dearest Mom,

In those few days I had with you I got a chance to tell you all about my sad and happy things just like my best friend and my real mom. Thank you so much my dearest mom. Know I am beginning my studies again. Yesterday my boyfriend (Dundul) and I had a very nice day!!!

With oceans of love, yours' loving daughter,
Namgyal

Much love to you, dear friends, and Happy Tibetan New Year to all,
Jane

P.S. Also enclosed are jpg photo files taken last year during Losar in Tibet. Just click on the files, then click Open to see the photos. They're not high resolution, but you'll get the picture...(See photos page 57-60).

From: Jane Wyeth
Sent: Monday, March 01, 2004 6:43 PM
To: Jane Bay
Subject: Re: Losar – Tibetan New Year

Oh Janie,

Here I am crying again, with the tears falling so much down my cheeks that they're plopping all the way onto my bare thighs. I'm sitting at my computer wearing my usual outfit when I'm at home alone – only a white extra-extra-extra large (for comfort and 'cause they shrink) Hanes T-shirt and my undies.

I kept smiling at so much of what I was reading – your cowboy boots, the cactus flower (obviously stuck debonairly in your hat), the tomboy quote, your throwing up immediately upon reaching the top of the stairs to your hotel room, and your story about Tommy giving up meat so his business would improve! (I just spoke with him only a few days ago — and he's never once mentioned to me in all these years, even though we speak regularly, that he and Rita were Namgyal's American godparents. Boy THAT was a surprise to read!).

And then my tears started — as soon as you wrote about having nightly after-dinner conversations during which she told you the story of her life.

Oh Janie, I loved the "technique" (if you will, but it's a crappy word, since the way you wrote was so loving and almost stream-of-con-sciousness rather than planned) of your including the e-mails you wrote each other at the very end. First, as I read yours to Namgyal, I could totally relate, as a mother, to what you were writing her upon your safe, but exhausting, arrival home. And of course, your adding that you hoped school had gotten off to a good start and that she'd reconnected with all her friends was exactly what every wonderful and loving mother would say to her daughter, even her grown up daughter.

Oh, but Janie, as soon as I read, "Dearest Mom," the tears started a-flowing, and they're dropping like balloons onto my thighs now again. And THEN when she wrote, "...just like my best friend and real mom..." Well, that was it. Except that very next sentence mentions her boyfriend!!!! (I did not know until that sentence that she had one). And as I read it, I felt the joy that only a mother can feel when she knows that her daughter is in love (or close to it, anyway). And then the "oceans of love".

Janie, Janie, Janie, my heart breaks yet again for you. I suppose that writing this book will be a kind of catharsis for you; yet writing it HAS to bring up so much of the pain that we all had hoped — by what you'd been writing us — had somewhat dissipated. I don't know how you do it.

Know, sweetie, that my love is with you always.
xxx Janie

From: David M. Petrou
Sent: Monday, March 01, 2004 7:21 PM
To: Jane Bay
Subject: Re: Losar – Tibetan New Year

Dearest Jane,

Thanks not only to the marvelously vibrant and animated photos you shared with your friends, but also to your loving and evocative writing, I have a real sense of how beautiful your daughter Namgyal was. I actually had goose bumps reading your excerpt from the new book you're writing as a living testament to her great spiritual strength and serenity. Of course, it also makes me feel your tragic loss all the more deeply, Jane.

If I were to become cynical, given the great tragedies in our own family life, it would make me think that all is about loss: loss of innocence; loss of youth; loss of profession or position; loss of health; loss of friends and loved ones. But because I am a person of great spiritual strength and a <u>real belief</u> in the indomitable resilience of the human spirit, I think life is more about what we gain: love, knowledge, friendship, beauty, faith. And I believe strongly that what you gained in your love for Namgyal and what she gained in her love for <u>you</u> is like a bright beacon that will never be extinguished and will be there, in your life, guiding your way forever.

Since I have your autographed copy of *Precious Jewels of Tibet*, I will eagerly anticipate the rest of your journey. May the beauty that is your love for Namgyal and her love sustain you as you reflect on her life and gift of her spirit.

Thank you, thank you, Jane, for sharing this with me. I just returned from my weekend in New York City, performing Beethoven's "Ninth" Symphony at Carnegie Hall, under the baton of Maestro Leonard Slatin and The National Symphony Orchestra. And that is the beauty and passion and joy that sustain my life. What a lucky soul I am.

With much love and compassion,

Your friend,
David xx

From: Ruth de Sosa
Sent: Tuesday, March 02, 2004 12:56 PM
To: Jane Bay
Subject: Re: Losar – Tibetan New Year

Dear Jane!

Thank you so much for forwarding all of this to me. I am so glad that you are writing another book. Your story is very magical and heart-warming...and in the e-mail from Namgyal sending you "oceans of love" I started crying knowing that her love was indeed as large as all the oceans on the planet…I, too, am still very sorry for all that has happened so unexpectedly…and grief visits again and again in different ways…

I trust also that the screenplay is still in the works…I would love to see all the colors, flavors and costumes shared with the world. Tibet and its people are very special souls and have much wisdom to impart to the West on a wider scale. And that your life, with how amazing it has been, also encompasses Tibet and now you are bringing and will continue to bring that message to a wider and wider audience of people at a time when the world so needs connection and spiritual encouragement.

Much love to you, Jane!
Ruth, sending you a big hug!

From: Lynne Hale
Sent: Tuesday, March 02, 2004 8:40 PM
To: Jane Bay
Subject: Re: Losar – Tibetan New Year

Dearest Jane,

I just got in from L.A. and wanted to read the message you had told me you had sent. I won't be able to see the photos until I get to work tomorrow but I wanted to read the text.

Your story is so beautiful. What I like about your writing style so much is the feeling that we are experiencing everything right along with you. There is so much sadness and loneliness in the world – it is uplifting to read about Namgyal sharing her thoughts that she carried in her head her whole life and the joy of being able to relieve her burden by finding a "best friend and mother" who would listen and give her counsel. If every child could find that person to love and listen to them, what peace we would have in the world.

She was surrounded by a loving family yet did not have anyone she could share her sadness with until you came into her life. When she signed her letters "with oceans of love" tears came to my eyes. Jane, if there was ever a story about destiny and one's journey in life—it is the story of Jane and Namgyal. You opened your heart to her and she came running in. You two had a bond across the world that was as strong as any mother and daughter. Love is so powerful.

Thank you for sharing your story with me. It is going to make a wonderful book. You could have just stayed in your house in Marin County, but instead, you went across the world to adopt a child who needed a mother.

Jane, I love your beautiful heart!
Lynne

From: Jane Bay
Sent: Wednesday, March 03, 2004 9:05 AM
To: Lynne Hale
Subject: Re: Losar – Tibetan New Year

Lynnie, it means so much to me that you have taken this story into your own heart. This is where I get the strength and courage to face this terrible loss and, hopefully, transform it into something that will be of benefit, not just to me, but to anyone who comes to know it. I am really truly grateful that you read it.

All my love,
Jane

From: Tina Mills
Sent: Wednesday, March 03, 2004 9:37 AM
To: Jane Bay
Subject: Re: Losar – Tibetan New Year

Thank you so much for giving me this bittersweet joy this morning.

The writing is sensational!!! You are such a good writer Jane – it just FLOWS so smoothly and is so informative (food, clothing, temperature) – and all so heartfelt. I can't wait for the book!!

Oceans of love to you!
T.

From: Jane Bay
Sent: Wednesday, March 03, 2004 9:55 AM
To: Tina Mills
Subject: Re: Losar – Tibetan New Year

Oh, Tina, thanks for the positive feedback. You know the process of writing is an intregal part of healing myself, and it does flow out of me. Every time I sit down to write one of these email missives, I light a lapis blue candle hand made by *Coventry Creations* with herbs of rosemary, benzoin, wormwood, heather, yarrow & lavender, and recite the "Inspiration" prayer that comes with the candle.

I call on forces higher than I, to release the energy that is held inside.
As my mind travels, guide it true. Inspiration is needed for what I am to do.
Creative forces shall flow through me. Understanding for all to see.
I call on thee in perfect trust and love, sending me guidance from above.
Harming none and helping all is how it shall be.
This I make true 3X3X3.

Oceans of love to you, dear Tina.
Jane

From: Tenzin Tsering
Sent: Wednesday, March 03, 2004 10:03 AM
To: Jane Bay
Subject: Gifts

Dear Mom,

Please do not worry about the gifts for our relatives. Mother-in-law recent back from China and did not find any suitable and fit clothes for Lhakyi as she is too big. Could you please bring her some clothes especially one or two different style of jacket with brown or black color which is wear by both man and woman and one should be a leather with all largest size and a jean with dark blue.

All the purchase fee mother-in-law will pay you back and I will send you some other list when I meet others.

Yours' lovingly,
Tenzin

From: Jane Bay
Sent: Wednesday, March 03, 2004 10:18 AM
To: Tenzin Tsering
Subject: Re: Gifts

Dear Tenzin,

I'll be happy to bring some clothes for Lhakyi. As you know, I'm a big woman, too, as are a lot of American women, and there are many styles available that will fit her.

Just let me know if you need anything else.

Love from your mom,
Jane

From: Tenzin Tsering
Sent: Wednesday, March 03, 2004 10:40 AM
To: Jane Bay
Subject: Re: Gifts

Dear Mom,

Another thing for Uncle Losoel is that vitamin capsule with high calcium for healthy bone and for eye sight. He has a capsule right now which is sent by one of his patient in the States and it is called cod liver oil capsules. Next thing my mother-in-law need some deep sea fish oil for curing blood fat and for gall bladder disease.

Most Tibetan including Uncle Losoel and myself have gall bladder diseases due to high fat nutrition as butter tea, meat. The disease which has compose stones in the gall bladder.

Last year I was terrible sick of gall bladder and in bed for some days with infusion. When I check at the hospital there is no stone in my gall bladder but it was extend larger size than usual and it is very painful.

Yours' lovingly,
Tenzin

From: Sushma Patel Bould
Sent: Wednesday, March 10, 2004 11:06 AM
To: Jane Bay
Subject: Re: Losar - Tibetan New Year

It is a rare and courageous gift to take the tapestry of one's personal suffering and offer that experience freely and openly to the world. One can only be touched and transformed by the alchemy of universal reflections in your writing.

Peace.
xo Sushma

From: Jane Bay
Sent: Wednesday, March 10, 2004 11:08 AM
To: Sushma Patel Bould
Subject: Re: Losar - Tibetan New Year

That's so beautiful, Sushma, it made me cry... Thank you for continuing to provide a sanctuary for my healing by receiving these emails.

From: Gordon Radley
Sent: Thursday, March 18, 2004 11:47 AM
To: Jane Bay
Subject: Re: Losar - Tibetan New Year

Jane,

All the photos are great (I think I have seen them before) but I especially love the "toast." Such love and joy in both your faces. A frozen moment in time that captures forever the essence of what you shared, as brief and yet intense as it was....

The excerpt was as captivating as I expect from your writing. Can't wait to read it all. Your commitment to writing is impressive and inspiring...

All my best,
Gordon

From: Jane Bay
Sent: Thursday, March 18, 2004 12:25 PM
To: Gordon Radley
Subject: Re: Losar - Tibetan New Year

Thank you, Gordon, for the positive feedback. I HAVE to write... I would have lost my mind if I hadn't had this means to process my grief. Losing Namgyal the first time resulted in *Precious Jewels*, and now, losing her to death will give birth to *Love & Loss*.

We had the yearbook party last night, and Anne is putting a copy in the mail to you today. Hope you enjoy my "Yearbook Swan Song," too.

Love,
Jane

From: Tsetan Khensur
Sent: Wednesday, March 24, 2004 2:25 AM
To: Jane Bay
Subject: How are you?

Dear Mom,

How are you? Today we marked the 43rd foundation day of
Mentseekhang in India in the presence of honorable minister of health
and finance C.T.A I could not stand among the three highest in my second year medical exam, but I able to hold position in the first division
with 88.8%. I am happy with my result and hoping to put what I
learned into practice when the time comes to deal with my patients.

As usual, we entertained our lecturers, doctors, and all other members
of our institution with different dances and songs of Tibetan, Hindi,
English and Nepali in the evening. Our main motive is to raise funds
for helping some poor patients and organization caring movement for
the cause of Tibet financially.

I am looking forward to see you this summer. That's all for today, take
care, with love,

Yours' lovingly,
Tsetan

From: Jane Bay
Sent: Thursday, March 25, 2004 5:33 PM
To: Howard Roffman
Subject: Chapters in my new book

Dear Howard,

Maybe it is better to read them in chronological order. The foundation
of the new book will be the emails I've sent out since Namgyal's
death, the emails and letters I've received in response, emails from
her the last two years of her life, emails from her brothers before and

after her death. I will weave the narrative between emails as flashbacks from the time *Precious Jewels* was published and I was reunited with Namgyal, until I come to the end of this story.

Writing is my salvation, Howard, whether it's good or not doesn't matter; it's what I have to do to process the grief.

Love,
Jane

From: Howard Roffman
Sent: Monday, March 29, 2004 8:28 AM
To: Jane Bay
Subject: Re: Chapters in my new book

Dear Jane,

Thank you so much for sharing these emails with me. I can see that writing is your salvation; it comes through very clearly in all the various pieces. When I look at all these materials together, what I see emerging is a powerful story about processing grief – the pain you experienced, your quest for healing, the help that those who care about you have offered through their words, and perhaps most fundamentally a search for meaning. I know how important this is for you, Jane, and it means so much to me that you have shared it with me.

Love,
Howard

From: Jane Bay
Sent: Monday, March 29, 2004 5:52 PM
To: Lisa Cooke
Subject: Thinking of you...

Dearest Lisa,

Please forgive my delay in responding to your email regarding the death of your dear friend. I was stunned to hear about what happened to her, and you and she have been in my thoughts and prayers so often ever since. I think it's harder to handle when death occurs so unexpectedly, and I hope you are getting through the shock of it without too much distress.

I hope you are finding ways to say goodbye to her with ritual or some type of ceremony to honor and consecrate the relationship you had with her, even something as simple as lighting a candle for her each evening when you come home. I still do it for Namgyal, and there is such a comfort in remembering her in the gesture. It also gives me the opportunity to talk to her each day, just to tell her that she will live on in my heart forever. I send you my deepest sympathy for the loss of your dear friend. Take time to mourn...

And I send all my love to comfort you.
Jane

From: Lisa Cooke
Sent: Monday, March 29, 2004 6:43 PM
To: Jane Bay
Subject: Re: Thinking of you...

Hi Jane,

You are so sweet. It's been a strange journey lately. The more I learn about brain aneurysms the more common they seem to be. They are so sudden and final. Like Namgyal, Laura was getting ready for the day and, then, suddenly, gone.

How are you? Have you been able to spend much time in Santa Fe? I hope that slowly the pain of your beautiful daughter's death is lessening and in its place is the warmth of all of the love you shared.

I think of you often. Thanks for your kind thoughts.

Much love,
Lisa

From: Lisa Cooke
Sent: Monday, March 29, 2004 6:55 PM
To: Jane Bay
Subject: Re: Thinking of you...

Dear Lisa,

I'm somewhat happily preoccupied with participating in Namgyal's cousin, Dr. Dickey's wedding the weekend of April 16, and eagerly anticipating my return to Tibet on May 16, bittersweet though it may be.

I'll probably have something to say about all this in an email letter before I leave, but for now, every day is better, and it is true that time heals all wounds, love heals the heart... I'm grateful for your love, and have so so much for you in return.

Yours always,
Jane

From: Paula Boam
Sent: Monday, April 05, 2004 7:01 PM
To: Jane Bay
Subject: Friends

Hey Jane,

I was just thinking about all of the things you have done for me, the kids, and most of all, Jeffrey. You have been such a wonderful friend. My heart breaks over your loss of your mom and your beautiful daughter.

Life... well, I have nothing wise to say. What can anyone say about life kicking you to the curb? I'll just say, I'm grateful you have been my friend.

My life is getting much better. For the first time the sun is shining and the moon is full. I'm strong again and it feels wonderful. I taking pictures again and feel like living. Thank you for standing beside me when I was at my worst. I am glad that I could share friendship with you. We were good for each other. Paulita and Juanita, lol. How perfect for two crazy girls. We sure made Jeffrey happy that night at Lucy's El Adobe Cafe right before he died.

I miss being friends with you like before, but life has its twists and turns. You will always be my girlfriend. A dear soul in my heart. You are my Juanita. And, I will always do anything for you. Having said all that, I hope everything is going well for you.

By the way, I'm in love with a boy from Kansas, lol. I'm crazy about him. He is the most gentle, sweetest and kindest soul ever. He was born in Kansas and lived some in Texas. He took me to NASCAR last weekend. We lived in a camper and I loved it!!!! Better than the Four Seasons Hotel. He had a bunch of friends there. We were all laughing and cooking.

We all walked down to the race and laughed so much. I just can't tell you how much I was meant for a simple life. I have never been more content. I love doing for others, and doing the right thing. With these people you do that all that time. By the way, he thinks I'm an angel, lol. I'm going to do everything I can to make him think he isn't wrong. And if he does find out...he won't care, lol.

I love you Juanita,
Paulita

P.S. He just loves the egg salad I make for you!

From: Jane Bay
Sent: Wednesday, April 07, 2004 1:09 PM
To: Paula Boam
Subject: Re: Friends

Dearest Paulita,

I am so happy to hear your wonderful news. I'm happy that you are embracing life again, and happy you have found someone to share it with, a good ole boy, at that.... And especially someone who appreciates your egg salad!!!!!

As you know so well, grief takes the life out of you, I mean look at how long it's taken since Jeffrey died to get where you are today, so I'm not saying anything you don't already know – from experience. But as I've said, we each have to grieve in our own way the loss of someone we love, and the way I'm dealing with the grief of losing Namgyal is by writing about it, just as I did when I lost her the first time and poured my heart out in writing *Precious Jewels*. I trust this process and know that if I hadn't had a spiritual practice and wasn't able to write, I would have lost my mind.

No one can save me but myself, and what I've needed since Namgyal died has been the space to be present with my feelings, not to bury them, or hide from any of the experiences I was going through, no matter how painful it was at any given time.

I didn't rely on therapy or anti-depressant drugs, and I am grateful to you, my dear friend, for your patience with me. I'm truly sorry that I can't be as close a friend to you as I've been in the past, but that doesn't diminish my love for you and the friendship that we have. That will never die...

I'm eagerly anticipating the trip to Tibet, Nepal, and India (May 16 – June 20) even though it will be challenging, both physically and emotionally, as I go to Mount Kailash to say goodbye to my beloved Namgyal.

You will be there with me in spirit, and in my heart always.

With oceans of love,
Juanita

From: Chin Rodger
Sent: Sunday, April 11, 2004 9:51 PM
To: Jane Bay
Subject: Peace and blessing – Easter Sunday evening

Jane Dearest,

The kids are tired out and in bed – I have a moment now – sending you great love and peace and blessings and joy too, bliss – "ananda".

We, Kim's closest best friends and our families, gathered today and shared a scrumptious Easter lunch – an occasion to remember our beloved Kim who left us last Easter Sunday. While the kids played, swam and a couple of the dads watched, we (moms) went upstairs and had our prayers – lit a candle each and said a prayer for Kim, but mostly for Art and the kids (for we all acknowledged that Kim does not need our prayers and strongly agreed that she is already in a place, in bliss) – it is very hard for him – he is struggling in every area.

We said our prayers, shared our memories of our time with Kim and cried our eyes out, chanted "om"... we concluded by my sharing of the poem that your emailed me, sent to you by your friend... "She was meant to be noticed by you" that was so perfect, so beautiful – it filled us with love, and comfort. So, thank you for sharing your journey so selflessly.

Here is something that came up, a paragraph I read somewhere, "Don't be dismayed at goodbyes...it is only a farewell before we meet again. And meeting again, after moments, or lifetimes is certain for us...."

Thinking of you, with great love,
Chin

From: Chin Rodger
Sent: Tuesday, April 27, 2004 10:32 PM
To: Jane Bay
Subject: "thank you"

Jane,

I want to acknowledge receipt of your donation, as well as George's donation towards my Avon Walk. I feel so encouraged by your loving support and great feelings behind your intention.

A journey – I'm blown away by the overwhelming support that I have been receiving – I put out my letter in the mailboxes of teachers and staff at our school and to the parents that I liaised with – within a week – they had generously offered their support. I'm so blown away – it is amazing how each of us can truly shine forth when a golden opportunity presents itself.

And my journey continues – Georgia's other best friend, Seth's mom, Adena (I am close to her and her family, too) is on her last days from a rare cancer (lymph) – she has deteriorated these few weeks – saw her Friday when I dropped Seth home – oh Jane – images of Kim on her last days flashed back – Seth is nine and his little sister Michaela is seven. I cried my eyes out when I left – somehow Georgia's and my journey seemed to be entwined in this – I know Georgia is a very evolved soul – but she is still a kid. And Scott, their dad – he is just hanging by the thread – barely able to hold on... Do include him in your prayers please, Jane.

Off to meditate a little then to bed, thanks again for your support. Please convey my thanks to dear George too.

Much love,
Chin

P.S. When do you leave for Tibet??? Soon – isn't it???

From: Jane Bay
Sent: Wednesday, April 28, 2004 10:01 AM
To: Chin Rodger
Subject: Re: "thank you"

Dear Chin,

Isn't it amazing how much love we receive when we open ourselves to others. I'm not surprised by the response you've received. Your beautiful heart is a beacon of light radiating out to everyone you meet. It is a honor to offer my support for your Avon Walk for Breast Cancer, especially because this terrible disease has personally touched so many people you love.

I leave on Sunday, May 16, and hope to send out another email before I go. You'll be in my heart and prayers all the way, and I will be happy to include Kim, Adena and their families in my prayers as well.

Much love, and blessings to you.
Jane

From: Chin Rodger
Sent: Wednesday, April 28, 2004 9:22 PM
To: Jane Bay
Subject: Re: "thank you"

Jane,

Thank you for your beautiful feelings – they can only come from a great heart – a great inner state.

And, thank you for your prayers. Adena passed on early this morning... With your blessings, I would love to share the poem "She was meant to be noticed by you" – at Adena's funeral service on Sunday.

Much love,
Chin

From: Jane Bay
Sent: Thursday, April 29, 2004 10:45 PM
To: Chin Rodger
Subject: Re: "thank you"

I'm so sorry, Chin, to hear of Adena's passing. Yes, of course, you may read the poem. It was written by Sarita Patel.

My heart aches for you, dear Chin. You've suffered two profound losses, and really the only comfort is having the experience of love with these precious friends who will live on forever in your heart. Time will heal the wound, and love will heal your heart...

Yours always, with great love,
Jane

From: Tenzin Tsering
Sent: Monday, May 03, 2004 6:45 PM
To: Jane Bay
Subject: Sorry for delay response

Dear Mom,

I am very sorry to response your email on delay due to the too much work. But anyway my waist is 30 inch and 36 length. I have another request to you that please bring small American gifts for Lhakyi's sister and her husband and also for their daughter as we are staying together in one home. Please bring clothes for Tenzin Monkyi that fit for the four year old children as she is quite big. Hope to see you sooner as May is already arrived. Thanks for your kindness and love to us. We really miss you a lot.

Yours' lovingly,
Tenzin

CHAPTER TEN

Mother's Day

From: Jane Bay
Sent: Monday, May 10, 2004 2:02 AM
To: Dear Friends
Subject: Mother's Day

Dear Friends,

On Saturday, April 17, Namgyal's cousin, Dr. Dickey Nyerongsha, and her new husband, Dr. Lobsang Rapgay, celebrated their marriage in Los Angeles with a traditional Tibetan wedding reception at the UCLA Faculty Club. That day also marked the ninth month since Namgyal passed away, the amount of time for the gestation of a baby, and I found in these two events a poignant reminder of the ebb and flow of life, love, and relationships.

The night before, Peggy Hitchcock and I hosted a "rehearsal dinner" for the happy couple who had actually gotten married "on-line" about six months ago. The dinner was held at the Olympic Connection, a Mediterranean style meeting/event center in West Los Angeles not far from Dickey and Lobsang's house. We had a feast of delicious Italian food. The tables were decorated with gold and burgundy tablecloths (the colors of a Tibetan monk's robes) and crowned with centerpieces of black-red roses in round glass fish bowls. The flicker of votive candles gave the room a soft, pink glow.

The sounds of the CD *Prayer*, a multicultural collection of ancient prayers and chants from many spiritual traditions, played throughout the evening. At Dickey's request, Peggy's partner, Allan Bayer, brought his clarinet and played along on several songs.

I wore a ton of Tibetan turquoise and amber jewelry and the green satin *chuba*, the traditional Tibetan dress, with the striped apron and gold brocade blouse that Namgyal's Auntie Drakpa had made for me last year in Lhasa.

At each place on the tables was a party favor in a small cardboard box around which Peggy and I tied thin burgundy, turquoise, gold, and fuchsia French ribbon. Inside each guest's box was a *tsa-tsa*, a small Buddha statue or relief image made of clay, either in the image of Shakymuni Buddha, Green Tara, or Chenrizig (the Bodhisattva of Compassion). Traditionally, *tsa-tsa* are used for meditation practice and are placed on altars, shrines, or other holy places. We gave Lobsang a *tsa-tsa* of Manjushri, representing wisdom, and Dickey, the Medicine Buddha, representing method. Lobsang thought it was a good union.

Midway through dinner, I made a few remarks about the occasion. I told the story about my spiritual friend, Losang Samten, inviting me to attend the Kalachakra Initiation and teaching by His Holiness the Dalai Lama about thirteen years ago before I began my studies of Tibetan Buddhism. I said, "Losang, wouldn't it be somewhat sacrilegious for a non-Buddhist to take this sacred teaching?" "No," he replied, "You can take it as a blessing." Okay, I thought, but I asked if he could recommend a book that would give me some information about it. He suggested Shantideva's eighth century *Guide to the Bodhisattva's Way of Life*. That elicited a chuckle from Peggy because this is a very complex text for anybody, much less a novice, as an introduction to Buddhism.

But I read it, rather the commentary of it, *Meaningful to Behold* by Geshe Kelsang Gyatso, from cover to cover and found it to be amazingly relevant to my own life today. One of the first things that struck me was the concept of *"recognition of all sentient beings as one's mother."*

The book spelled out a line of reasoning that went on to say, "The woman we presently recognize as our mother is such by virtue of our having been born into the world from her womb. Yet this is not the first

284

and only time we have taken birth. The continuity of our consciousness stretches back over infinite time and the births we have taken have been countless. As we have been born countless times it follows we have had countless mothers. Thus there is not a single being we meet who, over the incalculable expanse of beginningless time, has failed to be our mother."

"Therefore, if we see everyone we meet, friends, family, strangers, enemies, everyone, as having been our mother in one of our lives, we would honor her for giving us this precious life. She was our selflessly kind mother, feeding us with her own milk and protecting us from harm and fear. We would wish to repay her kindness, and never cause her harm." This concept was the beginning of my understanding of the interconnectedness of all beings...

Namgyal was only nine months old when her mother died. When she went to live with Dickey's mother, Dr. Tinley, it was Dickey who gave Namgyal her bottles of milk each day, and she who slept in a bed with Namgyal each night for many years.

When it became painfully clear that the Chinese government would not issue a visa for Dr. Tinley to come to the U.S. for Dickey and Lobsang's wedding reception, Dickey asked if I would be her mother. I was overjoyed...

Pasang Lhamo, Lobsang's ninety-two-year-old mother, brought her family's antique wedding jewelry that she and Dickey would wear at the reception. I had seen this type of necklace on a Tibetan doll that Rita and Tommy Sullivan had given me several years ago, but seeing the real thing on Pasang, and on Dickey in her red and turquoise satin *chuba* was stunning. She was a beautiful bride.

On our way over to the Faculty Club for the reception, Dickey pointed out that on the long strands of pearls, coral, and turquoise studded with diamonds, emeralds and rubies, were three 18 carat gold tools. One for picking your teeth, a pair of tweezers for pulling out whiskers, and a spoon to clean wax out of the ears. I guess you never know when you might need these things, but we had a good laugh about it. The Tibetans are such practical people.

At the reception, Lobsang's mother, Dickey, Lobsang, and I sat on chairs in a receiving line for the guests to participate in a Khata (a white silk blessing scarf) Offering Ceremony for the bride and groom. There were thankhas on the wall behind us, an altar on one side of the Buddha, and a table on the other side for a *chema*, a painted box with two compartments filled with ground barley flour (*tsampa*) and barley seeds, and a silver pitcher of holy water that Dr. Tinley had sent from Tibet.

Each guest was given five khatas and they would place the first one on the Buddha's altar, followed by placing one each around our necks. Having made the khata offering to the mothers, and the bride and groom, the guest would take a *chema* by pinching the barley flour between the fingers and throwing it up in the air, and then doing the same with the seeds. Then a small amount of holy water would be poured into the palm of the hand and sipped by the guest. If there was any remaining water in the hand, it was patted on the top of the head, to bless the guest as well.

Since there were 150 guests, we were almost completely covered in white gossamer by the end of the ceremony. It was an amazing experience being on the receiving end of such an outpouring of love. People gave me their congratulations on the marriage of my daughter, and I was honored that I could be there to represent Dr. Tinley to Dickey and Lobsang's family and friends.

Following the khata offering, we were wined and dined, and there were moving testimonials about Lobsang and Dickey, and great wishes for a lifetime of happiness together this time around. Then we were entertained by Tibetan and American folk singers, and by the end of the evening, even Dickey, who has a beautiful voice, took the microphone and belted out a traditional Tibetan song.

So the moral of this story is that every day is Mother's Day in Buddhaville.

Dickey's mother-in-law, Dickey and Jane at Wedding

Jane and Dickey at Rehearsal Dinner

This time next Sunday, I'll be on an airplane on my way to Lhasa, Mount Kailash, Nepal, and India, but I want to share the email Mother's Day greetings I received from Namgyal's brothers before I close.

Dear Mom,

Wishing you a very happy journey to the top of the world and good luck wherever you step during your journey.

You are so fortunate to visit GANG RINPOCHE (Mt. Kailash), the very holy mount of Buddhist as well as Hindus. May the blessings of the holy mount shower over you with everlasting happiness. Also, convey my hearty best wishes to my brother and his family. I miss them very much.

It is my pleasure to help you when you reach dasa (Dharamsala, India). Lastly, again wishing you happy and successful journey.

With love,
Tsetan

YAHOO! Greetings 🖼️

Yahoo! Greetings	with **american** 💙 **greeting**

Home | Favorites | Scrapbook | Outbox

Home > Holidays > Mother's Day 5/9/04 > Happy Mother's Day

Dear Mom,
No matter where you are we always love you and always prayer for you. wish you a happy mother's day and hope to see you soon. wish lots of love.

yours' lovingly
tenzin

Farewell for now, dear friends. You will be in my heart and prayers on this next Journey to the Roof of the World.

With Oceans of Love,
Jane

From: Lis Blackwell
Sent: Monday, May 10, 2004 8:57 AM
To: Jane Bay
Subject: Mother's day back at ya

Dear Jane – you are amazing – I am proud to be your friend. I truly enjoyed reading this letter and the accompanying letters from your Tibetan children. The description of the wedding is so beautiful. Thank you for sharing — I feel I was there.

I especially felt moved by the Buddhists' concept of interconnectedness.... "the woman we presently recognize as our mother is such by virtue of our having been born into the world from her womb. Yet this is not the first and only time we have taken birth. The continuity of our consciousness stretches back over infinite time and the births we have taken have been countless. As we have been born countless times and have countless mothers. Thus there is not a single being we meet who, over the incalculating expanse of beginningless time, has failed to be our mother."

"Therefore, if we see everyone we meet, friends, family, strangers, enemies, everyone as having been our mother in one of our lives, we would honor her for giving us precious life. She was our selflessly kind mother, feeding us with her own milk and protecting us from harm and fear. We would wish to repay her kindness, and never cause her harm." This concept was the beginning of my understanding the interconnectedness of all beings...

Happy Mother's Day back to you — a true mother you are.

We spent yesterday with Jules, Rachel and baby Max Mann along with the other stepmothers and birth mothers, grand steps and half sisters and step sisters et al, in Hamilton where Jules and Rachel live. I was hesitant and had a mini anxiety attack before leaving the car. However, it turned out to be very nice and when the three of us (Lexsea, Jeff and I) got back in the car we knew again that the only thing "to fear is fear itself…"

In the evening our dear friend Mike Cerre and his wife Jenna came by for a BBQ. Mike had just returned from Iraq and the reality of the war and atrocities being committed on and by humans to each other. We talked for hours about the sad situation and felt helpless. We all pray for some sanity before and on June 30th, the day Iraq regains its sovereignty.

Dear Jane — go out into the world safely. Take special care to come home with wonderful stories to share with the rest of us. Spread your love, but come home to us. If you get a chance please let me know the date of your return. We will have a celebration.

With my love,
Lis

From: China Galland
Sent: Monday, May 10, 2004 10:46 AM
To: Jane Bay
Subject: Re: Mother's Day

Dear Jane,

SO beautiful! And I'm so happy to have such delightful news of Dr. Lobsang Rapgay and Dr. Dickey. Perfect! How wonderful this is all turning out and how much I enjoyed your Mother's Day thoughts in "Buddhaville."

Also, you are making a great pilgrimage, one I still hope to make one day. Please take me with you in prayer. My husband, Corey, is having open heart surgery next week, May 18th and I would be grateful if you could remember him and also pray for his healing.

My daughter, Madelon, is actually still in India, where she has been since last September. She's in Manali on a retreat right now. If by any strange chance, your paths cross, please know who she is and introduce yourself. I'm sure she would love meeting you and you her. She is a dear and wonderful young woman!

Congratulations for once again turning out to be such a great mother, Jane!

Love,
China

From: Jane Bay
Sent: Monday, May 10, 2004 11:00 AM
To: China Galland
Subject: Re: Mother's Day

China,

I'll be in Chengdu, China on May 18th celebrating my sixty-third birthday with my dear friend, Mr. Fu Ching, at the Manjushri Temple, the oldest remaining Buddhist Temple in Chengdu. I will say special prayers for Corey at that time, and light incense for him and you as well. You will always be in my heart and prayers throughout this journey, but especially on June 3 at Mount Kailash for Sakadewa.

It would be wonderful to cross paths with Madelon, but it's unlikely as I'll only be in Delhi overnight on my way to Dharamsala to spend time with Namgyal's brother, Tsetan Khensur, and visit friends at Namgyal Monastery.

Au revoir, mon ami.

Love,
Jane

From: China Galland
Sent: Monday, May 10, 2004 11:30 AM
To: Jane Bay
Subject: Re: Mother's Day

Thank you, Jane, every prayer will help! I love being taken to Kailash with you by heart.

Re: Madelon, I know, very odd chance, but so many curious meetings occur, just wanted you to know. I don't even know when she'll be in Delhi. She is supposed to go to Dharamsala and visit our friend Tara Doyle who's running the Buddhist Studies program for Emory University. Maybe you'll bump into her there if she goes.

Have a blessed, blessed, and safe journey. You will be in my prayers as well. I will put your name on my altar and Happy Birthday!

Love,
China

From: Frank Wells
Sent: Monday, May 10, 2004 6:26 PM
To: Jane Bay
Subject: Re: Mother's Day

Dearest Jane,

I read your letter this morning, feeling like an invited guest on your special journey, and I am reminded of our pleasant conversation at lunch the other day.

As the three of us shared a meal together, contemplating life and sharing our experiences, we began a discussion of some of the world's religions, and the differences, and commonalities of these respective beliefs. I have thought of our conversation often since, and your recent correspondence has inspired some thoughts that I will now share with you.

I was born in Berkeley, CA — where my mother worked as a choir director for a large Unitarian church. It was the sixties, and it was a very diverse and progressive community with regard to organized religion. Sunday services often featured guest speakers from a variety of different backgrounds and religious faiths — from Buddhist Monks to Black Panthers. As a matter of course (and practicality), I spent many hours of my early youth roaming around this safe sanctuary, and it was there that I was first introduced to the concept of spirituality.

My mother is a deeply spiritual person, exposing her children to the richness of perspective that this outlook offers — while allowing us to find our own path. She remains my spiritual mentor to this day, and I have tried to raise my own children emulating her selfless grace.

There is a passage in the Bible that reads: "We are strangers, and sojourners." I believe that in each life we are born anew, cleansing us in innocence. We walk our path alone, following our heart in search of truth, and as each wonder is revealed we are enlightened and encouraged by the realization of that which has always been. These simple truths allow us to embrace and let go with grace and humility that sets us free.

In your letter you cited the concept of "recognition of all sentient beings as one's mother." When I consider these words, I find them to be intriguing and at the same time comforting. The idea that we are all family feels right to me, even if my own imperfect humanness won't always allow me to act as such.

I choose not to subscribe to any one organized philosophy, trying instead to learn as I go. My mother once told me "Be the student of life." Well, I am definitely a work in progress. Christian, Buddhist, or Atheist, if you follow your heart it will lead you down the path to truth…the universal message is love.

Wishing you a wondrous Mother's Day, on your journey to Buddahville (very funny). May you find what you seek.

With love and respect,
Frank

From: Jane Bay
Sent: Monday, May 10, 2004 7:40 PM
To: Frank Wells
Subject: Re: Mother's Day

Frank,

Thank you for sharing your wonderful, inspiring story with me. I feel quite humbled by the opening of your heart. My life is enriched by knowing you.

With love & gratitude,
Jane

From: Eleanor Coppola
Sent: Tuesday, May 11, 2004 6:05 AM
To: Jane Bay
Subject: Re: Photos for Mother's Day Message

Such a moving message and you do look sensational in your traditional clothing and beautiful jewelry! Have a wonderful trip!!

xxx

From: Lynda Beth Unkeless
Sent: Tuesday, May 11, 2004 8:33 AM
To: Jane Bay
Subject: Your maroon outfit for Tibet

Dear Jane,

This is the passage I was thinking of when I saw the maroon outfit you bought for your travels to Tibet.

It is from the book *Color in Your World* by Faber Birren, a color expert. The book was given to me by one of my clients, a European architect, who has a special interest in the impact of color in our everyday lives.

Maroon is red fire with the dampers regulated. (Because maroon is the author's favorite color, he looks upon it with not a small amount of bias.)

In the study of human personality, maroon holds an odd significance. It is passion tempered by conscience or adversity. It is ambition, bravery, strength whittled down by hard struggle and difficulty. It is all that is good in life, but good that is somewhat soiled and frayed in earning...

You are not reckless with your friends or the world. Consequently, you may be likable and generous. There is a possibility that you are a fairly great person at heart, one who has reduced intense red heat to the rich, deep glow of maroon. Although discipline may have been forced upon you, it also may have been fostered by your own purpose. You may have recognized at one time that red flames are quite a strain on others as well as on yourself.

If you have certain composure, it is not because of inflexibility of character; the qualities of red are still present. If you happen to be a saint, you are sure to have a glint of sin in your eyes. If you are a sinner, the expression on your face will bespeak atonement.

Does any of this resonate? Sorry I can't give you the context of red which he refers to in this passage — too lengthy to type all the info on red itself.

Thank you for sending me your "Mother's Day" email. Mother's Day can still be a difficult day for me. My father died on Mother's Day five years ago as if to make some comment on my mother's death by her own hand. Stuff still arises for me on Mother's Day, and last Sunday was no exception.

Love,
Lynda Beth

From: Chin Rodger
Sent: Wednesday, May 12, 2004 9:22 AM
To: Jane Bay
Subject: Re: Mother's Day

Jane,

Indeed, Meaningful to Behold — thank you for this reminder — for I was so captivated by the awesome truth in this when I first read it in your book *Precious Jewels* — I wrote it down in my journal last year. I am still awestruck by the all embracing message and truth it contains. Thank you, Jane — for being the constant ever guiding light...for all of us.

Many congratulations — truly — what joy, what joy!!! Sounds to me — your cup of joy is full to the brim!!! I love your Tibetan outfit — so full of colors — great wholesome colors — Georgia loves your Tibetan outfit too. It is such a shame here in the States that kids don't get to see and experience traditional costumes from other cultures. I was so blessed with my growing up in Malaysia. We are looking forward to our trip to Penang in the summer.

I wish for you, dear Jane — a great journey to the roof of the world — an auspicious journey. May it fill you with love and grace. I will be thinking of you and sending you blessings.

With oceans of love to you, too.
Chin

From: Fay David
Sent: Wednesday, May 12, 2004 11:36 AM
To: Jane Bay
Subject: Re: Mother's Day

Dear Jane,

Thank you so much for sharing this with me. It is so moving and beautifully written. As I read, I kept thinking how fortunate you must feel to share in the lives of these wonderful people and how fortunate they must feel to have you in their lives. I loved reading the Mother's Day wishes from Namgyal's brothers. They emote so much love and care for you!

I wish you all the best on your journey. You will be in my thoughts!

Love,
Fay

P.S. The pictures of you and Dickey are gorgeous! The richness of the traditional dress and jewelry is simply stunning.

From: Fu Ching
Sent: Thursday, May 13, 2004 12:44 AM
To: Jane Bay
Subject: greetings from Chengdu

Hello, dear Jane

Warm greetings from Chengdu to You and hope you are happy during the time. I think I can feel that from your photos in USA.

It will be so nice to meet you soon in Chengdu. I will be at airport to meet you and we can go to the nice restaurant and spend one beautiful birthday night with you in China.

Also, this time I know that you will have a pilgrim trip for you and for others. Wish you success and good health.

Any questions, please feel free to let me know.

Yours
Fu Ching

From: Melene Smith
Sent: Friday, May 14, 2004 9:15 AM
To: Jane Bay
Subject: Bon Voyage

Hi Jane,

I just wanted to wish you well on your trip to Tibet and India. I will think of you often while you are traveling and look forward to seeing pictures and hearing about your adventure.

I really enjoyed your stories and pictures of Mother's Day. Your traditional dress is fabulous and you looked very happy.

Give my love to Tenzin and family. Safe Travels!

Love,
Melene

From: Lucy Wilson
Sent: Friday, May 14, 2004 6:21 PM
To: Jane Bay
Subject: Re: Mother's Day

Hi Jane

Happy belated Mother's day to you from me, your child in a past life and mother in another. I love this concept.

You probably won't read this until you return from your trip so I welcome you back and can't wait to hear about your adventures.

Lucy

From: Patty Carlson
Sent: Saturday, May 15, 2004 12:22 AM
To: Jane Bay
Subject: Re: Mother's Day

Jane,

Thank you for sharing this lovely writing with me. I'm in awe of your "attention to detail" and impressed with how specific and descriptive you recall everything. Guess I'm getting more and more concerned as I get older (maybe it's really "busier"?) about my lack of recall! Anyway, your writing is fun to read – almost like being there. Love the description of color, names, details. What a gift you have. Don't you love those times when we're with friends and family and the Love is just pouring out of everyone? Nothing like it. Wish the world had so much more of it.

I feel for how special you must have felt being Dickey's mother that evening. What an honor. Especially with her being your daughter's cousin. As a mom to my two wonderful boys, I've struggled recently as their new stepmother tells them they are not to refer to me as their "real mother" in that household; I'm to be called their "other mother" or "Patty" by them over there. And they're to call her "Mommy" too. The name I'm most proud of. It's really pained me. But your writing adds a whole new perspective, one that I find quite soothing. Thank you, Jane. I will be pondering this concept. It's beautiful. And you're right, there's a bigger picture here… isn't there always?

Safe travels to you, Jane. See you when you return.

Patty

CHAPTER ELEVEN

Life & Death

From: Jane Bay
Sent: Sunday, July 18, 2004 7:00 PM
To: Dear Friends
Subject: Life & Death

Dear Friends,

I'm alive, and almost well. I'm sorry I haven't been in touch with you sooner since my return from Tibet, but I want to share with you now the latest chapter in my story. It's quite long, over ten pages, so print it out and read it at your convenience:

Altitude was a problem from the very first day I arrived in Tibet. By nightfall, I was vomiting and had diarrhea even though I was taking Diamox, a Western pharmaceutical to prevent altitude sickness. Namgyal's brother, Tenzen Tsering, arrived around nine o'clock that evening at the Lhasa Hotel with vials of a Tibetan medicinal elixir made from an indigenous flower, along with a case of Coca-Cola.

The next morning I felt much better despite a fitful night's sleep and a slight headache. I joined Bob Thurman and the Geographic Expeditions group that included my friends, Peggy Hitchcock and Tom Latinovich, in the dining room for breakfast around eight-thirty. I'd met most of group the day before when I boarded the plane in Chengdu. They were already on board en route from Beijing to Lhasa. It was a big group, twenty-five people of all ages, early twenties to over seventy. I made several new friends almost immediately, and I was eager to get to know them better on the trek to Mount Kailash.

We had three days in Lhasa (at 12,000 feet altitude) that I spent with Namgyal's family while the group went sightseeing during the day to temples and monasteries I'd visited several times on previous trips to Tibet. The nausea and tummy upset subsided, and each evening I joined the group for dinner and Bob's dharma talk.

But the morning we began our journey across the Tibetan plateau toward Mount Kailash, I was filled with foreboding. With every thousand foot ascent over the high passes, I found it more and more difficult to breathe. By the time we got to Yamdrok Lake, the sacred turquoise lake pictured on the cover of *Precious Jewels of Tibet*, I was throwing up in plastic laundry bags Tommy had taken from the hotel in Lhasa.

That night when we finally arrived in Gyantse (after eight hours of traveling on the poorest excuse for a road I've ever been on), Bob said he thought it might be wise for me to turn back, that there was no shame in not going on. I didn't really "feel" that bad and dismissed the idea outright. Maybe it was just car sickness. It was our first day on the road after all, and turning back was not something I would even consider.

The drive to Shigatse was long, but not as difficult, and the nausea, whether caused by altitude or car sickness, had ceased. We were met by the GeoEx trip leader, Sanjay, who had just arrived from Nepal. He wanted to stay a second day in Shigatse to acclimate himself. Several of us stayed behind with Sanjay and caught up with the group a day later.

When we arrived at camp, the group was gathered in the dining tent for dinner. We were greeted with cheers and applause. Bob said, "You're a brave woman, Jane." I thought, "Brave? Bravery has nothing to do with it, it's more like obsession." I was going to Mount Kailash for Sakadawa, the festival in celebration of the Buddha's birth and enlightenment, even if it killed me.

On June 3, the morning of Sakadawa, I woke up in the Darchen Guest House at the base of Mount Kailash with a raging sinus infection and bronchitis, barely able to walk more than twenty-five feet without having to stop to catch my breath. But it was the day I had been waiting for, one of the primary reasons I'd come back to Tibet. It was the day I planned to say goodbye to my beloved daughter, in her homeland, and serendipitously, the day Namgyal would be reborn into her next life — nine months from the forty-ninth day of her death.

The day before, Bob Thurman and the group had victoriously returned from their four-day circumambulation around the sacred mountain. We had a jubilant celebratory dinner. Bob read an excerpt from Lama Govinda's book, *The Way of the White Clouds*, about the bond that is created among brothers and sisters who share a pilgrimage to Mount Kailash, and to my wondrous surprise, they dedicated their kora around the mountain to me. By this gesture I felt connected to the mountain, and them, as one. I had shared their experience, and we were brothers and sisters on a journey to the roof of the world.

Bob had done a fire puja the second day of their kora that included prayers for Namgyal. Before they left, he asked if I had any personal items of clothing or photos of Namgyal to burn in the fire. I had the picture of Namgyal and me taken the year before at Yamdrok Lake with our arms outstretched, and the hat she was wearing in that photograph that her Auntie Drakpa had given me when I was in Lhasa. I gave both of these items to Bob to burn in the fire puja on the mountain. By all accounts, it was glorious.

I never planned to do the kora; just to get to the mountain was my goal. I had stayed behind at the Darchen Guest House to rest up for the remainder of the trip, but I could see Mount Kailash from the window outside my room. The four days the group was on the mountain I spent mostly sleeping, eating simple meals prepared by one of the Nepali cooks, and watching the white clouds. A driver and a young Tibetan woman named Pendon also stayed behind to look after me. I was happy, despite my deteriorating health.

The first night alone I was unsettled when a large Hindu contingent arrived from India, and someone tried to open the door to my room. Pendon slept with me for the next three nights, and it was a great comfort to be with her. She reminded me of Namgyal. One day we drove out to Tarboche, at the base of Mount Kailash, where there was a great prayer flag pole and a *mani* (stones piled on top of each other) shrine. It is the starting place for many trekkers, and it is a magnificent spot. I had made it to the mountain!!!!

On the eve of Sakadawa, with the full moon rising, I heard there would be a medical evacuation the next day after the raising of the flagpole at Tarboche for one women who had come off the mountain earlier with altitude sickness, and for another who had sustained a cut on the leg that wasn't healing. Given the current state of my own health, rested but obviously not well, I thought it would be better to join the evacuation to Nepal rather than continue with the group for another five or six days camping at Lake Manasarovar and backtracking over the roads from hell to Lhasa.

On the morning of Sakadawa when one of the cooks arrived with breakfast tea and a basin of hot water for washing, I asked him to get a message to our trip leader, Sanjay, that I needed to talk with him as soon as possible. I asked again when the cook returned to retrieve the cup and basin, and finally, Yam, our Nepali guide who was the Co-Trip Leader with Sanjay, showed up. I told him what I'd heard about the evacuation, and he said he'd get back to me. I'd already decided to cancel the India leg of my trip, and when Yam returned saying Sanjay had approved my going on the evacuation, I felt a great sense of relief and went over to the dining room for breakfast.

Bob, Tommy, and several other friends were already there. I told them about my plan. Everyone agreed it was a good idea, except for the concern that the Maoists in Nepal had called a general strike, planning to close the airport and hotels and to target tourists. We would have to travel through one of their strongholds on the road from the border to Kathmandu. The objective was to get to Kathmandu before the strike began in five days. But I wasn't too worried about it.

Around nine that morning, Sanjay came to me in the dining room to confirm the evacuation plans. We talked about airline ticket changes to get back to the U.S., and he mentioned that if the Maoists were causing any disturbances on the road, we'd have to take a helicopter from the border to Kathmandu. No problem. He asked me to go to the Western medical clinic as soon as I got there to be examined as part of the evacuation. No problem.

Then he said, "Are you packed? The cars are leaving at nine-thirty so bring your bags to the lobby as soon as possible." "What? I'm going to Sakadawa this morning. I was told the evacuation was later this afternoon AFTER Sakadawa." I was stunned...I said I wasn't packed, I had no intention of leaving before Sakadawa, that's what I had come all this way for, and I wasn't really that sick.

Bob said, "Jane, you don't need to go to Tarboche, you saw the full moon of Sakadawa last night. It's going to be crowded and dusty, and it's just the raising of the flagpole which won't happen until two-thirty this afternoon." Sanjay chimed in that the evacuation was happening at nine-thirty, and there would be no other opportunity to leave. If I wanted to go, now was the time. My head was spinning, I was dizzy, and I just couldn't think clearly. High altitude can distort one's perception, cause the thought processes to slow down, along with the breathing, and the old brain just doesn't respond like it should. I found myself doing what I rarely do in life. I let other people influence my decisions, and before I knew it, I was on the way back to my room to pack.

Bob offered to help, but when we got to the lobby, some of my bags were already there. How did this happen? Bob stayed with the luggage while I went on to my room at the end of a long hallway off the lobby. My day-pack and small suitcase with cameras, vitamins, toiletries, all the vital things, were still in the room.

At that moment, Nima, a tall, strikingly handsome Tibetan man in jeans and a black cowboy hat, who manages the guides from Wind Horse, our land operator in Tibet, came into the room. Nima, who had been sweet and attentive throughout the trip said, "Can I help you?" I just looked at him in disbelief at what was happening. He put his arms around my shoulders, I put my arms around his back, and for a moment he held me. "I'll miss you, Jane." "I'll miss you, too, Nima." "Are you ready?" "I guess so," I sighed. He picked up the bags and started to leave, then said, "When you come back to Tibet, will you bring me a watch like you gave

Wangdu?" I said I would, and together we walked out of the room. I had a bit of a crush on Nima, as did several other women on the trip who were of a certain age.

Wangdu is the general manager of Wind Horse, and I've known him since my first trip to Tibet in 1994. We've become good friends over the years. He invited Namgyal and me to his home last year for Losar, and I've gotten to know his family. I brought gifts for him and his son, and Nima had been with us when I gave Wangdu a gold *Star Wars* watch with a leather band and C-3PO's face on the time plate.

There was a great deal of commotion in the lobby when Nima and I got there. Bob was carrying my big Pullman suitcase to the Land Cruiser, but I stopped him, saying I needed to get something out of it, right away. He helped open the case, and rummaging around in the bottom I found what I was looking for — the *Star Wars* C-3PO watch I had planned to give to Tsetan Khensur, Namgyal's brother in India.

I rushed over to Nima, and handed it to him. "I won't be coming back to Tibet, Nima." He took the box, tucked it in his leather jacket, smiled and nodded. I knew this was the last time I would see him.

Then I was hustled out of the lobby into one of the Land Cruisers at the hotel entrance. Yam, Pendon, the young Tibetan woman, and two other women, one Chinese, one American, were already in the vehicles. Yam and I would be riding together; the other women were in the second car.

Just as I was about to climb into the back seat of the Land Cruiser, Sanjay come over to the car with a final bulletin about the evacuation. He said if we had to take a helicopter from the border to Kathmandu it would cost $2,000, which we'd have to pay in advance (split among the three of us who were evacuating), and there was also a possibility that the border could be closed if the Maoists were agitating before the strike, in which case we'd have to drive back to Lhasa.

The next thing I remember was looking over at Dechen Thurman, Bob's son for whom I had developed a great affection, standing on the steps of the Darchen Guest House with other members of our group who had spontaneously gathered to bid us farewell. His hands were folded in prayer and when our eyes met, I saw in his a look of deep concern. I mouthed, "Say a prayer for me," but no sound came out of my voice.

And we were gone, on the road away from Mount Kailash, away from the Sakadawa festival. In a matter of thirty minutes, a blink of an eye really, my dream vanished in a trail of dust as we headed out across the bleak, barren, high Tibetan Plateau.

To say I was in a state of shock would be a gross understatement. I couldn't speak for some time, and buried my head in my hands in disbelief. Finally, I asked Yam, "What did Sanjay say about the border being closed, I didn't understand."

Yam explained that we were going to drive like a bat out of hell for twelve to thirteen hours a day for the next two days over the roughest, most desolate, harsh terrain, with no roads most of the way, crossing mountain peaks over 16,000 feet to reach the Tibet/Nepal border before the Maoists' strike, with the possibility of having to drive all the way back to Lhasa for another five days over more high mountains and glacier peaks if the Chinese and/or Nepalese closed the border because of the Maoists' threats.

I went berserk. "You mean to tell me you're evacuating us (descending to lower altitude as quickly as possible) only to take us back up to Lhasa at 12,000 feet with another five days driving cooped up in this car? That's insane!!! Nobody in their right mind would do this." My diatribe continued toward Yam, who I must say remained calm and tried to comfort me throughout, all the way to Lake Manasarovar.

I was very angry. Angry primarily at Sanjay for not briefing me (and the other women) ahead of time, and for not thoroughly explaining exactly what the conditions were so we could make a rational decision about our own fate. I would never have agreed to go knowing fully what the possible outcome could have been. I got swept up in circumstances I couldn't control, and I think, probably due to oxygen deprivation in my brain, couldn't assimilate what was actually happening. I felt I'd made the worst decision of my life based on false information in the first place (the AFTER Sakadawa evacuation rumor), and a lack of communication from the trip leader about the consequences if the border was closed.

Lake Manasarovar is beautiful, but there was no joy in my heart in seeing it. By the time we got there, I was distraught and withdrew into a smoldering rage.

We drove on for several hours until reaching the Mayum-la Pass, a magnificent 17,000-foot mountain peak where we stopped for a break. The ubiquitous prayer flags that appear at many of the high passes in Tibet fluttered and rumbled in the gusting winds carrying their supplications to the heavens above. Yam had brought a string of prayer flags he intended to take to Sakadawa, and we decided to have our own flag raising ceremony here.

The other women stayed in their car, but Pendon took my DVD camera to record Yam tying the flags to the pole. I stood next to him, but when he said, "Jane is here to say prayers for her daughter Namgyal," I broke down and cried. He kissed the tears on my face, and had he not held me up, I would have collapsed in a heap on the ground. I could barely say the words, but Yam repeated them after me. "Namgyal, I pray for you to have a long and happy life, and that your new mother will love you unconditionally as my mother loved me. You will live on in my heart forever." When I looked at the DVD after returning home, just as these words were spoken a fierce wind came up and they were rendered indiscernible. Maybe it took such a powerful force of nature to get my message to her.

When we finally stopped for lunch, Rita, the Chinese woman who was the official evacuee, was incredibly weak from throwing up all morning. Yam had brought one of the oxygen tanks used on the kora around Mount Kailash, and he gave it to Rita, only to find after she took a few inhalations that the tank was empty. I had one last aerosol can of oxygen (about the size of a hairspray canister) in my daypack, and we shared it until it was gone later in the day. We ate our measly boxed lunch of hard-boiled eggs, apples, and crackers and got back on the road again. The "evacuation" was all down hill from there, in more ways than one.

We drove and drove and drove, all afternoon across the dusty, high desert stopping only to go pee-pee. Even with the windows rolled up, and wearing a Michael Jackson painter's mask, I was choking on dust. I also tied a turquoise bandana over my mouth and nose, to no avail. Finally, we came to a village where we hoped to find a doctor for Rita, and something to eat. No such luck. All we got were sodas, but I remembered I still had a bag of trail mix bars in one of my suitcases, and I managed to dig it out for a snack. It turned out to be the only food we would have for the rest of the day.

We hadn't been on the road again for more than an hour when the vehicle Yam and I were in broke down. At that moment, a streak of panic struck me like lightning. This evacuation could end up killing me!!!

The men who drive the vehicles up and down and around these mountains are amazing individuals. Physically strong and powerful, constantly alert, and skillful mechanics, your life is literally in their hands. Both drivers worked in unison on the repair that seemed to take forever to fix, but by the clock, was only about forty-five minutes.

We were running way behind schedule, and the rest of the drive was over more high passes on pencil-thin bumpy roads curving around mountains with over a thousand foot dropoff on one side and falling rocks and boulders on the other side. Forget about oncoming traffic. In some cases there wasn't more than five inches between us and the passing vehicle. I still have calluses on my right hand from gripping the handrail above the door trying to steady myself from all the jostling, in a desperate attempt to hold on to something secure. And it was getting dark. I felt like the typical child in the backseat asking daddy, "How much longer until we get there?" Yam said, "You don't want to know the answer."

Around ten o'clock, we could see a yellow glow in the distance, but it wasn't lights from the town of Saga, our destination. It was the full moon that appeared like a gigantic golden ball floating in the black sky slightly below us as we rounded a curve. I'd never seen anything like it, and it seemed so close you could almost touch it. I thought about all the times during the five years before Namgyal's death that I would go outside each month on the full moon and send a "message on moonbeams" to her in Lhasa. And so I did this night as well, wherever she was.

We finally reached Saga shortly after midnight, fourteen and a half hours after leaving Darchen. We arrived at a Tibetan guest house only to find that it was full up and closed for the night. My patience was at its end, and I barked orders to find us a Chinese hotel instead. The drivers came back shortly, and we proceeded toward the hotel, but the road was under construction. We had to walk about a block through the muddy mess to get to the hotel entrance. The two young Chinese women who greeted us were friendly and courteous. They even arranged for someone to make a pot of noodle soup for us to eat, but I was so exhausted I could only drink a few sips of the broth.

Pendon and I shared one room, and Rita and the American woman, Dale, shared another. The beds were comfortable, but the best thing about the hotel was that there were toilets. Granted, they were Tibetan toilets, a hole in the floor that you'd squat over to do your business, but they did flush, so the smell was tolerable. However, there was no running water in the sink, so the Chinese women brought a thermos of hot water and a washing bowl. I managed to wipe off some of the dust from the day's journey, and went to bed.

Next morning, I learned that Dale had slipped on water Rita accidentally spilled on the bathroom floor the night before, and she had pulled a muscle in her leg, now joining the ranks of the walking wounded.

After a breakfast of hot rice soup and hard-boiled eggs, we started our drive to the Tibet/Nepal border. Just outside Saga, we came to a ferry crossing at a narrow but deep river. There were dozens of cars and trucks in line ahead of us, and the ferry only carried three or four vehicles at a time. Things were not going our way. We waited three hours and forty-five minutes to get across.

The drive to the border took ten hours, with only one stop for food along the way at a Tibetan Tea House catering to travelers. They served packaged noodle soup to which we added boiled water, and we had apples and rice cookies with sugar on top that Pendon had gotten at a market before we left Saga. The soup was too spicy for me to eat, but I had enough with an apple and cookies and one of the Coca-Colas Tenzin had given me in Lhasa.

Throughout the trip, the Tibetan drivers sat separately for their meals. At the Tea House, our driver pulled a dried leg of lamb (mutton) out of a satchel bag, and with a bowie knife sliced long strips of meat and fat that he ate for his lunch. He didn't share it with the other drivers, and it was only partially eaten. When he'd had enough, the meat was put back in the bag, the knife wiped off with a dirty cloth, he finished his cup of butter tea and was ready to roll.

The driving seemed interminable. More dust and heat, cooped up in the car. I prayed for the nightmare to end. To place my mind somewhere else, I listened to Caetano Veloso's CD *Omaggio a Federico e Giulietta*, a live concert celebrating the life of the Italian movie director and his actress wife. It was the perfect distraction, and I listened to the joyful music over and over for hours on end.

We arrived in Zangmu, a sleazy border town controlled by the Chinese, at ten-thirty that evening, again with no dinner other than the trail mix bars. After we checked into the hotel, Yam ordered a Nepali meal that looked delicious, but my throat was raw from coughing, and the food was just too spicy to eat. I went to bed on an empty stomach once again.

Our rooms had working toilets (the kind you sit on) and showers, and the next morning I bathed for the first time in twelve days. I could wash the dust off my body, but not out of my lungs. I felt refreshed all the same. At breakfast, Yam gave us the news that the Maoists had cancelled the strike, and it would be smooth sailing, so to speak, to Kathmandu that morning.

We said goodbye to our Tibetan friends, and walked across the so called "Friendship Bridge" between the Tibet/Nepal border without a hitch, considering the chaos with hundreds of other tourists, Nepalis, big semi-trucks and vehicles trying to get to Nepal before the strike. Many were unaware that it had been called off the night before.

Several drivers from Far Horizons, the travel company GeoEx uses in Nepal, were waiting for us on the other side, and we started the drive to Kathmandu. The air was fresh and moist, and I could breathe again. Even though the roads were unpaved and bumpy part of the way, the Nepal countryside is lush with greenery, terraced fields, and waterfalls. It was a welcome sight.

Shortly before noon, we pulled into a village on the side of a hill, bustling with midday activity. Roadside shops selling brilliantly colored fabrics, appliances, furniture, novelties, and fruits and vegetables ran the length of the street. We stopped in front of an open-air restaurant preparing to serve lunch. Yam informed us that the drivers needed to take their "lunch break," but we would have to wait in the cars. He bought a bunch of unripe miniature bananas for us and joined the drivers in the restaurant. That didn't go over very well with me, but I was beaten down so low from the trip at this point, I didn't have the energy to say anything about it. I took the last remaining trail mix bars from my bag and went over to Rita and Dale's car. That was our lunch.

During the drive to Kathmandu, we were stopped at half a dozen Army checkpoints where our drivers had to present papers and in some cases show our passports. The checkpoints were small three-sided wooden shacks with corrugated tin roofs situated on the side of the road. Most were staffed by several soldiers in olive green khaki uniforms carrying submachine guns, and an army official to check the documents. These checkpoints were not present on my two previous trips to Nepal, and the situation was tense and unsettling. But not nearly as unsettling as seeing teenage boys roaming around the villages in Tommy Hilfiger clothing, toting the same type of weapons. I asked Yam what it was all about, and he said, "They're part of the civilian army." It was not a comforting response.

As soon as we arrived, Yam took Rita and me to the CIWEC Clinic, the Western Travel Medicine Center, next door to the Yak & Yeti Hotel where we would be staying. There, I met Dr. Johnny Yates, a young M.D. from Long Beach, California, who was a big *Star Wars* fan. I was diagnosed with acute mountain sickness, exacerbated by acute sinusitis and bronchitis. The good news was that my oxygen saturation was back up to 95% (it was between 71-74% in Tibet), but I was still having difficulty breathing, and my sinuses were bloody and inflamed even though I had just completed taking a course of Azithromycin (a very powerful 5-day antibiotic) that Bob Thurman had given me the night before *Sakadawa*.

Dr. Johnny felt additional antibiotic treatment was not needed at that time. He determined that I was medically fit to fly and advised returning home as soon as possible to see my personal physician for further evaluation. Okay, that sounded like a clean bill of health to me.

The first thing I did after checking in at the Yak & Yeti was make a reservation for dinner in the hotel restaurant. It was four-thirty in the afternoon. I'd stayed at the Yak & Yeti, an exclusive hotel with fabulous gardens and ponds, after returning from my first trip to Tibet in 1994, and I had been fantasizing for the past three days about the meal I would have when I got there. As an appetizer, I had a tall glass of fresh squeezed watermelon juice. I ordered a steak, baked potato with gobs of butter, garlic bread, and a salad. The food was as good as I remembered; however, there were no baked potatoes on the menu. The maitre d' recommended fried polenta cakes on a bed of sautéed spinach that turned out to be a delectable substitution. For dessert, I had a big slice of Black Forest chocolate cake with vanilla ice cream. I felt like I was back among the living.

After dinner I called my friend, Shana Chrystie at Geographic Expeditions. It was very early Saturday morning when I reached her in San Francisco. She had been in constant communication with Sanjay throughout the trip and knew all about my altitude problems. Shana had been in contact with my travel agent, Cathy Nilsen, who had already changed my airline ticket so I could leave the next day.

Panic set in as I realized I wasn't strong enough to leave early the next morning for thirty-plus hours of flying from Kathmandu to New Delhi to Frankfurt to San Francisco. I had a Business Class upgrade ticket on United that cost $200 to change, and Shana was concerned it would be nearly impossible to change it again, especially given the fact that it was the weekend. I gave her Cathy's cel phone number, and she said she'd get back to me as soon as she heard something, but there was a window of only twelve hours before I would have to leave on the scheduled flight, or forfeit the ticket and buy a full fare Business Class ticket to come home a day later.

After we hung up, I slipped into a series of mind games about money that escalated into a state of high anxiety. It went along the lines of: I spent all that money to go to Tibet for *Sakadawa* and got yanked away three hours before it began, I had to cancel my trip to India to see Namgyal's other brother and would have to fill out endless paperwork to get a refund from the traveler's insurance company to get reimbursed for those expenses, i.e., hotel, airfare to and from Dharmsala, car and driver, etc., and because I felt like hell most of the time, I didn't even get to go shopping at the Bharkor in Lhasa where I wanted to spend my money... ad infinitum.

When the phone rang an hour later, it was Shana. She had talked to Cathy, who had miraculously managed to get the ticket changed again, and I'd be leaving on Monday. For the first time on the trip, my luck was changing and the nightmare was almost over. I called Cathy immediately and through my tears, thanked her for saving my life. She said, "You had to go on this trip, Jane, but now we have to get you home." The flights back to the U.S. were blessedly uneventful. I slept most of the time but was still having difficulty breathing.

As soon as I got home, I made an appointment for the next day with my doctor, Al Oppenheim. He was shocked to see me two weeks before the end of the scheduled trip. I told him some of the gory details. He confirmed Dr. Johnny's diagnosis but felt the sinus infection was still a problem and put me on Cipro, another powerful antibiotic, and Albuterol, a steroid inhaler to help with the breathing. "This isn't the way it was supposed to happen, Jane, and you're not as well as you think you are."

He was appalled to hear what my oxygen saturation levels were in Tibet and said, "You went too high, too fast, and stayed too long." "What would have happened if I hadn't evacuated when I did?" I asked. Given what he knew about my condition at the time, he said, "You could easily have come down with pneumonia and died."

313

Dr. Al also thought I should have a chest x-ray, and I was shocked to learn it indicated the airways in the lower lobe of my left lung had closed down. This condition was created by shallow breathing at high altitude causing a lack of oxygen to the lungs. No drugs were prescribed to correct it, just deep yoga breathing exercises to push oxygen down into the lungs to force open the airways again.

But the nightmare wasn't over yet. The combination of the antibiotic and steroid inhaler created a petri dish condition in my mouth, and I woke up one morning with flaming blisters in my throat, on the roof of my mouth, and with my tongue covered with white fuzz. My lips were so swollen I looked like Angelina Jolie. It was a fungus infection, thrush/candida, that went down my throat into the esophagus. More heavy-duty drugs were required to kill the fungus. And my immune system was seriously compromised. I could hardly talk, or swallow, much less eat any solid food. I went to bed and lived on watermelon and mashed potatoes for over a week.

It wasn't long before I sank into an emotional low point in my life. I still had a lot of anger about the evacuation and was questioning why all this was happening when I received the following email from Shana.

> From: Shana Chrystie
> Sent: Monday, June 14, 2004
> To: Jane Bay
> Subject: Checking In
>
> Good to talk to you on Saturday. Sorry it was such a rough trip. I know it is disappointing to feel like you missed Sakadawa and, in retrospect, you wish you had stayed, but give yourself credit for what you did do. To have continued on the trip after being so sick in Lhasa shows a lot of strength, courage – and love for Namgyal. Stephen was telling me that when Bhagwati (his ex-wife) organized the Kailash Pilgrimage for Swamiji (a group of 150!) they told people to look at whatever happened on the trip as sadhana (practice). In this light, you did a big piece of work.
>
> Love,
> Shana

Practice in the Buddhist sense has to do with living life in accordance with the teachings of the Buddha. Working the Dharma, so to speak. But I felt disconnected from my spiritual practice. My mind was so agitated I'd rarely had the desire to meditate. What were the lessons I was supposed to learn from this experience? It couldn't be "Impermanence," I already knew about that one. It couldn't be "Patience," I'd been working on that for over ten years since one of my friends said I was graciously impatient. Was it about "Grasping and Clinging?" Why did I feel such a profound sense of disappointment about the trip?

Several weeks later, Lis Blackwell, a friend of twenty-two years, came over on a Saturday afternoon for a visit. It was a warm summer day. We sat at the kitchen table, sipping iced tea, as I told her the story about the trip. Lis, genuinely troubled by what she heard said, "Jane, you need to come to terms with this situation, it's not good for you."

Finally, I said I thought the problem I was having the most difficulty letting go of was that I had projected too much importance on saying goodbye to Namgyal in her homeland, at Mount Kailash, on Sakadawa, the day of her reincarnation. I wanted some kind of closure. I felt I had failed to carry out my mission, my purpose for returning to Tibet again within the first year since her death.

"You chose LIFE, Jane, and you feel guilty about it."

Lis' words rang in my ears. I had to ask her to repeat them to make sure I heard correctly. Did I choose LIFE by leaving Mount Kailash on June 3? Were there protector deities at the mountain that were looking out for me in a situation that appeared to be working against my best interest and my intention? Did the concern of my friends play into a divine plan to save my life? Did my own inner voice guide me to the evacuation? I needed to sit with these thoughts for a while, but during that afternoon with Lis, there was a subtle shift in my perception.

One morning on the way to work I heard the Rolling Stones song "You Can't Always Get What You Want" on the radio, and I realized I actually got what I needed.

I began to think about the three days in Lhasa I'd spent with Tenzin Tsering, Lhakyi, my precious granddaughter, Tenzin Monkyi, and Lhaki's family. When I looked at the DVD footage of the day Peggy Hitchcock, Tom Latinovich and I had lunch with the family, when Tenzin Monkyi and her cousin, Tenzin Saldon, did a song and dance for us, my heart opened up, and I could breathe again.

In his book, *Bodymind*, Ken Dychtwald writes about the breath.

> *In the terminology of yoga, our word breathing is translated as* pranayama, *and the word air is, roughly,* prana. Prana *also means 'life force.' The implication of this multiple meaning is that the air we breathe contains, in addition to life-supporting oxygen, a vital force that we ingest as we inhale. This pranic life force circulates throughout the body, moved by the pumping action of the heart and by the interaction of the diaphragm and lungs. In order for an individual to make full use of the life force that is available to her, it is necessary that she make full use of this breathing/living apparatus.*

And that's what I'm doing, I'm practicing breathing, and I'm glad to be alive.

This weekend was the first anniversary of Namgyal's death. A year can seem like an interminable amount of time when you're a child, but the year since Namgyal died seems to have passed more quickly than any other year in my life. I was surprised by the changing of the seasons, when holidays came and went, and birthdays reminded me that I wasn't getting any younger. At times, I felt I had nothing to look forward to without Namgyal in my life. We had such grand plans for the future. In a way, I'd been dreading this day, but when it arrived I was relieved. I had survived.

Dickey, her friend Cynthia Chang, and I had a fire puja for Namgyal on Friday night. We had dinner in the garden first, I showed them the DVD of Tenzin Monkyi and her cousin dancing and singing, then we had the puja.

Before we started, Dickey had placed a khata, a silk white offering scarf, on Namgyal's altar in my bedroom, and she wrapped another one around a log. We each separately held the log to infuse it with a silent prayer for Namgyal, then I placed it on the burning fire. I also put a second string of smoke bundles in the fire that David Riordan had given me the weekend Namgyal died that had been hanging from the roof outside my bedroom all year. As the fire burned, we sang Om Mani Padme Hum, lit incense and lined up dozens of tea candles (the ones in small round silver tins) on the brick steps from my room into the garden. It looked like the rows of butter candles one sees in every monastery in Tibet. We prayed, and we cried.

Cynthia brought her Lhasa Apso, a puppy from a litter Dickey's dog had shortly before her wedding. The puppy presided over the puja with the occasional diversion of digging and frolicking in the flower beds. Her name is Ping, the Chinese word for peace.

At the end of the puja, we spoke to Namgyal, each of us wishing her a happy life and telling her that our love will continue in this lifetime and for eons to come. I spoke last. I wanted to tell Namgyal that I was okay, and that I didn't want her to worry about me.

Jane at Tarboche – base of Mt. Kailash

Dechen and Bob Thurman—roof of the Johkang Temple
Photographer: Rich Martini

Puja fire burning of Namgyal's hat –
Mt. Kailash—Photographer: Rich Martini

I read a poem that pretty much sums up how I'm feeling about life these days, then I placed it on the burning embers.

After a While
Poem written by Veronica A. Shoffstall

After a while you learn the subtle difference
between holding a hand and chaining a soul

And you learn that love doesn't mean leaning
and company doesn't mean security

And you begin to learn that kisses aren't contracts
and presents aren't promises

And you begin to accept your defeats
with your head up and your eyes ahead
with the grace of a woman, not the grief of a child

And you learn to build all your roads on today
because tomorrow's ground is too uncertain for plans
and futures have a way of falling down in mid-flight.

After a while you learn that even sunshine burns
if you get too much.

So you plant your own garden and decorate your own soul
instead of waiting for someone to bring you flowers.

And you learn that you really can endure
that you really are strong
and you really do have worth

And you learn and you learn
with every goodbye you learn...

And so, dear friends, don't you worry about me either. I'm living one day at a time and learning every step of the way...

All my love to you,
Jane

From: Tsering Tenzin
Sent: Sunday, July 18, 2004 7:05 PM
To: Jane Bay
Subject: Namgyal's death anniversary

Dear Mom,

Namgyal's death anniversary was held in nunnery in the Pembo Valley and it went very well which was told by Uncle Losoel as it happened when we were in Shanghai.

I think you are better and recovered well and this yesterday we went to Nathang and Tashigang Monastery to give some donation for monks and tell them to pray for Namgyal.

Yours' lovingly,
Tenzin

From: Jane Bay
Sent: Sunday, July 18, 2004 7:11 PM
To: Tenzin Tsering
Subject: Re: Namgyal's death anniversary

Dear Tenzin,

I'm happy to hear the ceremony for Namgyal at the nunnery went well. I've sent you a very long email today about my trip to Tibet and the first anniversary of Namgyal's death. I hope you are able to read it. I will continue to pray for Namgyal all the days of my life, and keep an altar for her in my home, wherever I am. I am very happy to have known her, if even for such a brief time. She was a kind, compassionate, loving person, and I am proud to have been her mother.

All my love to you, Lhakyi and Tenkyi-la.

Your mom,
Jane

From: Goldie Hawn
Sent: Sunday, July 18, 2004 7:37 PM
To: Jane Bay
Subject: Re: Life & Death

Dear Jane!!

I'm in Awe of you! A journey into the deep. My love goes to you. Thank you so much for sharing this with me. I will always keep it close. These words have great value. xx and soo sooo glad you are home!

Lovingly,
Goldie

From: Kristine Hanna
Sent: Sunday, July 18, 2004 8:09 PM
To: Jane Bay
Subject: Re: Life & Death

Dear Jane,

I opened up this e-mail a little while ago and read it straight through. For most of the chapter, I had alternate feelings of anger, sadness, frustration, disbelief and shock.

When I got to the last few pages I started to feel relief at the end of the journey, but I also felt joy – for you, your life and who you have become as a person. You are absolutely amazing and I am proud to know you and call you my friend.

I started to cry when I reached the end and read about the fire puja, and then I read "Comes the Dawn" and cried some more. But the tears were not sad tears – they were tears of hope for Namgyal, for you, me, for all the people that we love and hold so dear. Thank you for sharing this chapter of your life in such an amazing way. It is truly a gift!

With love,
Kristine

From:	Tom Hunter
Sent:	Sunday, July 18, 2004 10:48 PM
To:	Jane Bay
Subject:	Life & Death

Dear Jane,

I am in Paris on holiday, and I awoke this morning an hour or so before I had planned to. I have been here a couple of days before my wife, our two best friends Larry and Sally and I go to the south of France to watch the Tour de France – a passion of ours and one of the world's greatest sporting spectacles. I was first annoyed that I had wakened early – today is a travel day for us and will be long (although nothing compared to what you endured!!).

Unable to fall back asleep, I went to my computer to begin drafting a memo for Tonik Barber at Lucasfilm. I had asked for a wake up call early this A.M. to do this work, so that Tonik would have it on her desk Monday morning in California. Well, here I was, awake even earlier, and began to think about some of the information I wanted to impart to my friends at LFL so they could advise George wisely.

But first, I should check my email....There among the spam messages was your email and the story of your trip to and from Mount Kailash. Ten pages or so I thought? No time to read this now, I've got to get to work, then shower, pack, check out, etc., etc. But then, it IS early... So I began to read and was again transported with you to the roof of the world. I was enthralled and absorbed by your tale, and more impressed than I can express by your courage and determination to complete the pilgrimage you set out in your daughter's honor.

About two-thirds of the way through your story a thought – at first quiet, but then as I read on, louder and more insistent, reverberated in my mind. "Jane," the thought went, "you must return now. Namgyal

322

is looking after you, is concerned for her mother's well being and is sending you home. She knows how deep your love is for her, and does not want you to risk your health further in an attempt to prove it to her or to yourself."

When I reached the point in your story where your friend Lis wisely and perceptively told you you had "chosen life," I understood. I am not a particularly spiritual man, but through you I have begun to experience more often the spiritual side of life and existence. Thank you for sharing your powerful story, thank you for heeding Namgyal's wishes and turning back. Thank you for choosing life. Do not be disappointed for those aspects of your planned trip that did not go as you had wished. Do not feel guilty for having chosen life. This path was determined for you, and you chose wisely.

I hope you have recovered physically and are feeling yourself again. I know you have recovered emotionally.

With love and best wishes,
Tom

From: Jane Bay
Sent: Sunday, July 18, 2004 11:07 AM
To: Tom Hunter
Subject: Re: Life & Death

Tom,

I love getting your email from Paris!!!

You may have noticed I sent out "Life & Death" around dinnertime here in California. I went downstairs to prepare my supper to be eaten in front of the TV as I always do on Sunday nights while I watch Masterpiece Theatre, my favorite program on PBS.

As I was getting ready for bed, I realized I hadn't turned off the computer. I went back upstairs to my little birdcage of an office and found your email reply glowing in the dark on my computer screen.

I think you're right, Tom. Namgyal was the angel looking out for me at Mount Kailash.

Enjoy the Tour de France.

Much love to you, dear friend,
Jane

From: Jacqui Louez
Sent: Sunday, July 18, 2004 11:53 PM
To: Jane Bay
Subject: Life & Death

Oh My Darling Jane,

I have just finished reading your letter. You have brought me to tears. I have to say that initially I was rather concerned reading it for both your physical and emotional state. By the time I had come to the end of your incredible journey I realized that you were indeed fine. I am so glad you had the courage to leave the mountain.

I don't know why these things happen to us. Why we are tested and pushed to such great lengths. I do know that once you make it out to the other side we inevitably become stronger, better people. I know you have been through more than any person should ever bear in the past twelve months but you did make it through. You are surrounded by people who love you and support you because you give back the same, if not more and unconditionally. I am so happy to hear that you are OK and that you made the trip for Namgyal.

When I was eighteen I was in a violent armed holdup. It was just two months before my HSC (the major exams for entry into University). I ended up having to have three operations on my spine because I was injured during the holdup. Once I emerged from the darkness the originally terrifying experience turned out to be the greatest gift. I have learnt to value life and every single day we are given on this earth. I have also learnt to tell people how I feel about them and not to hold back.

So, my Dear Friend, I am really proud of you for making it through this truly difficult time. I am really proud of you for communicating with all of your friends as you haven't been afraid to share what you have been going through.

Last but not least, I greatly value our friendship and your place in my life.

Love you,
Jacqs Xoxoxox

From: Lisa Cooke
Sent: Monday, July 19, 2004 8:44 AM
To: Jane Bay
Subject: Re: Life & Death

Dear Jane,

What an amazing experience! I am so thankful you are recovering and you came back in time to be safe.

What struck me from reading about your journey is the wonderful gift Namgyal keeps sending you. She fills your heart with such love that you were determined to make the difficult trip to Mt. Kailash to honor her, despite your illness. That kind of love is so rare in life, and it will beat in your heart forever.

It was very profound that your friend pointed out you chose life, and it struck me that you weren't being guided by the opinions of others to evacuate at all. That it was Namgyal guiding you towards life and showing you that while hers is gone, your life is still unfolding before you. And your life is as important to the many people who love you, as hers was to you. Helping you with this excruciating choice she gave you more closure than you could ever have received from a ceremony.

Because of my family's heritage, I read this Native American prayer at my grandmother's memorial. It is the Indian way of honoring the dead and processing grief.

Native American Prayer
Traditional

When I am dead
Cry for me a little
Think of me sometimes
But not too much.
Think of me now and again
As I was in life
At some moments it's pleasant to recall
But not for long.
Leave me in peace
And I shall leave you in peace
And while you live
Let your thoughts be with the living.

As someone who loves you, I thank you my dear friend, for choosing life.

XOXO
Lisa

From: Lynda Beth Unkeless
Sent: Monday, July 19, 2004 10:01 AM
To: Jane Bay
Subject: Re: Life & Death

"so...you decorate your own soul instead of waiting for someone to bring you flowers..."

Dear Jane,

I was always waiting for my mate,
wondering where is my mate?
and the moment I gave up that idea
and started to live my life
as the poem says
so as to decorate my own soul
was the beginning of the end of the pain
and the start of my most authentic life!

I am happy to know that you got through the first anniversary of her death virtually unscathed, and blessedly filled with the revelatory insights your email shares with us.

Stop the struggle.
Calm the emotions.
Rest in yourself.
Enjoy the rest of the ride of your life...

With love,
Lynda Beth

From: Noah Skinner
Sent: Monday, July 19, 2004 11:01 AM
To: Jane Bay
Subject: Re: Life & Death

Dear Jane,

Reading your e-mail made me feel like I was in Tibet sharing your experience with you. Neither of our adventures this summer worked out like we had hoped but at least we can say we did it and nobody can take that away from us.

Like Sterling Hayden says, "The years thunder by, the dreams of youth grow dim where they lie caked in dust on the shelves of patience. Before we know it, the tomb is sealed. Where, then lies the answer? In choice. Which shall it be: Bankruptcy of purse or bankruptcy of life?"

Jane, you will never be bankrupted in life and I truly admire you for that. Would it be okay to share this chapter with my parents? Please let me know. I'm sure they would truly like to read it. Take care.

Love,
Noah

From: Tom Latinovich
Sent: Monday, July 19, 2004 12:25 PM
To: Jane Bay
Subject: Re: Life & Death

Soulfully beautiful, Jane. Considering I knew all the details, I was also surprised to be so riveted by the story. Nice work!

Tom

From: Rich Martini
Sent: Monday, July 19, 2004 4:33 PM
To: Jane Bay
Subject: Re: Life & Death

What a fabulous email, Jane. Thanks for including me in it.

I bet no one's written to you about Sakadawa, and what you didn't miss. Honestly, Bob was right. Dusty, waiting endlessly while the trucks pulled the flagpole an inch further up in the air... all of it, from my pov, much less dramatic than your trip to Nepal. And the prayers at the top of the mountain, repeated by Yam, were obviously much more powerful than any you could have said at the ceremony.

First, the group of monks who were there were so ill equipped, and poorly trained, that they seemed bored with their prayers and instruments. I've recorded some prayers in the past (www.cdbaby.com/nechunkmonks) and I know when I hear ill trained, sloppy chanting. It really felt like they were there for the tourists, provided by the Chinese. The lead monk looked like a guy who was wearing regular clothes under his robes, and was bored silly. Yes, there were some unusual costumes from nomadic Tibetans who walked around the pole, but equally there were goofy tourists from the States, like the guy from Chicago who dressed up in full Tibetan regalia, and looked ridiculous in his outfit, but wanted everyone to see him. It reminded me of when the Dalai Lama pointed to some people in the audience in Pasadena and said (I'm paraphrasing) "I see some people wearing robes and other artifacts that Tibetan monks wear but there's no need to do so – unless you are born in Tibet, you can't actually be a Tibetan monk. Just be yourself."

I'm pretty certain the reason you were evacuated so quickly is because it was the right thing to do – God knows what might have happened had you been delayed longer – I may have told you, but two people from that Hindu group that you mention actually died from AMS – this according to Swamiji, the monk we spoke to at Manasarovar – they told him that they were not given adequate amounts of Diamox, two members of their group were hospitalized, and two died during their kora. So everything happened for a reason, as far as I can tell — you were able to make it to Kailash, and pass along those items for Bob to put into the fire puja – there's a long tradition of pilgrims going to Darchen and hiring Tibetans to walk the kora for them…I was just reading Govinda's *Way of the White Clouds* and he pointed that out as well. So think of that bizarre group of western pilgrims as those who did the kora on your behalf, like the long tradition it comes from.

Back to the Sakadawa ceremony – honestly, I felt trapped by the smoke, and the pushing and shoving tourists who wanted to move me off the spot I was standing on with my DV camera. Meanwhile Tenzin (Bob Thurman) was organizing his own trip to the inner Kora with this German photographer – everyone was scratching their heads – is he crazy? The German was telling him it was a "six-hour hike" but everyone knew that wasn't true… except Bob, who insisted on going. Dechen looked worried, we were all worried, and later that night, Bob didn't return. People thought he was hurt, or had been arrested – I actually felt him saying "I need a ride back to camp, but I am fine" in my inner voice…but he disappeared on that mountain. Didn't come back for thirteen hours, and we didn't see him until the next morning sometime. He was exhausted. He'd fallen six times and had scrapes and cuts all over him – but it was something he just had to do.

Anyways, the flags that were at the Sakadawa ceremony — since we were told not to bother putting them up during the kora – the day we were at the top of the pass was an "inauspicious day" and I said to Yam, "I came all this way, can't I just put up a flag, and tomorrow it will be auspicious?" and he said flatly, "Go ahead, but all the prayers associated with those flags will be meaningless." So I had to keep my long long line of flags until Sakadawa, which by the time we got there, there was a huge thirty-foot pile of flags – all brought by pilgrims. I gave mine to Nima and he took them to another guy who dumped them into this huge pile…along with a thousand others.

So I let that go – trying not to attach negative emotions to what happens in life – and later on, after the flag pole was up – (lots of cheering, but a bit anticlimactic) I walked over to the pole of flags to see what would happen to them and I saw these Americans trampling around the flags, looking for their own – but just walking all over them — and I heard this Tibetan say "Calm down, every flag that's here will be put up" – I don't speak Tibetan, but I know that's what the guy said, cause I heard it in my head more than anything else…and that seemed to calm the frantic tourists down…so I took some pix, and then offered to help this same Tibetan carry some of the flags over to the pole…and took a big handful and carried it over to him, while he climbed on top of the ladder and started to hang the flags – pulling them up from me, as a long long stream went through my fingertips…and there – at the end of this long stream, I saw a picture of my baby Olivia and my wife…I had accidentally actually carried over the very flag that I had made out of the thousands that were lying in a heap. Amazing. I took a picture of it and will enclose it in a later email for you.

Anyways, just a note to say loved your story, and agree that it was all about you learning patience, forgiveness, and acceptance…as we all learn those things – and as Swamiji said to us – it's not until you get home, much later, away from the strangeness of the Tibetan climate, food and clothing – that the affect of coming to Mt. Kailash and Lake Manasarovar begins to influence your life – and as he pointed out – not necessarily in the way you thought it would, but what the mountain thinks is good for you...

xoxoxox
'cardo

From: Gordon Radley
Sent: Monday, July 19, 2004 6:57 PM
To: Jane Bay
Subject: Re: Life & Death

Amazing...and beautifully told.

What I felt as I read your account was that your unplanned, and unexpected, and unwanted trip from Tibet to Kathmandu was a transformation journey that was your way to reach closure with Namgyal's passing. The hardship, the dust, the heat, the interminable ride, the lines at the ferry, the lack of food, this was your climb up Mount Kailash. Your anger subsiding into exhausted acceptance evidenced how you were no longer able or willing to be in charge and control. You had given up control in Tibet to others and events had taken over, taken over because you needed to take this journey and you never would have. The physical journey from Tibet to Kathmandu was the only way for you to experience the inner journey you needed to take to reach closure. But for your physical condition in Tibet you never would have let it happen, but once it did, you had to have a "cleansing" of your consciousness that took the form of a weakening of the resistances and immunities in your body. Even the dust was a way to purge your insides and cause you to "learn to breathe" (i.e. rebirth yourself) again. All your systems were letting down to take you to a different place inside you from which to come back. As you became weaker and more vulnerable and less "Jane" you actually were finding that place inside you that could unconsciously and unwillfully but most purely, wordlessly, and without intention say good-bye to and bless Namgyal's life.

Now it is not a process of "getting well," but finding a new and pure breath inside of you for the journey of your future that like this trip from Tibet will in its best form be unplanned, unexpected, and unintentional. As my Malawian friends always say, "reach well…"

Gordon

From: Jane Bay
Sent: Monday, July 19, 2004 10:49 PM
To: Gordon Radley
Subject: Re: Life & Death

Gordon,

It's always fascinating to hear your response because I'm just telling the story, and I don't actually know what it means when I'm writing. All I know is that I have to get the experience out of my system and into the world to be able to reflect on what it all means later.

When I read your response, it became perfectly clear that this is what it was all about. You've reflected my experience back to me in a way that allows me to look at it not with my mind, but with my heart, and I felt compassion for myself. I hope that doesn't sound too self-absorbed because you have given me a wonderful gift, and I'm grateful to you for it.

Thank you for your thoughtful and insightful reply, and the admonition to "reach well."

Love,
Jane

From: Lynne Hale
Sent: Tuesday, July 20, 2004 10:03 AM
To: Jane Bay
Subject: Re: Life & Death

Jane,

Your story was so beautiful! I felt I was on the journey with you. Thanks so much for sharing it. And that poem at the end is going into my book of favorites. I love it. I will read it many times over!!!!

You've gone through quite a transformation, my friend.

Lots of love,
Lynne

From: Jane Bay
Sent: Tuesday, July 20, 2004 10:36 AM
To: Lynne Hale
Subject: Re: Life & Death

So now you know the whole story. It's so funny, Lynne, all during this past year since she died, I asked Namgyal to come to me in my dreams, especially when I was in Tibet, but she never did. Last night after I finished writing this chapter, Life & Death, I dreamed about her...

It was a very short dream. Namgyal and I were in a house some-where, and she was holding a baby boy. He was playing with a mala (rosary) and I asked, "Is he your reincarnation?" She said, "Yes, Mom, he recognized my mala as his own." We were very happy to be playing with him and went on about our business. I don't remember anything else about the dream except that I was very happy for her.

xoxo
Jane

From: Nancy Harris
Sent: Tuesday, July 20, 2004 11:09 AM
To: Jane Bay
Subject: Re: Life & Death

Dearest Jane:

So glad to hear from you. I am in Bangkok writing reports after an exhausting two months through Europe fundraising. Francoise just joined me last week, and the first day she asked whether I'd heard from you. We were both very worried about your trip when we saw you. I am sorry I wasn't in Tibet during that time, I certainly could have tried to help.

I have no great words of wisdom, but a great appreciation that you are alive and that you write so well of your struggles with the downside of samsara. I find myself in similar states of darkness and all the role models for how to keep climbing from the wreckage are very precious.

As Francoise says to me, to comfort me when I really feel life is over and goals weren't reached and everything is very black, "It's not reaching the moon that's the point, it's the ways you use to reach the moon."

Please take good care of yourself and convalesce in quiet and serenity.

Much love,
Nancy

From: Jane Bay
Sent: Tuesday, July 20, 2004 11:15 AM
To: Nancy Harris
Subject: Re: Life & Death

Dear Nancy,

I'm so glad to hear from you. I never know if you get my emails, and I really wanted you to have this one. Actually, I'm doing well emotionally and gaining strength physically every day. I've come to a place of acceptance about Namgyal's death, and I think I had to go through that hell realm in Tibet to get there. I know you would have helped if you could, but this was my Karma, and even though it was a nightmare, I got what I needed after all.

Please give Francoise my love, and much love to you as well.
Jane

From: Nancy Harris
Sent: Tuesday, July 20, 2004 1:40 PM
To: Jane Bay
Subject: Re: Life & Death

Dearest Jane,

It's three A.M. but I'm still up, having a lot of trouble with sleep/wake cycles. Your letter keeps haunting me. Francoise is right here now, and says to you: "I'm very happy that you came back alive."

I am giving her your address now and she can write you directly. She is not only a fantastic worker born to help Tibetan children, but a life-saver to me. I am very lucky to have such a friend and co-worker on this very unusual path.

Hell realms indeed. Well, the point is to survive them. Here's to that! More later…

Much love,
Nancy

From: Margi English
Sent: Tuesday, July 20, 2004 3:53 PM
To: Jane Bay
Subject: Re: Life & Death

First of all — THANK GOD you are home!

What a journey, Jane. You are brave — I know you say obsessed — "driven" maybe. But I hope that you put all of that drive into your health. We all need you here. I've really missed you this time.

I am in Manhattan until tomorrow night and then return to Los Angeles. Hopefully we can speak over the weekend if you have time.

Much love,
Margi

From: Tenzin Bob Thurman
Sent: Wednesday, July 21, 2004 8:10 AM
To: Jane Bay
Subject: Re: Life & Death

Dear Jane,

My goodness gracious! What a time you had! I'm sorry the evac was so harsh, but the trip to Lhasa was the same, only five days instead of two! The reason for the rush and not waiting for the following day was both for your health and the concern over the Maoist shutdown. Sanjay did the very best he could. I think your final analysis comes close to it. Choose life every time!

Have you gotten through some parts of the *Infinite Life*? I think it will help, if you wade in there, bit by bit.

Love,
Bob

From: Jane Bay
Sent: Wednesday, July 21, 2004 9:44 AM
To: Tenzin Bob Thurman
Subject: Re: Life & Death

Good morning, dearest Bob,

Rich Martini sent a reply to "Life & Death" about his experience at Sakadawa, and from the sound of it, he probably ingested as much dust as I did. He also told me about your doing with the inner kora and how worried everyone was when you didn't come back at the expected time. I'm glad you survived with only cuts and bruises from your falls.

I know a lot of my anger about the evacuation was misplaced on Sanjay, and I do understand the circumstances, but I still feel the lack of clear communication was unfortunate. Peggy told me her trip to Nepal was as smooth as silk, so you just never know what you're gonna get…

When we were in Lhasa, Namgyal's brother kept picking up and reading parts of my copy of *Infinite Life* (that you had inscribed for me at the Herbst Pavilion event), so I gave it to him. He knows who you are, and was thrilled to have it. Needless to say, I'll order another one from Amazon, as I had just begun to read it.

Hope to see you soon.

Love,
Jane

From: Chin Rodger
Sent: Wednesday, July 23, 2004 11:09 AM
To: Jane Bay
Subject: Re: Life & Death

Dearest Jane,

I am so sorry to hear that you had such a hard and challenging trip. Would love to give you a huge hug.

As your friend Shana said it is all part of our sadhana and you have fulfilled your dharma even with a highest intention of going – not to mention enduring all you did…Namgyal is smiling down at you. The Bhagavad Gita said "…on this path effort never goes to waste, and there is no failure. Even a little effort toward spiritual awareness will protect you from the greatest fear…" (2:40)

Jane, you know in your heart that there are no goodbyes for you and Namgyal, wherever you are she will always be in your heart and you in hers. When you are in touch with your heart and she is in touch with hers (now in her new birth), you are completely connected, you are actually in God's heart. In that heart, you will know everything that you must know. In that union, in that love, you are together.

Know too that you are always in my heart – from the very first day I walked in your office so many years ago – there was so much great and warm energy radiating around you. You are full of love.

I am having a great journey with the Avon Walk – been on training walks with my walking buddies – a team of sixteen now – all beings full of light and love – their courage and love and support humble me – from a single gal, a new mom to a grandma of four...we have been walking between eight to sixteen miles weekly – I feel I must eat more nutritious food – not losing weight though. I'm still at same ol' ninety-nine lbs.

We leave this evening for our trip to Malasia. Tons to do yet. Enjoy the rest of your summer.

I send you great love and blessings. And love to you from Elliot and Georgia, too.
Chin

From: Fay David
Sent: Thursday, July 23, 2204 12:13 PM
To: Jane Bay
Subject: Re: Life & Death

Jane,

I read this through last night. Thank you so much for sharing your experience in Tibet and the realizations it brought you. I can't believe the difficulties you went through. But I was not in the least bit surprised about how you determinedly stuck it out and came through the experience with grace and new found understanding. I thought to myself, in a way, your harrowing experience in Tibet parallels your sorrow over the last year and how you have come through both with a deeper understanding of life and love. It is clear how your life and time with Namgyal are truly a gift.

Love,
Fay

From: Yam Gurung
Sent: Saturday, July 24, 2004 11:46 PM
To: Jane Bay
Subject: Re: Life & Death

Hi Jane,

Good to hear from you and receive your letter. I am glad to know you are well and doing fine.

Your letter was pretty much a full description of the trip. I wish you all had a better trip than it turned out to be. But I am sure when you look back at the trip after some time, perhaps you will find some positive aspects of the trip and you will enjoy cherishing the experience of the trip.

Re: your letter I think I should correct you with a couple of minor informations. One is that I do not represent Far Horizon, it is an Indian company. I work for Geographic Expeditions as a leader and I was the co-leader of the trip with Sanjay Saxena and the second one is that place we spent the night after departing Darchen is SAGA not SHEGAR as we did not go to Shegar at all. Actually these minor mistakes do not make any differences at all, I only felt that I should give you the correct info.

Otherwise how are you and how is your health now? I am fine here with my family. I went to Tibet again for three weeks for a trekking trip and am back to Kathmandu now.

This is all for now Jane. Pls. take care of yourself and stay in touch. Will definitely see you when I visit the U.S.

All the best,
Yam

From: Jane Bay
Sent: Monday, July 26, 2004 9:05 AM
To: Yam Gurung
Subject: Re: Life & Death

Dear Yam,

It was good to hear from you, and thanks for the corrections. I will change the manuscript accordingly because I do want it to be accurate. Writing that chapter for my new book was a great catharsis and has in fact allowed me to look at the whole trip with some perspective now. There are many wonderful experiences that I will cherish, especially the friendships I made, including yours.

Take care and hope to see you in the not too distant future in California.

Warmest regards,
Jane

When I went to Tibet in May, I took gifts for Tenzin and his family, but the jeans for him had been too small, and the leather jacket for Lhakyi had been too big. I had Tenzin take off the jeans he was wearing to get the correct measurements, and the exact style he wanted: Wranglers 34 – Western Strong Denim #13MWZ – 36 x 32. They were easy to find once I was well enough to go shopping again. It turned out Lhakyi and I wear the exact same size jacket, and I found a very stylish one for her that was on sale made of black leather with a faux fur leopard collar.

The other gifts I had taken to Tibet were all greatly appreciated, some due especially to the kindness and generosity of my dear friend, Lis Blackwell, and her daughter,

Lexsea Mann, who was at the time a senior at Drake High School located around the corner from my house. I had run out of time before I left, and asked Lis if she could pick out clothes for my granddaughter, Tenzin Monkyi (Tenkyi-la), and her cousin, Tenzin Saldon, Lhakyi's sister's little girl. I wanted to get jeans for the girls, and red, white, and blue (American flag colors) clothes that have been very popular in Tibet since 9/11.

Lis and Lexsea hit every store from one end of The Village Shopping Center in Corte Madera to the other, from Macy's to Nordstrom and everything in between. They selected two outfits for each child, complete from head to toe. And each girl got a pair of red Converse sneakers.

I had dinner with Lexsea, Lis, and her husband, Jeff Mann, a few nights before I left, and when I got to their house, Lis and Lexsea had added a few special items to the children's trousseau. One item was a pink satin dress with a white lace collar that Lexsea wore in second grade, and another dress (costume) made of pink and gold chiffon that Lis had made for Lexsea's first ballet performance. Liz also added a child's vest she had made for Lexsea out of an antique American quilt, to go with one of the jean outfits for Tenkyi-la.

I carried these gifts to Lhasa with a note from Lexsea to Tenzin Monkyi, and of everything I brought, Lexsea's clothes where the biggest hit. Tenkyi-la looked like a little Tibetan princess in the ballerina dress and was extremely pleased with herself.

Tenzin Tsering and Lhakyi bought Lexsea a Tibetan *chuba* (dress/robe) made out of exquisite silk brocade fabric, and Tenkyi-la wrote a thank you note to Lexsea that I carried all the way to Mount Kailash and back to the U.S.

The time I spent with Tenzin Tsering and his family was bittersweet. No one wanted to talk about Namgyal's death, and even though there were so many unanswered questions in my mind, I decided, out of respect, not to force the conversation. Being with Auntie Drakpa was the most difficult. She cried every time I saw her during the three days I was in Lhasa. Finally, on the last day, she opened up, and through her tears, we shared our grief over the loss of our beloved daughter.

Lhakyi and her sister, Sonam Llamo, and their husbands and daughters live in the home of Lhakyi's mother, Sonam Chopel. I had been to her home several times during both visits to Tibet in the last year, and her gracious hospitality was endearing.

The day before I left Lhasa to go to Mount Kailash, Uncle Losoel and Sonam Chopel had prepared a magnificent feast for Peggy Hitchcock, Tom Latinovich, and me. It was that day I learned that Lhakyi's great-grandfather had founded Mentseekhang, the Tibetan Medical College in 1916. Lhakyi is a doctor, and I was surprised to hear that she is also studying western medicine at the University in Lhasa. Though we never had a conversation in English, I'm sure Lhakyi speaks some, and understands a lot. She showed us her clinic in her mother's home where she sees patients.

Before we left Sonam Chopel's house, she invited us to their shrine room to have a *chema* (offering blessing). It was a ritual I had done so many times with Namgyal during Losar, and it was an honor to be invited to do it.

We took pictures in the shrine room where Sonam Chopel presented me with a gift in a long red felt box. I opened it to find a 1950s gold man's wristwatch cradled in the white satin fabric lining. On the inside lid of the box were two Tibetan words written in gold ink.

"Mom, this watch belonged to the Panchen Lama. He gave it to Lhakyi's father before he died in 1989."

The words written in gold were the Panchen Lama's name.

The Panchen Lama is Tibet's second-ranking spiritual leader. He is the moon to the Dalai Lama's sun. On May 14, 1995, the Dalai Lama announced that six-year-old Gendun Choekyi Nyima was the reincarnation of the Tenth Panchen Lama. Shortly after this announcement, Gendun Choekyi Nyima and his family are reported to have been taken from their home in Tibet to Beijing, and their whereabouts have been unknown ever since. The Chinese installed their own Panchen Lama at Tashilumpo Monastery in Shigatse. Amnesty International considers Gendun Choekyi Nyima to be the world's youngest political prisoner.

Lhakyi's mother had given me a family treasure.

From: Lis Blackwell
Sent: Tuesday, July 27, 2004 5:35 PM
To: Jane Bay
Subject: note from Lis

Hi Jane,
I am thinking the email Lexsea sent to Tenzin did not go through because of the zip/pics??? Anyway, here is the letter part and we attached the two photos you liked.

Dear Tenzin, Lhakyi and Monkyi,

Greetings from California!

I was so excited that Jane brought back the beautiful *chuba* for me. It fits me perfectly and I love the colors and the pattern of the fabric. This was very thoughtful and generous of you to get for me and to have Jane bring it back. Here are two photos of me wearing it in the backyard at my home.

I am also very happy to see the pictures of Monkyi wearing my two dresses from when I was young. To imagine they are now on a little girl in Tibet is simply amazing! Tenzin Monkyi is very beautiful.

Thank you again.

Your friend,
Lexsea Mann

Tenzin Monkyi in Lexsea Mann's ballerina dress
Photographer: Jane Bay

Lexsea Mann in Tibetan chuba
Photographer: Lis Blackwell

From: Jane Bay
Sent: Tuesday, July 27, 2004 5:45 PM
To: Tenzin Tsering
Subject: Note from Lis Blackwell & her daughter Lexsea

Dear Tenzin,

Hope you received the photo files and Lexsea's letter. I'm forwarding her letter in case you didn't get it.

Much love from your mom,
Jane

From: Joanne Shenandoah
Sent: Wednesday, August 11, 2004 11:40 AM
To: Jane Bay
Subject: Re: Life and Death and Jane

Greetings Jane!

What an incredible adventure. I'm pleased you are now home and healing. My thoughts and prayers were with you on that journey. I had wished I could have gone. I cannot imagine the physical and mental exhaustion that it entailed. The Iroquois say we must have seven layers of skin to endure life's challenges and challengers. You endured! Your story made me laugh and made me cry. You have been through an adventure of a lifetime and one that will certainly enrich the life of others.

Miss you, Jane. Won't be at Indian Market with all its glory this year...but hopefully our paths will cross soon. Hugs to you!

Love,
Jo

From: Melene Smith
Sent: Friday, August 13, 2004 9:27 AM
To: Jane Bay
Subject: Here's to Life!

Hi Jane,

I was relieved to get your email about your trip to Kailash. When I heard you returned early I thought maybe you didn't get to see the holy mountain. Your account of your trip suggests you were disappointed you missed Sakadawa but I am so pleased and impressed that you got to see and spend time at Kailash. I am so glad you chose life! I know how difficult it is to think and how easy it is to just take what comes at high altitude but it sounds like you on some level knew the right decision to make. I hope you are feeling better and the pilgrimage experience has improved with time. Sometimes I think you don't give yourself enough credit. I know how difficult it is to travel and be comfortable in Tibet and you rose to the challenge. The description of the ride to Gyantse and then to the border brought back memories for me and I too felt a little queasy. Even to attempt what you have is very commendable and just amazing.

Your love of the country, its people, culture and spiritual tradition is truly realized by your commitment to travel there as often as you have. Namgyal I am sure is proud of you and realizes and appreciates the efforts you have made in her memory. I know she too would want you to be safe.

I was happy to hear that you got to spend time with Tenzin and his family and the image of Tenzin Monkyi and her cousin singing and dancing brought a smile to my face. I remember the girls having such open and happy faces. Did you happen to get to see the mural for Namgyal? I would love to hear about it and see a picture if possible.

I would love to hear more about your trip and see pictures. Maybe we can get together next month? I again am glad you are home safe and feeling better.

"There is the risk you cannot afford to take,
and there is the risk you cannot afford not to take."
        —Peter Drucker (and the wisdom to know the difference)

Love,
Melene

From: Paula Boam
Sent: Monday, August 16, 2004 4:17 AM
To: Jane Bay
Subject: Hey Juanita

Thank you for all the updates. Reading about your last journey was very scary though. Jeffrey would have read it and told you that it was pretty frightening, but it makes for a great story.

I miss you Jane. I have been very busy this summer. We have completed two cooking shows and they are on all the time. The cable people really love Katie and me. The girls are fine and Dash is my angel.

But the big news is...I got married. Yep, his name is Richard Bickford and he lives in Kansas. I've been there most of the summer. I'm very happy and he will be moving here next June. He has to wait until his daughter graduates from high school. Dash really loves Rick. Everybody does. He is so kind, loving and such a gentle person. Well, that's enough from me. Give my love to everyone.

I love you and miss you,
Paulita

From: Jane Bay
Sent: Monday, August 16, 2004 10:37 AM
To: Paula Boam
Subject: Re: Hey Juanita

YOU GOT MARRIED? Oh my god, that's fantastic!!! You have to tell me more details, I mean I want to know EVERYTHING, but all I can say is I am soooo happy for you. Glad to hear about the cooking show, too. Hope you'll be doing more episodes.

Well, I made it through my first year of mourning for Namgyal, and as intense and scary as the trip to Tibet was, it was in fact exactly what I needed. I'm now concentrating my energy on putting the new book together which I hope to send to the publishers in the near future.

You have been on my mind so much these last two weeks. I've been home recuperating from knee surgery, again, on my left knee from a torn meniscus, just like the right knee only this time in two places, and with other complications. The injury happened two weeks after I had taken the last of the antibiotics and antifungal drugs for the secondary health problems from the Tibet trip. When it rains it pours, I guess.

I'll never forget how wonderful you were cooking and taking care of me when I had my first knee surgery, and how much fun we had. That's probably why I recuperated so quickly before. Just not the same this time around. Anyway, I'm off to physical therapy, then a couple of hours in the office this afternoon.

I really miss you, too. I'm ready to engage in the world again, and hope we can get together sometime this fall. I'd love to see you and catch up on everything that's happened in your life during this past year.

I love you, dearest Paulita.
Jane

From: Benina Gould
Sent: Sunday, August 29, 2004 1:06 PM
To: Jane Bay
Subject: Re: Life & Death

Hi Jane,

How are you feeling? I have been so concerned about you, but as you know Dickey is in Tibet, so no reports from her in the last few weeks. I gather if you are politicking you are better. I read the description of the trip and what a journey (by the way it will make a great chapter in your book) although endings never seem to be the way we envision them. I guess that is the real message of impermanence. I have been listening to tapes by Howard Culter interviewing the Dalai Lama and chapter seven of *The Art of Happiness* is excellent.

Hope to see you soon and visit the ranch.

Love,
Benina

I had read *The Art of Happiness: A Handbook for Living*, written by Dr. Howard C. Cutler, that recounts extensive conversations he had over a period of years with His Holiness the Dalai Lama, but I took it down from the shelf and dusted it off to refresh my memory. Chapter seven is about the value and benefit of compassion. It's about the ability to identify with the pain and suffering of others.

At the very first teaching I took from the Dalai Lama, His Holiness gave a commentary on Shantideva's *Guide to the Bodhisattva's Way of Life*. He explained the importance of generating Bodhichitta, the aspiration (wish) to achieve enlightenment to benefit all sentient beings. Bodhichitta is a Sanskrit word that means "awakened heart."

In chapter seven of *The Art of Happiness*, the Dalai Lama gave a meditation on compassion:

> So...let us meditate on compassion today. Begin by visualizing a person who is acutely suffering, someone who is in pain or is in a very unfortunate situation. For the first three minutes of the meditation, reflect on that individual's suffering in a more analytic way – think about their intense suffering and the unfortunate state of that person's existence. After thinking about that person's suffering for a few minutes, next, try to relate that to yourself, thinking,

'that individual has the same capacity for experiencing pain, joy, happiness, and suffering that I do.' Then, try to allow your natural response to arise – a natural feeling of compassion towards that person. Try to arrive at a conclusion: thinking how strongly you wish for that person to be free from that suffering. And resolve that you will help that person to be relieved from their suffering. Finally, place your mind single-pointedly on that kind of conclusion or resolution, and for the last few minutes of the meditation try to simply generate your mind in a compassionate or loving state.

What I've come to understand by doing this practice is that we can either let the circumstances of our lives harden us so that we become increasingly resentful and afraid, or we can let them soften us and create the ability to keep our hearts and minds open to suffering without shutting down. By letting the pain of the world touch our heart, we can turn the pain into compassion. And that compassion can be of benefit to oneself as well as others.

> With a wish to free all beings
> I shall always go for refuge
> to the Buddha, Dharma, and Sangha
> until I reach full enlightenment.
>
> Enthused by wisdom and compassion,
> today in the Buddha's presence
> I generate the Mind for Full Awakening
> for the benefit of all sentient beings.
>
> As long as space endures,
> as long as sentient beings remain,
> until then, may I too remain
> and dispel the miseries of the world.
>
> The Bodhisattva Vow

From: Jane Bay
Sent: Friday, September 03, 2004 9:15 AM
To: Tsetan Khensur
Subject: Hello from California

Dearest Tsetan,

I was so pleased to hear about your successful trip collecting herbs despite the poor weather conditions. I hope you have not seriously injured your back. Can you have acupuncture for it to relieve the discomfort?

I must admit this summer has been very difficult. The complications from Acute Mountain Sickness I experienced in Tibet took almost six weeks to cure, then I injured my left knee and had surgery to repair the torn meniscus on August 2. I was in bed for a week, but am recuperating very quickly much to the surprise of my doctor/surgeon. I'm still walking with a cane, and I don't expect any further problems even though it will not be completely healed for another two months.

I'm planning to go to Santa Fe, New Mexico, for a week's vacation from September 4 – 12. Mostly just to rest and relax visiting with friends. The weather is wonderful this time of the year in the high desert, and it reminds me very much of Tibet, warm during the day and cool in the evening, indicating the coming change in the seasons.

I've started putting the pieces together for my new book. I've been thinking about Namgyal so much lately, and I miss her very much. I don't think that will ever change, but the sadness of losing her is not as painful. Working on the book is bringing up all of the feelings I had for her, and I feel a lot of gratitude to have known her if even for such a brief moment in time. I'm sure you miss her, too.

Work at Lucasfilm is very busy as we're preparing for the release of the last *Star Wars* movie. George is in London now shooting the final scenes, and by the end of the year, the media campaign will begin. This is the end of an era that started twenty-seven years ago. Before you were born....

Take care of yourself, dear Tsetan. Know that you are always in my heart and prayers.

With much love from your mom,
Jane

From: Tsetan Khensur
Sent: Saturday, September 4, 2004 10:15 AM
To: Jane Bay
Subject: Re: Hello from California

Dear Mom,

It is so nice to be back in Dharamsala and I am thinking how wonderful it would be to be back in Tibet where I really belong. Here the weather is good and I have been busy in washing my clothes as you know it was raining during the trip and no chance to get dried even if washed. Manaly is considered as a valley of apples and the people mainly live on selling apples where we get apples at a very low rate, so I bought few for friends and I would surely bring the best for you too if you were somewhere near.

The class will begin from 6 Sept and it is again the time for us to work mentally more, it is a little boring but overcome easily.

The problem with my back is gone gradually at the moment of my arrival at Dasa, nowadays I am completely fine. It is wonderful and happy to know that you are recovering very rapidly, but it is more important to take very good care of yourself even if symptoms of your sickness disappeared as sometimes symptoms put us in trouble, you know it well.

Wishing you a happy vacation. The prayers for your and Namgyal's eternal happiness are always in my heart.

With love,
Tsetan

From: Sylvia Boorstein
Sent: Monday, September 06, 2004 2:25 PM
To: Jane Bay
Subject: Hello from Sylvia

Blessings again on your project, and your words, "I am beginning to look forward to each day," echo in my mind as the sound of the heart's recovery.

Sylvia

From: Gail Currey
Sent: Tuesday, September 07, 2004 6:26 PM
To: Jane Bay
Subject: Life & Death

I assumed that the title "Life & Death" referred to your spiritual journey on contemplating the spiritual rebirth of your daughter. I knew it corresponded to your travels but somehow didn't directly associate it being about your travels. Having made this assumption, I waited until I was well rested and in a contemplative frame of mind before sitting down to read it. So on a hot but beautiful and quiet Sunday I sat down on our outside deck to read your writing. BAM

The next thing I know I am sharing your anxiety, your frustration and your nauseousness as I read through your harrowing adventure. I cannot imagine actually living this. It was difficult enough just to read about it.

Thankfully you have survived not only physically but actually were able to turn the events into something life affirming for yourself and for others. I am sure that your daughter would be proud of your strength and your choices.

Thank you for sharing,
Gail

From: Tenzin Tsering
Sent: Tuesday, September 21, 2004 12:54 AM
To: Jane Bay
Subject: Jeans and diet medicine

Dear Mom,

I am looking forward to getting my jeans pant and Lhakyi's diet medicine. When are you going to send me? I am so excited but do not hurry on it and take your time. I am so sorry to make you so many troubles when you are so busy and take care for your health. How is your knee right now? I hope it is getting better.

When I heard about what happened at Kailash I feel very sorry about it that your breathing was so difficult when you speak out. But you made your dream true and I am so proud of it.

Last week I met my nephew from Canada and his Canadian girlfriend too and we enjoyed a day together.

With lots of love and hugs.

Yours' lovingly,
Tenzin

From: Mark Advent
Sent: Monday, October 04, 2004 11:49 AM
To: Jane Bay
Subject: Hi from N.Y.

Hi dear Jane,

I re-read your "Life & Death" email on Friday en route to N.Y.

What an experience!! And just think, I almost joined you on it. I would have opted to cut the trip short...and would have traveled back with you to look after you.

My thoughts are that you saw things such as the moon in front of you as you never saw it before. What an incredible sight that must have been. And sending messages on moonbeams is enchanting to me to think about. It must have been a profound impact on understanding the universe and our place in it.

I hope that you are well. I think of you a lot and regret that we still have not gotten together on a mutually suitable place and time. I have been working the globe and have several large projects set to announce by the end of the year.

Just know that you are being thought of this beautiful day, and that you always have a friend who holds you in his thoughts and prayers.

Love from your friend,
Mark

From: Jane Bay
Sent: Monday, October 04, 2004 12:02 PM
To: Mark Advent
Subject: Re: Hi from N.Y.

Dearest Mark,

You are a true friend, and neither time nor distance can erode the warmth of feeling between us.

Love always,
Jane

From: Jane Bay
Sent: Sunday, October 03, 2004 5:05 PM
To: Tenzin Tsering
Subject: Package Mailed

Dear Tenzin,

On Friday, I mailed a package by Global Express through the U.S. Post office in San Rafael, California to you c/o Tibet Poverty Alleviation Fund. It will take about a week to ten days to arrive, so you should check with your office around October 8. The tracking numbers are: ED362450157US. PS Form 2976-A label # CP428052009US.

There are four pairs of Wrangler jeans for you. Two blue, one black, and one brown. They are the exact measurements of the jeans we measured in Lhasa at Auntie Drakpa's house. They are called Wrangler 34 "Western Strong Denim" #13MWZ size 36 x 32. I have ordered two lighter colors for you and will send them when I get them.

In the package is a leather jacket with faux fur collar for Lhakyi. I think it will fit her. I have also sent two boxes and a few extra packets of the diet powder to mix with water to make a diet drink. She should have five (5) drinks per day, one every two to three hours but NO FOOD for one (1) week. She will lose approximately eight to ten pounds. Then she should go on a diet of fruits, vegetables and meats/chicken/fish but no bread, rice, barley, or noodles for three (3) weeks, also eating small portions every two-three hours apart. She should lose another eight to ten pounds during that time, and can continue with this diet until she loses the amount of weight she wants to lose.

If she likes the diet drink, I will send her more of it, but she must try it first. She could then repeat the above instructions. I have personally tried this product, and know that it is safe and she will lose weight.

Please let me know as soon as you receive the package.

Much love to you all from your mom,
Jane

From: Tenzin Tsering
Sent: Sunday, October 03, 2004 8:19 PM
To: Jane Bay
Subject: Re: Package Mailed

Dear Mom,

Thanks for mailing your parcel and your love. You already sent four pairs of jeans for me and so please do not send lighter jeans next time. Other four will last many years. I am still in the process of my passport and may get it in November so I can meet Tsetan in India.

We are all leaving to India including Uncle Losoel, mother-in-law, Lhakyi and Tenzin Monkyi. We decide to take Monkyi with us.

Yours' lovingly,
Tenzin

From: Tenzin Tsering
Sent: Saturday, October 09, 2004 12:41 AM
To: Jane Bay
Subject: Re: Package Mailed

Dear Mom,

Yesterday I did receive your parcel including four jeans, one leather jacket, one hat, two boxes of diet drinks, and some pictures. Every clothes are fit exactly for me and Lhakyi, even black and brown jeans is fit to her very exactly. We are so happy to receive such good things and thank you very much for your concern and kindness.

With lots of love and hugs, yours' lovingly,
Tenzin

From: Celeste Bonfiglio
Sent: Monday, October 11, 2004 9:10 AM
To: Jane Bay
Subject: Life & Death

Hi Jane,

Please forgive the tardiness of this reply. I have just now have had the opportunity to read the chapter you sent me. I really look forward to being able to read the whole book.

The experience you wrote about is difficult even to imagine. My husband was reading along with me and kept on asking if it was really true. We live in such a materialistic atmosphere here in Marin, and I think most of us forget how much more there is to learn. Having is one thing, but doing is something altogether different. Thank you for sharing your experience. It is truly inspirational.

Hope this finds you well and happy,
Celeste

From: Jane Bay
Sent: Monday, October 11, 2004 9:32 AM
To: Celeste Bonfiglio
Subject: RE: Life & Death

Dear Celeste,

Happy to hear you and your husband were able to read Life & Death, and YES, every single word of it is all too true. I'm just beginning to understand and appreciate the experiences I had in Tibet this summer and, of course, will be writing more about that in the narrative of the book.

I am feeling better, almost back to normal but still having some discomfort from the knee surgery. It's taking a little longer than I had expected to heal, but I'm getting stronger both physically and mentally everyday.

Looking forward to seeing you again soon,

Love,
Jane

From: Tenzin Tsering
Sent: Sunday, November 07, 2004 8:21 PM
To: Jane Bay
Subject: Trip to Nepal - India

Dear Mom,

Actually we were planning to leave on the last flight to Nepal that was supposed to stop at the end of November, but somehow it has already stop flying at the end of October, so we are planning to leave at the end of November or first week of December depending on if my papers are processed and for our daughter.

Hopefully my papers will be process quickly this month due to the great initiative from my wife's struggle. We are planning to leave by overland to Nepal and hope these days there are less checkpoints. We are planning to stay there for three months and probably back to Tibet in March.

In terms of money we are planning to put all in the waist belt. It is a habit for Tibetans.

Hope to chat with you in a later stage.

With lots love, yours' lovingly,
Tenzin

From: Jane Bay
Sent: Sunday, November 07, 2004 10:11 PM
To: Tenzin Tsering
Subject: Re: Trip to Nepal - India

Dear Tenzin,

I hope you are successful in getting your papers, and I understand how difficult it is. I think it is very important for you to see Tsetan Khensur.

I hope and pray you have a safe journey and return to Tibet with no problems. Please keep me updated on your plans.

With all my love, your mom,
Jane

CHAPTER TWELVE

The Endless Knot

From: Jane Bay
Sent: Thursday, November 11, 2004 6:44 PM
To: Dear Friends
Subject: The Endless Knot

Dear Friends,

The Endless Knot is commonly known as the Buddhist symbol that represents unending love, good fortune, and the interconnectedness of all beings, but more about this auspicious symbol later.

Since my last email, I have been recuperating from knee surgery and am just now getting back on my feet, both literally and figuratively speaking. I'm happy to report that my health problems resulting from the trip to Mount Kailash have improved considerably and, as James Brown would say, "I feeeel good."

I've decided on a new title for my book: *LOVE & LOSS – A Story About Life, Death, & Rebirth*. And there's one more story I'd like to tell you from the chapter entitled The Endless Knot:

Recently, I went to New Mexico for the weekend to see my spiritual friend, Losang Samten, the former monk from the Dalai Lama's monastery, who took me to the Tibetan Children's Village in Dharamsala, India, where I met my daughter, Namgyal Youdon. Even though we have spoken many times on the phone during the past sixteen months, I hadn't seen Losang since Namgyal died.

Shortly after the knee surgery, which was much more complicated than had been anticipated, I was at one of the lowest point in my life in terms of physical and mental well-being. And I was in a lot of pain. I was also struggling with the proverbial question, "What is my purpose in life?" I longed to see Losang, and when I called he said, "I'm always here for you, Jane, why don't we get together in Santa Fe."

Losang was in New Mexico to construct a Tibetan Sand Mandala (a painting made of colored sand) at the Albuquerque Museum. That is where I first saw a sand mandala when Losang and the monks from Namgyal Monastery constructed the Kalachakra Mandala shortly after I met them at Skywalker Ranch over fifteen years ago. I was struck by the synchronicity of these events and felt an eager anticipation to be reunited with Losang at this time and place.

Much to my dismay, Southwest Airlines misplaced my luggage during the flight from Oakland to Albuquerque on Thursday night. I spent all day Friday sorting it out in Santa Fe and didn't arrive at the Albuquerque Museum until seven o'clock that evening, missing the ceremony for the dismantling of the mandala.

I was somewhat frazzled when I arrived, but Losang greeted me with open arms. I was escorted to a seat in the front row of the hall just as closing remarks were about to be made by the curator of the museum. Following the traditional offering of khatas and complimentary remarks, a Mantra Healing Concert began with a performance by Tenzing Tsewang, also a former Namgyal Monastery monk, and Losang's friend.

Tenzing told stories about his nomad family in Tibet and sang traditional folk songs while playing the Tibetan *Dranyen*, a three double string lute instrument. He played a bamboo flute, used Tibetan bells, and did deep voice mantra chanting. Losang accompanied him on a bamboo flute for one song and demonstrated a Tibetan ritual dance during one of the chants. Towards the end of the program, Tenzing invited the audience to participate in singing a mantra-healing chant with him. It was the Mantra of the Medicine Buddha. The Tibetan words were written in the program along with a brief description in English.

Before we began, Tenzing talked briefly about the Medicine Buddha and pointed out a picture of the lapis blue deity on the cover of his CD *Mantra Healing – Tibetan Sounds of Purification*.

Then he said, "Visualize the Medicine Buddha in your heart. If you're not a Buddhist, just visualize a lapis blue marble at the center of your heart. You don't have to be Buddhist to sing the mantra, or for it to have a beneficial effect on you."

He went on to say, "As you sing the words of the mantra, visualize a ray of blue light streaming out from your heart filling your entire body, then visualize that light filling this room, and everywhere outside the building, all over the state and country, and covering the whole planet to heal yourself and all sentient beings."

It was a tall order, but the audience responded wholeheartedly.

TAYA THA
OM
BEKHA ZAYA BEKHA ZAYA
MAHA BEKHA ZAYA
RAZA SAMUNG GATE
SOHA

TAYA THA: Gone beyond (beyond Samsara & Nirvana)
OM: Empowerment of Buddhas
BEKHA ZAYA BEKHA ZAYA: Medicine Buddha, Medicine Buddha
MAHA BEKHA ZAYA: Greatness of Medicine Buddha
RAZA SAMUNG GATE: King's Transmission
SOHA: Dissolve in me

An interpretive translation of the prayer is: "Thus, hail to the body, speech, and mind of the Buddhas: The King of Healing, of Great Healing, the Fully Exalted One. Thus, O King of Healing, of Great Healing, The Fully Exalted One – may your blessings consecrate us."

As I chanted the mantra along with the audience, my heart opened and I felt a lightness of being for the first time in a very long time. And it felt good.

After the performance, Losang introduced me to Tenzing. I told him about Namgyal's death and my trip to Mount Kailash, which is not far from his family's nomadic encampment in Western Tibet. At the concession table, I bought his CDs *Mantra Healing, and Lotus Hand – Tibetan Grooves* that he called Tibetan fusion. Tibetan chanting, singing and instruments fused with screaming Santana guitar riffs and western musical orchestration. I listened to both CDs on the drive back to Santa Fe that night, and almost continuously the rest of the weekend.

Before leaving the museum, I confirmed an appointment to meet with Losang the next day for a private meditation session at my house. Having traveled on pilgrimage with Losang to sacred Buddhist sites in India, Nepal, and Tibet, we have meditated together many times in many places over the years. I needed to reconnect with my spiritual friend. This was the primary reason for going to New Mexico.

Losang mentioned he was doing a sand mandala demonstration at Galerie Züger just off the Plaza in Santa Fe on Saturday morning, if I wanted to come.

"I'd love to since I didn't get to see the mandala you made here at the museum. What mandala was it?"

"The Eight Auspicious Symbols," he replied.

The next morning when I got to Galerie Züger, I could hear the sound of the *chakpu*, (funnel instrument rubbing together as the colored sand pours onto the mandala board), floating out to the sidewalk before I entered the gallery. People were milling about, some gathered around a tall pedestal table where Losang was making a small mandala about the size of a large pizza. He would stop from time to time to talk to people about what he was doing. When I reached the table, I saw that Losang was constructing The Endless Knot, one of the Eight Auspicious Symbols in Buddhism.

The eight Buddhist auspicious symbols consist of: a parasol, a pair of golden fish, the great treasure vase, a white lotus, the right-turning conch, the endless knot, the banner of victory, and the wheel of dharma (Buddha's teaching). These symbols of good fortune represent the offerings that were made by the gods to Shakyamuni Buddha (Prince Siddhartha) immediately after he attained enlightenment.

Sitting down on a red leather loveseat situated on a landing two steps up from the floor of the gallery, I had a bird's-eye view of the mandala. The endless knot overlaps without a beginning or an end, symbolizing the Buddha's endless wisdom and compassion. It indicates continuity as the underlying reality of existence, and symbolizes the endless cycle of death and rebirth until illumination. I was mesmerized by the exquisite beauty before me.

Some time after Losang finished the mandala, the Gallery Director suggested he go ahead with the dismantling ceremony. It is a customary practice. To my surprise, Losang motioned for me to come to the pedestal standing opposite him. He began the dismantling process by pinching bits of sand between his fingers from a band of lotus blossoms that encircled the mandala, dropping the tiny grains in the center of the endless knot. He then invited me and the few remaining observers in the gallery to do the same, as well as pinching bits of sand from each of the ten geometric enclosures within the intertwined lines of the endless knot.

When this step was completed, using a foam brush, Losang swept sand from the outer edge of the mandala to the center, cutting a two inch swath through the brilliantly colored painting. He handed me the brush and, following his lead, I swept sand to the center, then passed the brush to the person on my left, who did the same until all the sand had been swept to the middle of the mandala board. Losang scooped it up with his hands, putting the sand in a plastic baggie, and went into an adjoining room. I don't know what happened to the sand after that. Usually it would be disbursed into a body of water to bless the water and all the creatures in the water, but this wasn't a typical situation where a mandala would have been consecrated or created as a meditational practice. It was a demonstration, yet participating in its dissolution was a profound experience. A great lesson on impermanence.

We arrived at my little casita located a few blocks from the Plaza around three o'clock, just as the afternoon sun drenched the adobe walls of the house with golden autumn light. We lit incense and candles all around the living room, and settled in to begin the meditation.

Losang said he would be chanting a Dorje Namjom purification med-itation, and at some point in the practice, he would give me instruc-tions about visualizing certain deities and would touch my crown chakra, the third-eye chakra, throat chakra, and then the heart chakra which in the Tibetan Buddhist system represents the highest level of consciousness. He had a Tibetan Bell and used a book of Tibetan *Sutra* (scripture) to recite the chant.

As the chanting began, the stress and tension in my mind and body began to relax. I let go of all words and thoughts, and surrendered to the moment. My body and mind dissolved down into a deep meditative state in which I was completely unaware of my surroundings except for the soothing sound of Losang's deep mellifluous voice. I had no sense of my body or the clothes on my back, or sitting on the couch, or the candles burning or the smell of incense. Nor the sound of cars and people on the street, or birds singing in the trees.

Sometime during the meditation, Losang said, "Visualize the Dalai Lama, and all the Buddhas and Bodhisattvas, and Dakinis (the sky walk-ing deities who represent the feminine aspect of one's 'Buddha nature') in front of you, their healing energy and light flowing into your body."

As the chanting continued, he touched the four chakras, and I felt a concentric ripple of warmth radiated out from each point.

When the chanting stopped, I had the sensation that Losang was stand-ing behind me. He blew his breath into the opening of my crown chakra, and I experienced it as liquid gold, honey-colored nectar that flowed down into my heart, transforming my awareness into the energy of total bliss.

We sat in silence for several minutes. When I opened my eyes, Losang was sitting in the leather armchair next to the couch, smiling. So was I. I told him about my experience. Until that time, I had no knowledge of Dorje Namjom.

Dorje Namjom is a major meditational deity of the highest yoga Tantra in esoteric Tibetan Buddhism. It is the root of all tantras. Losang explained after the meditation that great yogis and practitioners for thousands of years have relied on Dorje Namjom to purify their body, speech and mind. As there are many unseen factors that control the life of human beings, there are, consequently, mysterious illnesses and diseases prevalent in today's modern world that medical science and technology are helpless to relieve. The practice of Dorje Namjom can dispel all negativity, remove obstacles, and cure illness and disease. It's a healing meditation.

Then Losang asked, "What happened on your trip to Mount Kailash?" As I told him the story of "Life & Death," the previous chapter in the book, it appeared that his eyes filled with tears.

Late in the afternoon, I drove Losang over to the James A. Little Theatre where Tenzing Tsewang and Fernando Cellicion, the internationally renowned Native American (Zuni) flute player, singer, performer and recording artist (who had recently returned from performing in Mongolia) were rehearsing for a benefit concert that evening.

Just before we arrived at the theatre, I reached over to touch Losang, and he took my hand in his and kissed it. No words were spoken, but I felt unconditionally loved.

The concert was magical. Tenzing and Fernando had never met before the rehearsal but immediately bonded as brothers. They were from the same soul tribe. As I luxuriated in the richness of these two musical traditions intertwining, I had an awakening to the interconnectedness of all beings. It was like a light bulb turned on in my consciousness, and I could see clearly the true nature of reality. I felt connected, and it felt good. I realized I was back among the living.

On the plane returning to California I finished reading Robert Thurman's book *Infinite Life*, and I want to share some of it with you:

The Buddha taught that immense positive potential exists within each and every one of us, just waiting to be unleashed. We are naturally full of love and compassion since we have labored long and virtuously through many lives to become human beings. Now, with our highly advanced life-form relatively free from negative instinctual drives, we are poised and ready to pursue the path to total bliss that is enlightenment.

When you take responsibility for it, you can consciously, and therefore more accurately, aim yourself toward the achievement of a secure state of bliss for yourself and for others. You gain a sense of connectedness with all life that gives you great strength. You become determined to develop positively. You realize how tremendously meaningful is the slightest action, word, or even thought, and so you take ever more care to be virtuous in your acts of body, speech, and mind.

Contemplation is the essential balm we can use to heal ourselves, to restore our sense of purpose and meaning while acknowledging the liberation of infinite life. Once we learn to control our minds, we can recreate ourselves as happier, more evolved beings – individuals free from self-preoccupation, greed, immorality, anger, despair, distraction, and attachment; individuals full of self-confidence, compassion, goodness, tolerance, creativity, serenity – and, above all, love. Contemplative serenity enables us to make the most of our infinite life, being present and aware to the full, moment by moment for all time.

When I read these passages, I thought, this is my "purpose" in life, to live in this way, and I committed myself to an *Inner Revolution: Life, Liberty, and Pursuit of Real Happiness*, to paraphrase the title of another Thurman book.

As a mother, I don't believe there's such a thing as closure with the death of a child. I didn't really lose Namgyal when she died because her consciousness is still alive within me, in every cell of my being.

And so, dear friends, as I finish this chapter of the book, let's celebrate life and remember, love is all you need.

All You Need Is Love
The Beatles (Lennon/McCartney)

Love, love, love, love, love, love, love, love, love.
There's nothing you can do that can't be done.
Nothing you can sing that can't be sung.
Nothing you can say but you can learn how to play the game.
It's easy.

There's nothing you can make that can't be made.
No one you can save that can't be saved.
Nothing you can do but you can learn how to be in time.
It's easy.

All you need is love, all you need is love,
All you need is love, love, love is all you need.

Love, love, love, love, love, love, love, love, love.
All you need is love, all you need is love,
All you need is love, love, love is all you need.

There's nothing you can know that isn't known.
Nothing you can see that isn't shown.
Nowhere you can be that isn't where you're meant to be.
It's easy.

All you need is love, all you need is love,
All you need is love, love, love is all you need.

All you need is love (all together now)
All you need is love (everybody)
All you need is love, love, love is all you need.

All my love to you,
Jane

Click on this link to see The Eight Auspicious Symbols:
www.Karmapa.org.nz/prayers/teach/symbols.html

From: Jane Wyeth
Sent: Thursday, November 11, 2004 7:36 PM
To: Jane Bay
Subject: The Endless Knot

Dear, dear Janie,

Every time I read one of your e-mails about life, I marvel not only at your incredible ability to write so beautifully but also at how very very wise you have become. If I weren't so secure, I'd feel intimidated about how much you know, compared to me. As it is, I just get prouder of you all the time.

Of course Namgyal will live in your heart forever. Because of how you have shared her with your friends, she willl also live in our hearts, too.

I hope it's not disrespectful for me to write that I feel you and I, like Tenzing and Fernando, are from "the same soul tribe." I'm not sure what you meant by the expression, but I THINK you meant that they were much more than just kindred spirits. Did you make up that expression or hear it somewhere else? I would love to know, because I want to tell my two best girlfriends that THAT's why we love each other so....)

Love, love, love, love, love,
Janie

From: Jane Bay
Sent: Thursday, November 11, 2004 8:51 PM
To: Jane Wyeth
Subject: Re: The Endless Knot

Dear Janie,

I always look forward to your reply because you have interesting observations and responses to the writing. I hope you didn't feel I was showing off about my experiences, or my understanding of very esoteric knowledge. Tibetan Buddhism is confoundedly complex, however, I learned a long time ago, from Losang and the Dalai Lama, that the most important aspect of Buddhist practice is the cultivation of a good heart and compassion. That's what I hope to convey, and at the same time give the reader a taste of the richness of Tibetan culture and Buddhism.

The phrase, "from the same soul tribe," was coined by Stephen Dinan, the poet, writer and political activist whose writing I find eloquent and enticing. He wrote *Full Succulence*, the poem in "100 Days," one of my previous emails. I don't even remember the context in which I heard it, and I think it is about more than just kindred spirits.

I've always felt that even though by outward appearances, education, family background, spiritual tradition, etc., people may be very different, yet inside we are all from the same soul tribe. We are intrinsically connected to one another and share a common desire — to love and be loved. And at the level of the soul is love.

Love you Janie,
Jane

From: Judy Nelson
Sent: Thursday, November 11, 2004 9:09 PM
To: Jane Bay
Subject: Re: The Endless Knot

Dear Jane:

My eyes are filled with loving tears after reading this. I want you to know that your descriptions allow this reader to experience the joys of enlightenment. How clearly you display unanswered questions with the answers, if you know what I mean.

Thank you so much for sharing this with me. I hope this is one chapter you will read at your book tour. It is quite profound and will indeed have an impact on all who read or listen to you read it.

Congratulations, my friend. I'm so proud and happy for you. Your life is rich with blessings.

I love you,
Judy

From: Jane Wyeth
Sent: Friday, November 12, 2004 8:27 AM
To: Jane Bay
Subject: Re: The Endless Knot

Dearest Janie,

I absolutely did NOT feel that you were showing off about your experiences or your understanding of very esoteric knowledge. Goodness gracious, why would you think that? You are so incredibly humble about what you know and how you know it. Anyway, any intelligent person would understand that you're merely telling others about your experiences and what you've learned to help others in their own journey. You know as I've written you a number of times, that I personally have learned so much from you that it helps me in my own journey through this life and the next.

I'm not surprised that it was Stephen Dinan who coined the phrase "from the same soul tribe", as I remember being taken aback previously (though can't remember the specifics) of how intuitive he was when you quoted him before.

I'm so pleased that your surgeon pronounced you "healed", at least in his opinion. Yes, time will finally heal all the swelling, etc., and you'll eventually be your old self (and I don't mean in a chronological sense). I hope you've decorated your cane with a pretty silk flower or two…

As my mom used to say about everything that wasn't going according to plan, "You'll be fine." I quote her comment to myself on a regular basis. Mummy was SUCH an optimist. Most people would say she was just in denial. But her attitude certainly helped her deal with a lot of stuff in her own life.

Xxx Janie

From: Lis Blackwell
Sent: Friday, November 12, 2004 8:30 AM
To: Jane Bay
Subject: Re: The Endless Knot

Dear Jane,

Thank you for the endless knot. I want to feel that! It makes me happy to know you are better. Maybe lunch tomorrow, Saturday? I wish I could go to the R. Thurman talk, but have told my neighbor I would come to a get-together with her. She invited me two weeks ago….

The endless knot is so beautifully written. I love the images of the colored sands coming together in the middle of the mandala…I love the image of your pain dissolving into blue light.

Nothing new here and maybe that is why I am so "quiet"…still recovering from the election…but, hanging in there.

With love,
Lis

From: Laila Cook
Sent: Friday, November 12, 2004 11:18 AM
To: Jane Bay
Subject: Re: The Endless Knot

Dearest Jane,

Thank you for sharing that story and especially for including the link to the symbol. Your description of it was so beautiful, and I was curious to learn more.

I am happy that you had such a healing experience in Santa Fe and wish you a feeling of unconditional love from everyone in your life.

I love you from Oregon. Can't wait to read the book, and I love the new title.

xo,
Laila

From: David Petrou
Sent: Friday, November 12, 2004 1:02 PM
To: Jane Bay
Subject: Re: The Endless Knot

Jane, dearest,

Your emails, and this next chapter – sent me on a cold, rainy, and especially dreary almost mid-November day in Washington – have been like tiny, laser shafts of life…and hope…and sunshine, following so sad an election outcome, not to mention so much uncertainty and change in my own life.

Your story empowers me to believe that my story, too, will have a happy "ending" – that will truly be, in fact, a new beginning in my own life. Thank you so much for your friendship and for sharing your amazing journey with me and your other dear friends.

And yes, your new title has struck just the <u>right</u> aegis under which your entire odyssey belongs. May you continue to heal and may we see each other sometime very soon...

With appreciation and much love, dear Jane.
David

From: Susan O'Connell
Sent: Friday, November 12, 2004 3:25 PM
To: Jane Bay
Subject: New title for your book

Dear Jane,

The new title is universal — and describes both the disease or *dukka* of loss and the medicine of love.

Warmly,
Susan

From: Roger Christian
Sent: Saturday, November 13, 2004 3:50 AM
To: Jane Bay
Subject: Re: The Endless Knot

Dearest Jane,

Wanted to reply to you so many times, but am in madness here in Istanbul. I was in London as had to run away and think straight and my HD Indian movie *American Daylight* was in the London film festival. We had such a huge response, two full houses. It is now invited to Rome, Marrakesh, Goa, Paris, Dubai, Tribeca film festivals, so a small low budget movie, the first with a story about modern India and call centres, mostly a love story about the east and the west coming together and understanding about love is hopefully getting out. Take a look on <u>www.americandaylight.com</u>

You are amazing Jane and your journey is as Buddha and Christ and all the philosophers and teachers show us that we have to go through the pain and abandon all and dis-attach from all negatives and at the end the gift is love and silence. Why is it so hard and painful for some of us is certainly not karmic, just is as Krishnamurti so beautifully phrases it. Your last letter is very touching and may God bless you.

Love,
Roger

From: Laurie Bauman
Sent: Saturday, November 13, 2004 12:45 PM
To: Jane Bay
Subject: Re: The Endless Knot

Dear Jane,

What a beautiful and transformative story. It fills my heart at a time that has been tough – my best friend's mother, who was my second mother – died a couple of months ago and so I have been dealing with love and loss and some of the issues as to why it was important for me to find a second mother. Life does continue, and those we love who have left us here leave it a richer place. That is reason enough for celebration.

I look forward to seeing you in Santa Fe.

Much love,
Laurie

From: Chin Rodger
Sent: Sunday, November 14, 2004 6:39 PM
To: Jane Bay
Subject: Re: The Endless Knot

Jane,

I love the new title – deeper and more expanded – love, rebirth...

Thanks for all of your messages – especially the last email about your amazing auspicious experience – you truly have experienced what we would call the "blue pearl" experience – a great moment of initiation – only one with a very heightened awareness, very pure and only with the grace of a Master will one have an experience like yours. Indeed you are truly blessed, dear Jane.

I hope your knee will feel better and heal – joint disorders/operations take longer to heal. Continue to infuse every cell of your body with the mantra – more beneficial than any treatment you can have.

Friends have been urging me to start a Malaysian Satay Express cafe – I make the best most authentic satay anywhere, from my grandma's recipe. However, it will take a huge capital start up. I feel more comfortable in a service/giving profession, but like you said, as long as we are consciously living in joy and bliss – that is our seva, our selfless service, so it's just a thought for now.

Anyhow, dear Jane, have a great week ahead. I shall be meditating on your mantra for you to heal quickly and get back comfortably on your feet.

With great love and blessings,
Chin

From: Patty Casado
Sent: Monday, November 15, 2004 10:44 AM
To: Jane Bay
Subject: Re: The Endless Knot

Dearest Janie,

As always, your words, which are filled with your spirit and heart, take my breath away. Thank you for sharing your thoughts, experiences and life with me. It is a reminder of the work in front of me.

Always in my heart,
Patty

From: Jane Bay
Sent: Monday, November 15, 2004 10:54 AM
To: Patty Casado
Subject: Re: The Endless Knot

My dearest Patricia, you are part of the Endless Knot in my life, and always in my heart as well.

Love,
Jane

From: Mark Advent
Sent: Monday, November 15, 2004 11:15 AM
To: Jane Bay
Subject: Re: New title for my book

Dear Jane,

Thank you for sharing the new title of your book with me. I love the subtitle… "Life, Death, and Rebirth," but I am not sure about "Love & Loss." The first thing that popped into my head was "Better to Love & Lose" — A Story About Life, Death, and Rebirth.

I just felt I needed to share that with you. I know that you will take it in the spirit that I am sending this to you. It's just another thought.

Much love,
Mark

From: Jane Bay
Sent: Monday, November 15, 2004 11:31 AM
To: Mark Advent
Subject: Re: New title for my book

Thanks for the feedback, Mark. You're not the only person who has voiced that concern. I've thought about it a lot, and what I've felt is that there is no one who hasn't loved and lost. Many people get stuck in the "lost" part as I very easily could have myself, so the subtitle is a hint of what the book is about: rebirth.

There is life after death, not just for the person who has died, but for the loved ones left behind who must go on living, and hopefully living in the moment with a greater sense of joy. Does that make sense?

Love,
Jane

From: Mark Advent
Sent: Monday, November 15, 2004 11:37 AM
To: Jane Bay
Subject: Totally Makes Sense!

Dear Jane,

Thanks for sharing that with me! It really does make sense and believe me, there is NOT a lot of info, or books or people talking about "exactly that!" Losing something and having to go on...is one of the most...transforming concepts of all. I went through it with my father who was my best friend and rock. It was unbelievable what I saw my mom go through, too. The title now makes more sense and thanks for letting me share my thoughts with you!

Love,
Mark

From: Kitty Courcier
Sent: Monday, November 15, 2004 9:54 AM
To: Jane Bay
Subject: Re: The Endless Knot

Hey Sister,

Thank you for sharing your trip to Santa Fe. I'm so glad you and Losang had that time together. Jane, to those around you, you have always had a sense of purpose. I continue to be amazed and inspired by you.

xoxo,
Kitty

From: Jane Bay
Sent: Monday, November 15, 2004 11:46 AM
To: Kitty Courcier
Subject: Re: The Endless Knot

Sweetheart, I could not have gotten through this without you. You were there for me every step of the way from the moment Namgyal died, and you took care of me as only a sister could, but more than that, you are my best friend.

I love you, dear sister,
Jane

From: Sandra Lovelace
Sent: Monday, November 15, 2004 4:30 PM
To: Jane Bay
Subject: Re: The Endless Knot

Jane,

After reading "The Endless Knot," an inexplicable sense of wellbeing, connection or connectedness, perhaps even a little joy remains with me. To transform that level of healing through your personal experiences is powerful. Your description of pure honey, golden light flooding through the top of your head, during the Dorje Namjom purification meditation, is the sweetness of God-honeylight.

I remember the first time I uttered the sound of "OM". With that sound and in that moment, a portal into timelessness or divine continuity opened, and has never closed.

Love,
Sandra

From: Tsetan Khensur
Sent: December 8, 2004 4:49 AM
To: Jane Bay
Subject: Hello

Dear Mom,

How are you? So far I have finished my oral test, but the written test is still haunting me and I am preparing for it with all my energy.

The new calendar for 2005 was produced by Mentseekhang here in Dasa (Dharamsala). If it is needed, please let me know and I will send it to you. It is my pleasure to do so.

Take care, with love.
Tsetan

From: Jane Bay
Sent: December 8, 2004 11:06 AM
To: Tsetan Khensur
Subject: Re: Hello

Dear Tsetan,

Life is very busy this time of year here at Lucasfilm, but we do get a two-week break for Christmas and New Year's, so I will be going to Santa Fe on December 18 and will return to the office on January 3.

I'm glad to hear you've finished the oral test and let me know how it goes with the written test. I know Tenzin Tsering and family are on their way to see you in India. I'm so happy they will be seeing you soon. You are going to fall in love with your little (well, not so little, actually) niece, Tenzin Monkyi. She is an adorable child and is very funny, too.

You may remember from my email story "Mother's Day" that Dickey asked me to be her mother at the ceremony when she married Dr. Lobsang Rapgay in April. I'm sorry to tell you that Dr. Rapgay's mother, who was 93 years old, passed away yesterday in Los Angeles. Dickey and Lobsang live there now, but Dickey still has Tibetan medicine patients here in Northern California — Berkeley, San Francisco, and Napa mostly. She will be up here next week, and we will have a fire puja for her mother-in-law at my house, as we have done so often for Namgyal and your father.

Good luck on your written exam and let me know when Tenzin Tsering and family arrive in Dharamsala.

Much love to you from your mom,
Jane

From: Melene Smith
Sent: Thursday, December 16, 2004 3:36 PM
To: Jane Bay
Subject: Nice seeing you

Hi Jane,

Just a note to tell you how much I enjoyed seeing you at Chrissie and Jim's Tamale Party – it had been a while. I know you are going to Santa Fe for the holidays, and I want to wish you a very Merry Christmas and Happy New Year. I know Christmas Day is your grand-daughter's birthday – so Happy Birthday, too!

I have attached a favorite Lhasa photo celebrating female friendships. Merry Christmas.

Love,
Melene

Two women walking around the Bharkor – Lhasa, Tibet
Photographer: Melene Smith

From: Jane Bay
Sent: Thursday, December 16, 2004 3:45 PM
To: Melene Smith
Subject: Re: Nice seeing you

Dear Melene,

What a beautiful picture – it makes me want to go back to Tibet with you and walk arm in arm around the Bharkor with these magnificent women to celebrate <u>our</u> female friendship.

Tenzin Tsering, Lhakyi, Tenkyi-la (the birthday girl), Uncle Losoel, and Lhakyi's mother are leaving Lhasa today to go to Nepal and India for three months to see Namgyal's elder brother. They're driving overland, in the dead of winter across the Himalayas, so pray for their safe passage.

Best wishes for a happy holiday. Pray for peace in the New Year.

All my love,
Jane

From: Tenzin Tsering
Sent: Friday, December 24, 2004 4:58 AM
To: Jane Bay
Subject: Still in Nepal

Dear Mom,

We are now in Kathmandu with great stressful lifestyle that all the borders in Nepal are closed. Nobody knows when it will be safely open due to the Maoists strike. We are so worry about that as yesterday the Maoists burned eighteen Nepalese trucks with essential commodities on highway to Indian and Nepal border.

Our visa is just for sixty days and nearly one month is going to finish soon. Extension of visa in Nepal is so expensive and costs about 3000 rupees for one month, and if we need more than two month it costs even more.

Tomorrow is Tenzin Monkyi's birthday (three years old) and we are going to celebrate it in a very simple way.

We wish you a Merry Christmas and Hapy New Year. Once you receive my email, please make contact soon.

Yours' lovingly,
Tenzin

A Greeting card for Dear mom from tsetan

Dear mom,

Wishing you a New Year filled with new hope, new joy and new beginnings.

wishing you a very happy and succesful new year. may your dreams come true in the coming new year.

tsetan.

From: Tsetan Khensur
Sent: Sunday, January 2, 2005 4:08 AM
To: Jane Bay
Subject: Hello

Dear Mom,

How are you? I hope you have enjoyed a lot during your holidays.

I am staying with my Uncle Losoel, brother and his family in Dharamsala. They arrived here on December 29 at 9:00 PM, but they are not able to have the audience of His Holiness in Dasa due to a new rule ordered by the Indian government. We are preparing to leave for Bodhgaya before January 20, and we are hoping to have the audience on January 23.

Probably, I am going to Nepal with them after having the audience of His Holiness and I think I can help them during their trip.

Tenzin Monkyi is so cute and she talks about you a lot. In the beginning she seemed very shy to see me, but now she is very close to me and makes me a little bit tired to fulfill her different funny wishes.

My brother changed a lot physically, but his nature of being silent has never changed. His wife and mother-in-law are very kind and helpful. I am very grateful to them for helping my father and sister Namgyal when they were in need of help.

I am happy to see that Uncle Losoel loves me so much and is very affectionate to all the relatives. He is not my father, but his love and care for me is worthy and equal to my father. I hope I can pay him back as soon as possible.

Wishing you a very happy and wonderful New Year.

With love,
Tsetan

From: Jane Bay
Send: Tuesday, January 3, 2005 7:32 PM
To: Tenzin Tsering
Subject: How are you?

Dear Tenzin,

I have been in Santa Fe for two weeks for Christmas and New Year's holiday and didn't get your email until I returned to the office. I was very relieved when I heard from Tsetan that you arrived safely in Dharamsala.

I'm also worried about your financial situation and I want to wire money to you through Western Union. I checked the web and there are many places in India (especially in New Delhi) where I could wire the money. Please let me know asap where to send it.

Wishing you all a safe trip to Bodhgaya. I went there in 1994 with my spiritual friend, Losang Samten, when he was still a monk at Namgyal Monastary in Dharamsala. Losang is going to the monastery in February for a six-week retreat, but unfortunately you will have left India by that time.

I know Tsetan is very happy to be with his family again.

Much love to you all, your mom,
Jane

From: Tsetan Khensur
Sent: Tuesday, January 25, 2005 8:58 PM
To: Jane Bay
Subject: Bodhgaya

Dear Mom,

We are now in Bodhgaya and ready to leave for Nepal on January 28. We reached here on January 20 and Uncle Losoel and all family members of my brother got the opportunity to have the audience of His Holiness on January 25. There were about a thousand people from Tibet to have the audience.

I think we will arrive in Nepal on January 29 and have to stay there until Losar. This is all for today. I will email you when I arrive in Nepal.

With love,
Tsetan

From: Jane Bay
Send: Wednesday, January 26, 2005 11:10 AM
To: Tsetan Khensur
Subject: Bodhgaya

Dear Tsetan,

I am so happy to hear the news from Bodhgaya that Tenzin Tsering and family were able to have an audience with His Holiness. Please keep in touch with more news when you get to Nepal. And travel safely.

My love to you all, your mom,
Jane

From: Tenzin Tsering
Sent: Tuesday, February 8, 2005 1:48 AM
To: Jane Bay
Subject: Thanks for your kindness

Dear Mom,

Thanks for your concern and kindness. Don't worry about us, we are in enough financial shape now. We got a real visit from H.H. in Bodhgaya and received a certain compassion blessing.

We are staying in Tibet Guest House in Kathmandu with Tsetan. Today is the first day to access internet and phone for a week since we got to here. The Nepalese King shut down for security reasons because of the Maoists rebels.

With much love, yours' lovingly,
Tenzin

From: Jane Bay
Sent: Tuesday, February 8, 2005 12:43 PM
To: Tenzin Tsering
Subject: Re: Thanks for your kindness

Dearest Tenzin,

Happy New Year – Losar – February 9, 2005.

I have been so worried about you and your family being in Nepal since the King declared martial law, no telephones, no travel, etc., and hope you will be safe in the Tibet Guest House.

It is terrible how greedy some people are at the India/Nepal border, and I suppose you will face the same situation when you leave Nepal to return to Tibet. But I'm glad to hear your financial situation is okay.

I'd love to hear what you are doing in Nepal. Have you gone to Bodhnath to see the stupa there? It is very beautiful. Also, try to visit Swayambunath in Kathmandu. There is a branch of Namgyal Monastery at Swayambunath that I visited with my spiritual friend, Losang Samten, when we were in Kathmandu several years ago.

Please know that you and all your family and relatives will be in my Losar prayers for your good health and prosperity in the coming New Year.

Much love from your mom,
Jane

From: Tsetan Khensur
Sent: February 10, 2005 5:14 PM
To: Jane Bay
Subject: Nepal

Dear Mom,

We all are in the best of our health and I hope you are doing great in everything. Nowadays we are in Nepal and I think I can't go back to India until March as my bro Tenzin's mother-in-law had undergone a minor eye surgery, and it might take time to be healed completely.

I'm sorry for not being able to mail you earlier, but as you might know every communication system was shut down in Nepal due to the Maoists strike until yesterday. I will try my best to keep in touch with you.

Lastly, wishing you a very happy Losar. Uncle Losoel and all the family members are wishing you a very happy Losar, too!!!!!

With love,
Tsetan

From: Tenzin Tsering
Sent: Sunday, March 13, 2005 6:09 PM
To: Jane Bay
Subject: Back in Tibet

Dear Mom,

The situation at Nepal border was very difficult. Nepalese take lot of money from Tibetans to get access to cross border, but we are back in Tibet safely on March 3. I am back at work today.

Tenzin Monkyi is sent to kindergarden this week with Lhakyi's sister's daughter. In the daytime she is in the school and come back to home around 5:30 PM. Right now she is so eager to going to school.

When we were in Bodhgaya, we heard great speech from HH and especially about education for the children is the future for Tibet.

Yours' lovingly,
Tenzin

From: Jane Bay
Sent: Monday, March 14, 2005 10:50 AM
To: Tenzin Tsering
Subject: Re: Back in Tibet

Dear Tenzin,

I'm glad to hear you and your family arrived safely back in Tibet. The situation with the Maoists in Nepal is truly frightening.

It's wonderful to hear that Tenkyi-la is excited about school. Please keep me posted on her activities.

With all my love, from your mom,
Jane

CHAPTER THIRTEEN

A New Year

The magic of New Mexico is never more perceptible than during the Christmas and New Year's holiday season. Rooftops all over town are crowned with electric *Farolitos* (little lanterns) giving off a soft amber glow. Every year on Christmas Eve in Santa Fe, Canyon Road is closed at sunset. The street, art galleries, and houses from Paseo de Peralta up to Camino del Monte Sol are lined with traditional *Farolitos*, a votive candle set into a layer of sand in a small brown paper bag. The fragrance of pinion wood, burning in bonfires that dot street corners along the way, wafts in the crisp winter air. Christmas carolers linger by the fires as they stroll up and down the street. You'll find a cup of hot, spiced wine and a basket of *Biscochitos*, anise-flavored cookies, being offered by many storekeepers for those who need a respite from the cold.

I spent Christmas Eve, as I've done so many times in the past, with my friend Judy Broughton at her annual open house on Canyon Road. We had gone together to a Windham Hill Concert at the Lensic Theatre the evening of the Winter Solstice. Judy, whose marriage had recently ended, and I were brought to tears on more than one occasion by the spirited music, especially when Barbara Higbie sang Joni Mitchell's song, "River," accompanying herself on a Steinway grand.

> *It's comin' on Christmas, they're cuttin' down trees.*
> *They're puttin' up reindeer and singin' songs of joy and*
>   *peace,*

Oh, I wish I had a river, I could skate away on...

The song goes on to lament the loss of a love, and the lack of snow, but a few nights after the Solstice there was an abundant snowfall in Santa Fe, and we had a white Christmas.

The day after Christmas, I went up to San Juan Pueblo for the annual Turtle Dance held in the village plaza to honor the Winter Solstice. It's a line dance with only male dancers, young boys to elders. They were clothed scantily in white wool skirts held up by leather belts studded with round bells with floral bandana scarves tied around their necks, along with turquoise and shell necklaces, and buckskin moccasins. Each dancer wears an elaborate headdress made out of a painted gourd adorned with shimmering blue/green bird feathers, and a tortoise shell strapped behind the right knee. The dancers carry a rattle in one hand and evergreen branches in the other.

The dancers come out of the kiva in silence, with the children last. The dance doesn't begin until everyone is lined up and the song is started by an elder in the center of the line. There are several clowns walking around the line who tease and taunt the dancers and spectators alike. I was mesmerized by the sound of the bells, the singing, and the dancers' feet pounding on Mother Earth.

In their book, *Medicine Cards – The Discovery of Power Through the Ways of Animals*, Jamie Sams and David Carson write, "In Native American teachings, Turtle is the oldest symbol for planet Earth. It is the personification of goddess energy, and the eternal Mother from which our lives evolve. We are born of the womb of earth, and to her soil our bodies will return. In honoring the Earth, we are asked by Turtle to be mindful of the cycle of give and take, to give back to the Mother as she has given to us."

Turtle...Great Mother,
Feed my spirit, clothe my heart,
That I may serve you too.

After the Turtle Dance, I stopped by Norma Naranjo's house nearby at San Juan Pueblo. Norma had catered an event I attended at the Governor's Mansion honoring Native American artists the night before Indian Market this past summer. She calls her company "The Feasting Place – Connecting Earth and Spirit."

Norma is married to a man named Hutch from Santa Clara Pueblo, and I met them shortly after Indian Market when Marcia Keegan and Harmon Houghton invited me to go with them up to Hutch's cornfield at Santa Clara just north of Black Mesa. Marcia was going to photograph the corn that was ripe and ready to be picked.

The invitation was irresistible. I hadn't been in a cornfield since I was a teenager on my mother's family's farm in North Carolina. We arrived mid-afternoon, and the hot sun had flooded the field in glistening, bright light. The earth smelled rich and moist, and a warm breeze rustled through the thick rows of corn stalks. The green husks seemed almost translucent, and the yellow kernels were ready to burst with sweet milky juice. Norma asked if I knew how to tell if the corn was organic or not, and I replied that I didn't.

"If it doesn't have any worms, it isn't organic."

Sure enough, we found a worm or two in the ears that were picked that afternoon and carried back to Norma and Hutch's house.

They invited us to stay for dinner and we gladly accepted. Norma had made a peach cobbler that morning with peaches picked off the tree in her front yard, and she had baked Indian bread in the horno (a beehive-shaped, outdoor adobe oven) Hutch had built in their back yard. She gave us jars of peaches and apricots she'd put up, and fed us a feast of beans she had cooking on the stove all day - green chili stew, an apple and cucumber salad, and the peach cobbler with vanilla ice cream. Norma is into feeding people's spirits, and she had fed mine.

Before we left that evening, I asked Norma if she would cook for my New Year's Eve party. My spirit had been nurtured by Norma and her family. I wanted a traditional Native American feast and to share my experience with friends and family. It has been a year and a half since Namgyal died, and I'm healthier, physically and emotionally.

Grieving takes as long as it takes, but I'm back among the living again. I survived the worst possible thing that could happen to a parent, the death of my child. But, Namgyal's death has given me the gifts of grief, and out of that experience has come a renewed sense of purpose and commitment to live life to the fullest every day for as long as I live.

New Year's Eve was something of a "coming out" party this holiday season. Norma made Chicos (an Indian corn and pork stew), vegetarian green chili Posole, pinto beans, Calabacitas (cooked yellow squash and zucchini with onions, tomatoes, and corn), green chili chicken enchiladas, beef and vegetarian red chili tamales, a cucumber and avocado salad, and, of course, fresh baked Indian bread served in a willow basket Hutch had woven for her. For dessert, she made an Indian prune pie, which is made of two flaky pie crusts with a thin layer of prune paste between the crusts, and Natillas, a sweet, white pudding.

My sister, Kitty Courcier, and her partner, David Samuels, came from California for New Year's. Kitty roasted a sixteen-pound free-range turkey, just to make sure we had enough protein on the table for those folks embracing the low-carb lifestyle.

The buffet table was decorated with evergreen branches, we lit dozens of colored candles all over the house, David made a pinion fire in the living room fireplace and outside on the brick patio in the cheminia (an outdoor ceramic pot with a tall chimney), and the champagne flowed freely. Everyone loved Norma's cooking, and a good time was had by all. Several people took Norma's card to have her cater for them sometime in the future. It was truly a feast to be remembered, and a celebration of life. We welcomed in the New Year with full bellies and full hearts.

On New Year's Day, Kitty, David, and I drove down to Santo Domingo Pueblo to attend a Corn Dance. As I parked the car in front of the church just inside the pueblo, I remembered when, fifteen years ago, I'd brought Kitty to Santo Domingo on Christmas Eve for midnight Mass, not long after her late husband had committed suicide.

Following the traditional Catholic Mass, all the pews were removed from the church, and people went back to their homes. We were with Reno Myerson, who took us to a room off to the side of the altar where bowls of food were laid out on a long wooden table. We were invited to eat, and sat down at the table while Reno went over to the kiva fireplace and had a smoke (hand rolled cigarette tobacco) with several elders.

Around three o'clock in the morning, the dancers, dressed as deer and buffalo, came out of the Kiva and into the church that was now packed wall to wall with people. A path was parted down the middle of the room for them, but it was shoulder to shoulder people and dancers, with the dancers moving forward and backward just a few inches at a time.

Maybe it was the lateness of the hour or the heat emanating from all those bodies packed into the little church like sardines, but I was so dizzy from the experience I nearly fainted. The dancing went on until dawn, and we drove back to Santa Fe as the sun was rising. Kitty and I slept almost all of Christmas Day that year, but the experience had been a turning point in Kitty's healing from the loss of her husband.

This was the first time she'd come back to Santo Domingo, and she felt comfortable being there.

I was still walking with a cane, a consequence of the knee surgery this past summer; however, I was pain free thanks to the miracle of a cortisone injection in my left knee shortly before coming to New Mexico for the holidays.

We worked our way through the narrow corridors between the adobe buildings to the plaza in the center of the pueblo. The dance was in full swing when we arrived, with over a hundred men, women, and children, some as young as four or five years old, dancing in deep concentration.

The group of singers was quite large, and the drumming and song were strong and clear. The Turquoise Clan and Squash Clan alternated dancing cycles all day from early morning until sunset every day for twelve days during the Christmas/New Year's season.

As each clan entered the plaza, a flag bearer led the way, holding up a very tall vertical banner embroidered with corn stalks fastened to a heavy wood pole. The pole was topped with brilliant colored bird feathers indicating which clan was dancing. The singers and drummer followed the procession, then stood to one side as the dancers worked their way around the plaza in a series of intricate dance movements.

The Corn Dance is usually held on feast days throughout the year. Corn is a staple of the Native American diet and is also considered the germ of life. The Corn Dance during the holiday season is a prayer for the fertility of crops in the coming year, a spiritual reseeding and fertilization of the earth.

Kitty and David wanted to be closer to the dancers and walked down to the plaza where there was a group of people, mostly Anglos, standing in front of one of the houses. I stayed back by the rows of lawn chairs belonging to the residents of the pueblo.

After a while, I asked an older woman if I could sit in one of the empty seats until the owner came back to the dance, and she said it would be okay. A young woman and her baby sat next to me, but as I started to get up she said I could stay so I settled in and continued to watch the dance in silence, absorbing the sound and energy that radiated out in a concentric ripple from the dancers and singers on the plaza.

It was unusually sunny for a New Year's Day. I'd been to Santo Domingo many times in the summer for the Corn Dance, but this was the first time I'd been to one in the winter. It was easy to slip into a meditative state, and I sat very comfortably for over an hour until Kitty came over to say she needed to go to the bathroom. The older woman behind me said Kitty could use the bathroom at her house which she indicated was just a few yards from where we were sitting.

Further to my surprise, she asked if we wanted to come to her house to eat (which is a special honor), and we immediately accepted her kind invitation.

"That's a nice necklace you have. I make jewelry and maybe you'd like to see it."

I said I would, and as soon as the round of dancing finished, we went with the woman to her house.

Her name was Clarita Tenorio, and the house had been left to her by her mother who passed away three years ago. She said she missed her mother very much. I mentioned that our mother had died a little over five years ago.

"Not a day goes by that I didn't think about her, or make one of her recipes, or tell one of her stories," I said.

Clarita showed us a photograph of her mother, when she was ninety-two years old, whose hair was stark white. Her mother had been blinded by diabetes for many years. There were other family photos around the house, and I noticed an armoire filled with distinctive Santo Domingo pottery. They were made by members of Clarita's family, but she and her late husband were fetish carvers, not potters. Their specialty was horse fetishes, some of which she showed us on a necklace she was wearing.

Clarita's home was warm and cozy, decorated with other Indian artifacts and material. We sat at a long picnic table covered with bowls of food, some of which she quickly reheated for us. There was red chili beef stew, mutton stew, Jell-O salad, fried chicken wings, beef rolled in fried tortillas, hot dogs, chocolate cake, and pitchers of fruit punch. Children were coming and going.

One of Clarita's grandchildren, a boy about twelve years old, came in after a round of dancing by the Turquoise Clan, and plopped down in an easy chair in front of the television to watch cartoons during a brief rest between dances.

While we ate, Clarita showed us some of the jewelry

she'd made, and I bought a coiled wire bracelet of turquoise and spiny oyster shell that I immediately put around my wrist. She was sitting at the head of the table to my right where we were doing our business when the conversation changed. Her eyes welled up with tears.

"We had another tragedy this year. My granddaughter died. She drowned in a bucket of mop water, over there in that room, pointing to the living room. I'm a born-again Christian, and I pray she's gone to heaven."

It was a freak accident that happened when the baby, just a toddler, was playing with the mop, and when she sat in the bucket, somehow she had slipped down below the water line. Her older brother, who was in the room where we were eating, heard her splashing in the water, but by the time he got to her, she was gone.

As I listened to Clarita's story, an electrical current shot through my body similar to what I had experienced when I learned of Namgyal's death, and for a moment, I was too stunned to respond. All I could say was, "I'm so sorry. I'm so sorry."

Kitty, who was sitting to my left, said, "I'm a born-again Christian, too, and Jesus has a special place in heaven just for children."

After a few moments, I said, "I'm a Buddhist." I told Clarita about the Jizo Ceremony for children who have died, and said I would do this ceremony in memory of her granddaughter after I returned to California sometime during the New Year.

Clarita showed us a photograph of her granddaughter, whose eyes were bright and whose smile was big. We talked a little longer about her sadness, but I didn't tell her about Namgyal. We exchanged phone numbers, and I said I'd call her the next time I was in New Mexico.

Finishing our food, we thanked Clarita for inviting us to share in her family's New Year's feast and said goodbye as she went back to the Corn Dance. We headed toward the car to return to Santa Fe but walked in silence for a few moments.

"You know, Janie, there was a healing that took place back there for both of you. She picked you to share her grief with, and you were ready to receive it."

Later that afternoon we went over to Marcia and Harmon's house for their annual New Year's Day party to have black-eyed peas and pork for good luck, which is a Southern tradition that Kitty and I are quite familiar with, having had a mama from North Carolina and a daddy who hailed from Georgia.

Half a dozen monks from Drepung Loseling Monastery in India were at the party, and they blessed the food with a traditional Tibetan New Year's prayer for good fortune in the coming year.

And so it goes, the cycle of Life, Death, and Rebirth continues with the beginning of a new year.

From: Jane Bay
Sent: Monday, April 11, 2005 1:04 AM
To: Dear Friends
Subject: A New Year

Dear Friends,

Yesterday afternoon I went out to Muir Beach to Goat-In-The-Road, a place for Buddhist practice that was founded many years ago by my meditation teacher, Yvonne Rand. I was there to participate in the Jizo Ceremony for Children Who Have Died, as I had done for Namgyal on the occasion of the forty-ninth day from her death.

It was an opportunity to gather together to acknowledge and mourn the death of children from abortion, miscarriage, stillbirth, and death after birth. We would make offerings and say good-bye in a ceremony of remembrance and letting go, with the intention of nurturing and tending both the beings that have died and those beings who continue to live. On this occasion, I was there to make an offering in memory of Melina Tenorio, the granddaughter of Clarita Tenorio of Santo Domingo Pueblo in New Mexico.

Participants are asked to bring a piece of red cloth, scissors, needle, and thread. Both men and women are welcome, and there were fourteen people present including Yvonne. I didn't have any red cloth, but was able to select something from a basket of fabric remnants that Yvonne had on hand.

I found a piece of heavyweight red T-shirt material that felt a little like suede and cut a vertical rectangular section that included the hem. The hem became the top border of the banner I was making, through which I tied a piece of red string (that had been blessed by the Dalai Lama) at each corner to make the hanger. I cut the fabric in strips to make fringe along the bottom and attached a piece of white paper to the back of the cloth with an inscription written in pencil in memory of Melina.

I brought a prayer feather given to me many years ago by Reno Myerson that I attached with red thread across the top border of the small banner.

Yvonne invited us to use flowers, herbs, leaves, and stones from her garden to embellish our offerings. I pinched four small Cecile Brunner rosebuds from a bush right outside the Zendo and bound them together in a cluster with red thread. Using another small piece of red string, I tied the roses at the top of the piece of string that served as the hanger for the banner.

At the appropriate time during the ceremony, we placed our offerings on an altar where there were statues from many different religious traditions. I placed my banner on a porcelain statue of Mary whose hands were folded in prayer. I slipped the red string over her hands, and the rosebuds became a bouquet in her arms. The ceremony had been performed in silence except for Yvonne's instructions, but at this point we were able to speak.

I whispered, "This offering is in memory of Melina Tenorio, beloved granddaughter of Clarita Tenorio of Santo Domingo Pueblo."

I couldn't contain the tears that streamed down my flushed cheeks.

Enclosed is a Word doc of the final chapter to *LOVE & LOSS – A Story About Life, Death, & Rebirth*. The title is "A New Year."

Thank you all, dear friends, for your unwavering commitment to be there for me as I explored the depths of loss since Namgyal's death. I could not have navigated the emotional waters of this journey without you.

I love you,
Jane

From: Richard Nelson
Sent: Monday, April 11, 2005 1:08 AM
To: Jane Bay
Subject: Re: A New Year

Jane Darling,

Congratulations and thank you for the beautiful insights and observations. Judy and I are well, happy and full of love, and sending you same.

God bless you Cornwoman.
Richard

From: Joanne Shenandoah
Sent: Monday, April 11, 2005 1:35 AM
To: Jane Bay
Subject: Sekon (Greetings)

Sekon Dear Jane,

Nice to hear from you. I am glad you are doing what you do... it is soooo healing.

I am still here in Iceland and so anxious to get home. My daughter's father passed on Friday. What a shock, and I'm anxious because the funeral is tomorrow and my family are filling in for me. My wonderful husband, Doug George, will take her. Tomorrow, I will walk to the ocean and put my tobacco there with all these beings in mind.

The filming is going very well. People seem to like my acting abilities, but it is a strange feeling on the set. I guess some five people or so have lost loved ones this past week. Today, I will sage everywhere. The strange part of the film is this week, too. I have to pronounce someone dead, give morphine, snuff out that person, and then I get in a big fight with the other woman in the film. Sounds rather scary... huh? But, my one big paragraph in the film came off without a hitch. I was so happy about that. What an experience.

Thank you for keeping me posted on your amazing activities and for helping to bring healing to our planet. It's an honor to know you.

Love,
Jo

From: Joanna Lovetti
Sent: Monday, April 11, 2005 7:48 AM
To: Jane Bay
Subject: Re: A New Year

Dear Jane,

Thanks for sharing your experiences at the ceremony. I was online early this morning to get a work message out, and was pleasantly surprised to find yours. It came at just the right moment.

I'm feeling a little like a boxer before a big match these days. And a lot like I'm always getting myself in these situations where I'm having to be more of a grownup than I know how to be at any given moment. But, I couldn't help feeling in your making of the banner and prayers for lost children that the child in Jane was emerging as a beautifully nurtured spirit, who was happy to share the comfort and joy with others.

The last conversation Adam and I had before we went to sleep last night was about the difference between child-ISH and child-LIKE. To maintain the child-like spirit as an adult is so important, losing the child-ish attributes ruled by the self-centered ego.

Living here (Madrid, New Mexico), I have found with Adam, a world outside my driven ambition. That world stops and accepts an unexpected spring snowstorm, by running out and playing in it. That world leaps about with the dog and children. That world is grateful to be here taking in the beauty, despite the fears of a lost civilization.

So, you see, once again your timing is impeccable, dahlin'. Take care, my dear friend.

Love, always…
Joanna

From: Lucy Wilson
Sent: Monday, April 11, 2005 9:26 AM
To: Jane Bay
Subject: Re: A New Year

Dear Jane,

Thank you for coming to my art exhibit. You looked radiant – perhaps because your little surgery was so successful. And thanks for sharing your writing. I love the bit about Turtle being the oldest symbol for Mother Earth. I'm always fascinated by those kinds of myths – especially when they relate to animals, perhaps because I also like to paint the same creatures.

Love,
Lucy

From: Patty Casado
Sent: Monday, April 11, 2005 4:18 PM
To: Jane Bay
Subject: Re: A New Year

Dearest Janie,

Thank you for sharing your life wisdom with me. Today I received a message from Sacramento that the mother of my dear friend, Marie Moretti, had passed away on Saturday.

As the lamas are finishing the Shi-Tro Mandala, I am preparing to go north to be with her, with a heart that is not as heavy thanks to your words.

You are always in my thoughts, prayers and most especially in my heart.

I love you,
Patty

From: Tenzin Tsering
Sent: Sunday, May 22, 2005 7:02 PM
To: Jane Bay
Subject: Star Wars in Lhasa

Dear Mom,

This month is totally advertising from different media about the Episode 3 and it is now playing in Lhasa at new cinema hall. It is amazing and happy that many people going there to watch. I recently saw the *Star Wars 3* F1 racecar on TV, and saw George Lucas and some cast people. Looked like advertising for the film.

We are trying to watch film soon, but we are so busy at moment. I will be in Lhoka tomorrow and Lhakyi will be on night duty for two days in hospital for twenty-four hours. Her job is also very tough now.

Yours' lovingly,
Tenzin

From: Jane Bay
Sent: Monday, May 23, 2005 10:30 AM
To: Tenzin Tsering
Subject: Re: *Star Wars* in Lhasa

Dear Tenzin,

This is really amazing. I knew the movie was going to be released in China, but I didn't realize it would actually be playing in a theatre in Lhasa.

Hope you get to see it soon.

With love from your mom,
Jane

From: Tenzin Tsering
Sent: Thursday, June 30, 2005 6:44 PM
To: Jane Bay
Subject: We really miss you a lot

Dear Mom,

Looks like long time not chat with you. How are you these days? Here in Lhasa recently it is very hot at moment. Tomorrow is a very special day – it is Lhakyi's birthday on July 1.

Tenzin Monkyi is growing a lot in terms of skills of art like singing and dancing and recitation. We are so happy about her growing.

Anything that you would like from Lhasa just write down to me and I will send to you. I hope you are in the sound health and enjoyable life, too.

Take care of yourself, and we really miss you a lot.

Yours' lovingly,
Tenzin

From: Jane Bay
Sent: Tuesday, July 5, 2005 7:16 PM
To: Tenzin Tsering
Subject: Re: We really miss you a lot

Dearest Tenzin,

I am so sorry I haven't been able to email you for such a long time. I have had many projects at work due to the release of the last *Star Wars* film.

I'm sending DVDs of all the *Star Wars* episodes except Episode 3 that you recently saw in Lhasa. That film will be on DVD in November, and I will send it too so you have a complete set of all six *Star Wars* films.

I'm also sending *Star Wars: Revenge of the Sith* baseball caps and T-shirts for you, Lhakyi and her sister and brother-in-law, and cloth lightsabers and dolls of Darth Vader and R2-D2 for the girls. I'll send these to your office and let you know when the shipment will arrive in Tibet.

All my love to you, and the family,
Jane

Tenzin Saldon and Tenzin
Monkyi with Star Wars stuff
Photographer: Tenzin Tsering

The End of Mourning

From: Jane Bay
Sent: Sunday, July 17, 2005 5:36 PM
To: Dear Friends
Subject: The End of Mourning

Dear Friends,

Two years ago today, July 17, 2003, my beloved daughter, Namgyal Youdon, died in Lhasa, Tibet. Since that time, I have sent out many emails about my relationship with her during the last five years of her life, and the consequences of Namgyal's life and death on my life.

I received many replies to my email letters, and I've used some of your responses, along with emails from her brothers before and after her death, and the emails that Namgyal and I exchanged during the last two years of her life to create the foundation of the new book. I've written brief narratives that are interwoven throughout the emails to complete the story. It's sort of an "Email Diary."

Shortly after I sent out the email entitled "Love & Loss," I received a reply from Sylvia Boorstein, some of which follows:

> I thought, as I read, 'I wish I could read this description of the Jizo ceremony to my class.' I know about it, of course, and what happens there, but a personal account is always so much more moving. And the rituals of the fire ceremony, as I read them, were evocative for me of the religious ceremonies

I know that honor passings, and it is confirming to know, this is what human beings do. They say "good-bye" in ways that sanctify a relationship and its ending.

And, I thought as I read your sentence about the lightness of being, at the end, that it is so important to notice that moment of relief, and tell other people about it. I won't, of course, say anything of what you've written unless you tell me it would be all right. And, telling would be extra. You have been healing to me already.

Blessings,
Sylvia

When I first read Sylvia's message, I realized that I had to share, or give away, the experiences I was going through as part of the healing process, and, of course, I was glad for her to read it to her class. Soon, the book began to take shape without my even realizing what was happening. I needed to "tell other people about it," as Sylvia said.

And so, I'm writing you today, on this day of noting Namgyal's passing, to say my final "good-bye" and formally mark the end of mourning the loss of my beautiful daughter. I spent yesterday at Spirit Rock Meditation Center in celebration of Jack Kornfield's sixtieth birthday.

All throughout the day, I was reminded of the gifts of grief I have received in loving and losing Namgyal Youdon, and I celebrated her life as well. What a blessing she was, and always will be, in my life!!!

Since Namgyal's death I have come to a deeper understanding of the preciousness of life. I have taken to heart the Dalai Lama's admonition "to do a systematic study and analysis of the human death process as a cautious and practical preparation for the inevitable" – my own death.

Each night before I go to sleep, I practice dying by letting go of all my attachments, to friends and family, possessions, as well as my physical body, and I surrender to the nourishing care of the cosmos.

I am reminded of the words of Alan Jones, an Episcopal priest, who speaks of his daily practice in the art of "contemplative dying" in *Graceful Passages: A Companion for Living and Dying* that so eloquently express my own experiences of this process.

> In my tradition we try to practice dying every day so that we may be fully alive. What I understand of my prayer life is to place myself on the threshold of death, to participate in my dying, so that I may live each day and each moment as a gift. What I cultivate is a grateful heart; each moment then becomes a new thing. My gratitude comes from the sheer gift of life itself.

LOVE & LOSS – A Story About Life, Death, and Rebirth is dedicated to YOU, my dear friends, who held me in the arms of compassion throughout the writing. Your love and support encouraged and nurtured the telling of this story. May it be of benefit to all.

With love & gratitude,
Jane

P.S. The last thing I want to mention is that I have <u>deleted</u> everything you told me "in confidence" and anything I felt was politically or personally too sensitive in your life. If you have any concerns about what you have written to me, I will be happy to send you the pages of the manuscript that contain your email.

> *May all sentient beings have happiness*
> *and the causes of happiness.*
> *May all sentient beings be free from suffering*
> *and the causes of suffering.*
> *May all sentient beings never be separated*
> *from sorrowless bliss.*
> *May all sentient beings abide in equanimity*
> *free of bias, attachment and anger.*

Sources

Praise for
Precious Jewels of Tibet
by Jane Bay

"Bay is the Buddhist pilgrim as Everytourist, with videocam and portable compact disk player, meeting the ancient verities of the East in the search for enlightenment. 'Easier said than done,' she observes...a touching account of the inner journey and transformation of an 'overweight, middle-aged tourist.'"
Mary Grace Butler—*New York Times Book Review*

"A story of personal redemption. Jane Bay shares intimate details of her fears, sicknesses, and even her Western weakness for extravagant shopping and it's this frankness that lends authenticity and adds emphasis to her anguish over what the Tibetan people have endured."
Beth Ashley—*Marin Independent Journal*

If you would like to contact the Author regarding *LOVE & LOSS - A Story About Life, Death, and Rebirth,* visit her website.
www.JaneBay.com